Y0-AAM-404

PORTABLE  C

Henry Rabinowitz
Chaim Schaap

Prentice Hall, Englewood Cliffs, New Jersey 07632

Library of Congress Cataloging-in-Publication Data

Rabinowitz, Henry.
  Portable C / Henry Rabinowitz, Chaim Schaap.
    p. cm.
  Includes index.
  ISBN 0-13-685967-4
  1. C (Computer program language) I. Schaap, Chaim. II. Title.
QA76.73.C15R33 1989
005.13'3--dc20   89-32464
                                    CIP

Editorial/production supervision: *bookworks*
Cover design: George Cornell
Manufacturing buyer: Mary Ann Gloriande
Prentice Hall Software Series, Brian W. Kernighan, Advisor

The author gratefully acknowledges use of the following trademarks and
registered trademarks:
  UNIX is a registered trademark of AT&T
  IBM and PC/AT are trademarks of International Business Machines
  MS-DOS is a trademark of Microsoft Corporation
  VAX, PDP and DEC are trademarks of Digital Equipment Corporation
  Motorola M68000, 68020, 68030 are registered trademarks of Motorola, Inc.
  Intel 80286, 80386 are registered trademarks of Intel Corporation.
  Univac is a trademark of Unisys
  Macintosh is a registered trademark of Apple Computer, Inc.
  Sparc is a trademark of Sun Microsystems
  Ada is a registered trademark of the United States Government, Ada Joint
  Program Office

© 1990 by Delft Consulting Corp.
Published by Prentice-Hall, Inc.
A Division of Simon & Schuster
Englewood Cliffs, New Jersey 07632

The publisher offers discounts on this book when ordered
in bulk quantities. For more information, write or call:

  Special Sales
  Prentice-Hall, Inc.
  College Technical and Reference Division
  Englewood Cliffs, NJ 07632
  (201) 592-2498

Printed in the United States of America
10 9 8 7 6 5 4 3

ISBN   0-13-685967-4

Prentice-Hall International (UK) Limited, *London*
Prentice-Hall of Australia Pty. Limited, *Sydney*
Prentice-Hall Canada Inc., *Toronto*
Prentice-Hall Hispanoamericana, S.A., *Mexico*
Prentice-Hall of India Private Limited, *New Delhi*
Prentice-Hall of Japan, Inc., *Tokyo*
Simon & Schuster Asia Pte, Ltd., *Singapore*
Editora Prentice-Hall do Brasil, Ltda., *Rio de Janeiro*

Portable C

CONTENTS

PREFACE

C compilers exist for a greater diversity of computers than compilers for any other single programming language. The enormous potential market for software written in C is one of the reasons why programmers choose C as a programming language. Yet, as you have probably discovered, it is easy to write programs in C that encounter much difficulty in moving to another computer.

Whether you are accustomed to programming in an MS-DOS environment, a UNIX environment, or in other environments, this book will teach you how to write *portable C*, a style of programming that will enable your C programs to port more easily between diverse environments. The book can help you in several ways: by giving a set of rules that contribute to portable programming, by showing examples of programs that fail to be portable, by explaining the different kinds of subtle environment dependencies that can hamper program portability, and by introducing the C-World, a model of the execution of C programs that is independent of any actual environment. We also show how to design data structures which can be used to transmit data between computers of diverse architecture.

This book grew out of a course designed by the authors for AT&T Bell Laboratories. The book can be useful for

- Programmers who want to improve their coding style and make it more portable.

- Programmers who have to port other people's code, which may not have been written with portability in mind.

- Project managers and administrators who want to design project-wide and organization-wide standards for C programs.

- Language experts who want to improve their understanding of issues involved in portability.

This period of computer history is one of standardization. The battle to standardize software development interfaces is seen at all levels: operating systems (POSIX, X/OPEN, SVID, OSF, OS/2), windowing interfaces (X11), programming languages (ANSI C), "look and feel" of user interfaces, etc. In order to make the most of the potential wide markets introduced by these emerging (and competing) standards, programmers need to be aware of portability considerations in their programming style. C is a language that permits access to these emerging large markets, without guaranteeing portability to diverse environments. Thus the programmer needs to be aware of subtle environment dependencies that can creep into code, and how to avoid those dependencies.

The rules in this book attempt to create a balance between a wide universe of portability and a useful common subset of the C language. If we choose too wide a universe of environments, the resulting subset of the language becomes too poor to use. If we choose too rich a subset of the language, the universe of portability may be too small. In particular, we attempt to take into account the innovations of *ANSI C*, showing which of its useful features can be incorporated into portable C. You may find that the balance achieved by our rules is too restrictive or too generous for your needs. The rules must be seen, then, as advisory; they are the basis for your organization to determine its own language standards.

Examples of nonportable code are printed in white on black:

```
printf("%d %d\n", *p++, *p++);
```

Sections of code which have been corrected to make them portable appear on a grey background:

```
printf("%d %d\n", *p, *(p+1)); p += 2;
```

Portability is not a science like physics that flows directly from a set of axioms. It is often easier to give examples of what is *not* portable than to write rules that determine what is. Moreover, the language continues to evolve, even as this book is being written. We expect that future changes in the language and in the machines on which it runs will necessitate changes in the rules of this book. We hope that you will write us with your own experiences of portability problems, so that we can keep this book up to date in future editions. Please write to us c/o

```
Delft Consulting
15 West 72nd Street, Suite 9M
New York, New York 10023
```

or via electronic mail on usenet at

```
{allegra, cmcl2}!delftcc!chaim
```

This book was typeset by the authors using our own macros together with a variety of software packages including More and MacDraw on the Macintosh, and troff, tbl, psfig, and TranScript on a Unix-based system.

We would like to thank Delft Consulting Corp. for providing the computer and printing resources used to produce this book. Jim Euchner of NYNEX Corporation generously allotted time for Henry Rabinowitz to work on the book. Tom Veden helped give this project its initial start. We are grateful to Brian Kernighan, Sam Kendall, George Holober, Morey Antebi, and Marc Rochkind for their careful reading of our manuscripts and their helpful advice. The many contributors to usenet's bulletin board `comp.lang.c` provided useful ideas. Bob Ernest offered typesetting advice. Our editors Ed Moura, Karen Fortgang, Lisa Garboski, and Paul Becker helped us bring this book to print. We also thank Etti Schaap, Jahanshah Moreh, and Richard Azzolini for their support and forbearance—and Talia, Noam and Ariel for their fun diversions—during the years that this book was written.

Henry Rabinowitz

Chaim Schaap

Portable C

CHAPTER 1
INTRODUCTION

1.1 Why is portability a problem for C programmers?

Since its creation in 1972, the C programming language has become one of the most popular languages for software development. Its use continues to grow due to its combination of efficiency and portability. C approaches the efficiency of assembly languages while retaining the portability and maintainability of high-level languages. C compilers now exist for machines ranging from microcomputers like the IBM PC to supercomputers like the Cray. Portability offers the possibility that a software product developed in C will have a wider market and a longer lifetime than a product developed in the assembly language of a particular machine.

C's efficiency makes it an especially appealing software development language for the booming personal computer market. Although many PC programmers in the past have programmed nonportably, content with the vast market for PC software, the current proliferation of PC operating systems and models makes portability a greater concern.

Programmers who have chosen C for its power and portability sometimes find themselves dismayed when C programs do not move easily from one environment to another. They soon realize that nontrivial problems await the would-be writer of portable C code. Since C can get closer to the machine architecture than most other high-level languages, it is possible to write code that is highly *non*portable.

Portable means movable, but what is to be moved? Most often, it is the source code of the program that we wish to move from one kind of machine to another. We recompile the program on the second machine's compiler, and wish to have it run on the second machine in the same way it ran on the first. In reality, the program will often require modifications before it can run identically on the second machine.

Moving, modifying, and recompiling a program is called *porting* the program to a second environment. How much modification can a program require and still be called portable? An hour—a day—several months? The size and complexity of the program and especially its level of machine dependence affect how long the port will take. An operating system, inevitably tied closely to the architecture of the machine it runs on, will take longer to port than an application program such as an inventory system. The most generous definition of portability calls a

1

program portable if less time is required to port it to a new environment than to rewrite it from scratch in the new environment.

1.1.1 Environment dependence and dialects

Programs fail to port because they contain environment dependencies or because they use a different dialect of C than that supported by the target compiler.

In the definition of portability, we speak of porting a program from one *environment* to another. Each environment consists of both hardware—the computer—and software—the associated system programs. For a program to be portable, it must not depend on features of a particular environment, or if it does, such dependencies must be well isolated and parameterized. Thus portable code is environment independent. When we speak of environment, we mean both the *translation environment*, in which the code is compiled, and the *runtime environment*, in which the compiled program executes.

The translation environment includes the preprocessor, the compiler, the linker, and often the standard libraries. Each of these components of the translation environment may differ from one environment to another, causing portability problems. Some machines have a variety of compilers available; each presents a slightly different environment for the programmer. Similarly, the choices of preprocessor, linker, and libraries all affect the translation environment, even given a fixed choice of machine.

The operating system in the runtime environment presents a set of system calls that can be used by the application programmer or by the standard libraries. The runtime environment may contain libraries for dynamic binding. The runtime environment also includes the program startup and termination sequences.

The translation and runtime environments may involve two different kinds of machines in the case of a cross-compiler. More frequently, the translation and runtime environments involve the same machine. The translation and runtime environments may be one single environment in the case of an interpreter. The translation and runtime environments may use different operating systems, even if they use the same hardware.

Environment dependence, dependence on features of the machine architecture, the translation software, or the runtime software, is the main obstacle to portability of code. For example, when a program relies on certain features of a computer's architecture that are not shared by other computer architectures, such as word size, or order of bytes in a word, it loses portability due to *machine dependencies*. C is more prone to machine dependencies than other languages because it lets programmers "get their hands dirty," for example, by allowing bit manipulations and pointer manipulations with very few restrictions. It is precisely this "dirty-hands" aspect of C that makes it so popular compared to more elegant but fussy languages like Pascal.

When a program relies, as inevitably it must, on system calls or standard library functions that differ from one operating system to another, then it loses portability due to *operating system dependencies* or *library dependencies*. This problem is almost unavoidable since C is a small language, requiring function calls to perform such basic operations as input/output, dynamic storage allocation, and string handling—operations that are already embedded in other high-level languages. Library incompatibilities are among the most frustrating of problems encountered in porting C code.

When a program relies on certain nonstandard features of a given C compiler that are not shared by other C compilers, such as the amount of padding between members of a structure, it loses portability due to *compiler dependencies*. Some compiler dependencies arise from unspecified aspects of the C language itself. The definition of C leaves certain features unspecified so compiler implementers will be able to choose the most natural implementation for their machine.

The C language itself has changed over time, and with the arrival of the ANSI standard continues to change. Thus, code that relies on features of a specific dialect of C can be nonportable due to *dialect dependencies*.

1.1.2 Kinds of portability

We can distinguish several kinds of portability: *source code portability*, *data portability*, *binary portability*, and *locale portability*. Most of this book is about source code portability: how to write portable C code. Sometimes, however, it is not the *code* we wish to port but the *data* it produces. We want the output of a program on one machine to be used as the input to a program on a different machine. Achieving data portability is discussed in §4.11 and in §8.3.

Binary portability is the ability to run an executable version of a program in more than one environment, without access to the source code. We do not discuss binary portability standards in this book. Locale portability, also called *internationalization*, is an aspect of binary portability that is achieved when programs can adapt at runtime to different language and national environments. The goal of internationalization is that a single executable program should be able to work in different countries and adapt its input and output to locale-specific conventions including different languages, character sets, collating sequences, representations of money, numbers, time, and date. The goal of locale portability is addressed by features of the ANSI and X/OPEN standards, discussed further in §9.11.

1.1.3 Three examples of nonportable code

Is C portable? It depends how you write it. Portability is assumed to be an advantage of high level languages. Yet the ability of C to get close to the machine makes it possible to write code that is nonportable.

This book emphasizes a positive approach to program portability—a set of rules to follow that will help you write portable programs. But to appreciate the problems that nonportable code can cause, let us look first at three examples of portability pitfalls—apparently normal-looking programs that can cause trouble in certain environments. Take a moment to look at each example and figure out why it is not portable. What environmental features does each example depend on?

What will the following example print out?

```
main()
{
    char i;

    for (i = 5; i >= 0; i--)
        printf("%d ", i);
}
```

On an IBM PC, the example would print

```
5 4 3 2 1 0
```

which is what we would expect. But on an IBM 370 series mainframe, the example would print

```
5 4 3 2 1 0 255 254 253 252 251 250 249 248 247 246
```

and would in fact continue printing numbers indefinitely in an infinite loop.

The environment dependence in the example is the use of type `char` for variable `i`.

`char` i;

In some environments, like the PC, `char` is a signed type, while in other environments, like the 370, `char` is an unsigned type. In environments where `char` is unsigned, the loop will never terminate, since `i` is never less than 0.

To make the code portable, we can change the declaration of `i` to

`int` i;

since int can take on negative values in all environments.[1] For further discussion of the use of char to represent small numbers, see Chapter 4 and §5.2.

The second example contains a common portability error. The code intends to test if the first argument on the command line begins with a –, which denotes a command option or flag.

```
main(argc, argv)
int argc;
char *argv[];
{
    /* Is first command line argument an option? */
    if (argv[1][0] == '-')
        process_option(argv[1]);
    . . .
```

The code works fine on a VAX and on an IBM PC/AT running Microsoft C, but will cause "Segmentation fault (core dumped)" on a Sun 3 machine if the user supplies no command-line arguments.

By convention, a null pointer follows all the valid argument pointers in the argv array. If the user provides no command-line arguments, argv[1] is a null pointer. Since argv[1][0] is the same as *(argv[1]), we are attempting to de-reference a null pointer. That is not allowed in C. The result of de-referencing a null pointer is undefined in portable C.

A portable version of the code is

```
if (argv[1] && argv[1][0] == '-')
    . . .
```

or equivalently

```
if (argc > 1 && argv[1][0] == '-')
    . . .
```

The proper use of the null pointer is discussed in §7.3.2, §7.3.3, and §7.3.4.

The third example contains code to print out its version number. What portability problems can you find in the example?

---

[1] In ANSI C we could declare i as

    signed char i;

but that declaration would not be portable to non-ANSI environments.

```
#define VERSION "1.03"   /* keep version number as a macro
                          * to make changes easy */
void prVersion();

main()
{
    prVersion();
    ...
}

/* print the program's version number */
void
prVersion()
{
    static char outmsg[20] = "Version #";

    printf(strcat(outmsg, VERSION));
}
```

On a PC/AT using Microsoft C with the "small model," the code compiles and executes as expected.

```
C> msc /AS ver.c
C> link ver
C> ver
Version #1.03
C>
```

However, using the "large model" causes strange output.

```
C> msc /AL ver.c
C> link ver
C> ver
&‡□SQWV"Φ( ΘΦ•Θ|Φ|
C>
```

Compiling and running the same code on the same machine under System V Unix causes "Segmentation violation--core dumped."

The code exemplifies a frequent type of portability problem: failure to declare an external function. C assumes that unless otherwise declared, every function returns an int. However, in this case, **strcat** returns a pointer of type char *.

```
    printf(strcat(outmsg, VERSION));
```

In environments where int and char * are the same size—such as the PC/AT using the small model—the code works, but only by accident. The example fails on the PC/AT using the large model, because there `ints` are 16 bits while pointers are 32 bits. The program checker **lint** can detect this problem.

The best way to prevent such problems is to declare all external functions in a header file (or at the top of the file in which they are used). To make this example portable, you can include a header file that contains the declaration for **strcat**:

```
extern char *strcat();
```

In an ANSI environment, the file **string.h** contains a declaration for **strcat**. In a non-ANSI environment, create your own **string.h** and put the declaration for **strcat** in it.

A portable version of the example is then

```
#include <string.h>
#define VERSION "1.03"   /* keep version number as a macro
                          * to make changes easy */
void prVersion();

main()
{
    ...
```

1.2 How this book can help you write portable code

1.2.1 The approach of this book

Rather than just listing a bunch of things not to do, this book provides a set of simple positive rules that will enable you to program in a more portable style. The rules define a style of C programming that we refer to as *portable C*.[2]

It is impossible to prove a program absolutely portable; someone can always invent a new computer or compiler that will violate the conventions of all known code. Given the variety of machines that have C compilers already, no matter what set of rules we adopt for portable programming, there is bound to be some machine or compiler that violates those rules. Thus we must make certain *practical assumptions* about the universe of machines to which we will be porting code. For example, there may be some environments in which a `short` cannot hold the number 32767. However, such machines are so unusual that we can

---

[2] Note the *portable C* style described in this book has nothing to do with the *Portable C Compiler*. The latter is an AT&T compiler designed to port easily to many machines. The Portable C Compiler currently implements [SVPG RefMan] C.

make a practical assumption that in all environments we are likely to encounter, a `short` *can* hold 32767. We need to make certain practical assumptions lest portable C become strictly a "lowest common denominator" for all C environments; we do not want to make portable C so restricted that it loses its power and practicality. Those are, after all, C's virtues.

There are two kinds of rules in this book: rules that handle differences among dialects of the C language, and rules that would hold even if everyone programmed in the same dialect.

Because there are different dialects of C, the rules of portable C attempt to establish a common subset of all the dialects. However, we didn't want to rule out all the valuable features of newer dialects just to promote portability to environments with older dialects. Portable C is based on the C defined in the original "C Reference Manual" [K&R], with additions from later dialects, including ANSI. In general, if a later feature provides valuable functionality, and can be emulated in older environments that lack that feature, then we include it in portable C. Thus, portable C includes extensions to [K&R] such as type `void`, since `void` can be emulated by type `int` in environments that lack it. Portable C also includes or emulates ANSI features such as standard header files containing function prototypes (see §3.1). We assume that C compilers and code will head in the direction of ANSI C, so portable C strives to be compatible with the ANSI standard.

In designing the rules for portable C, we sought to balance several—often contradictory—goals.

- The rules should be easy to remember and use. The enforcement of some rules could even be automated by a computer program analogous to **lint**.

- The rules should be consistent, as much as possible, with existing practice. We do not wish to create a radically different style of programming.

- Portable C should retain all the powerful and useful features of C, including features implemented only in newer compilers and ANSI C. It should not be a "lowest common denominator" of C dialects.

- Similarly, portable C should not assume a "lowest common denominator" of environments. Portable C should port to as wide a variety of environments as possible, but it is necessary to make some practical assumptions about the universe of environments to which we want to port.

- The rules should promote modern programming style, modular code organization, and strict typing. We have been influenced in these directions by ANSI C and C++.[3]

---

[3] Stroustrup, Bjarne, *The C++ Programming Language*, Addison-Wesley, 1987.

Portable C is not a new standard or a new dialect; rather, it is a style of programming in C whose purpose is to achieve wide portability of source code without sacrificing ease of programming. The rules actually make the language simpler by limiting the kinds of statements you can make in C.

The book motivates the rules by cautionary examples drawn from experience, like the three examples shown earlier in this chapter. It helps to know what practices to avoid in order to know how to program portably. The more you are aware of the variety of machine architectures, the less you will be likely to assume that the environment in which you program is typical of all others.

However, you cannot be aware of all possible environments. If you finish this book with a sense of the portability rules and how to use them, you will be able to program more portably, even if you forget the rationale behind the rules.

In addition to rules that define portable C, this book offers a number of "style suggestions"—optional guidelines to promote good programming practices that do not specifically affect portability.

Your company or project can use the rules as the basis for devising your own company-wide or project-wide standards for C programming.

1.2.2 Porting code written by others

It is one thing to port code you have written in a portable style, but quite another when you are faced with porting someone else's code. Since you have no assurance that they coded with porting in mind (and they probably did not), you have to try an *ad hoc* series of steps in order to get the code to work in your environment. Since you may have to port other people's code, it is necessary for this book to discuss all the pitfalls of machine dependencies that you must avoid. Even though by following the rules of portable C you are unlikely to fall into the erroneous usages, you must be aware of them when dealing with other people's code. (See §9.10).

1.2.3 Creating an organizational standard

Ultimately, you will have to decide on your own dialect for C programming. It is a good idea for every organization that programs in C to set up a standard of its own, both to ensure a consistent style for maintenance, and to enhance portability. One possible style sheet is given in [Lapin]. In setting up a standard for C programming, an organization should consider the potential universe of environments to which the programs may have to port. For example, will the programs always live in an MS-DOS environment? Can you assume your programs will always run on ANSI-conforming compilers? Can you assume that your program will run only on 32-bit machines?

You cannot always predict the future of a program, yet each programming group must assess the tradeoffs between the benefits of a wide universe of portability, and the usefulness of assuming particular constraints on that universe. For example, programmers within AT&T may feel that UNIX System V can be taken as a given in their environment, and later find themselves porting code to an MS-DOS machine or a BSD machine or a Macintosh.

As part of establishing your own organizational standards, it is a good idea to create a header file with certain definitions that will be used as part of your organization's standard. The header file **environ.h** should include all definitions that are specific to your environment, but not specific to any particular application.

In addition to making your own organizational header file, it is useful to have an organization-wide library to contain commonly used functions. Such a library limits the need for each programmer to "re-invent the wheel." An organization-wide library of functions can also aid portability by encapsulating certain environment-specific functions in higher-level functions that are independent of the environment. For example, you could write a general function to do raw-mode input from a terminal, which would call at a lower level the routines of the specific operating system to achieve that input. (See §9.1.)

1.2.4 Basic rules of portable C

We now introduce the basic rules for writing portable C. Subsequent chapters will introduce their own rules, which make these rules more concrete as well as illustrating the use of these basic rules. The basic rules can be reduced to three principles:

PORT1: *Be explicit; don't rely on defaults of the language.*

C has many defaults. It is a tolerant language. Although C compilers have lately tended to be less tolerant about such matters as type conflicts, C can tolerate some dangerous or meaningless code. The best way to avoid this problem is to be explicit: in casting operands of operators, in casting arguments to functions, in casting return expressions in functions, in declaring functions with a return type, in declaring functions before using them. This principle is intended to promote strict typing, and attention to the use of types in C.

PORT2: *Don't rely on the representation of the value of data objects.*

The way a given environment represents the value of a floating point number, a pointer, or a codeset character is likely to differ from the way another environment represents the same value. Portable C uses an abstract machine, removed from the particularities of any given environment, as its way of picturing the representation of data objects.[4]

PORT3: *Identify, isolate, and parameterize environment-dependent code and definitions in separate source or header files. Include* **environ.h** *in every source file.*

The minimal approach to portability is to identify environment-dependent code with comments. But you can do more. To the extent that your program must depend on features that are part of your environment, the environment-dependent parts of your code should be isolated in special low-level library routines, insulating them from the rest of your code. Header files are also a good place to hide environment dependencies. For example, you should create an **environ.h** file to contain the environment-specific #defined constants and typedefs necessary for your code. We call these #defines and typedefs *parameterized* constants and types. They depend on the particular environment for their definition.

This book cannot describe every unusual and bizarre kind of computer architecture. The list is too long, and will only grow over time, outdating any list we could provide. That is why we provide instead a set of rules for programming.

1.3 Standards and portable C

Historically, one reason for the proliferation of C dialects has been the absence of a formal standard for the C language. The language called "C" is in fact a set of dialects that have evolved over time. The ANSI C standard XJ311 should help to remedy the drifting divergence of C dialects. However, the draft ANSI C standard (at this writing) is still far from universal implementation. At least a few years will pass before the majority of C implementations comply with the ANSI standard. In fact, the ANSI committee has chosen to introduce new features as part of its "standard" with which no pre-existing compiler is in compliance. Thus ANSI C is in effect a new dialect of the language which must compete with existing dialects. Until ANSI achieves widespread acceptance, the *de facto* standard remains Kernighan and Ritchie's "C Reference Manual," which appears as an appendix in their definitive book *The C Programming Language* [K&R, First Edition].

However, even the [K&R] Reference Manual is not the last word in C, because it was amended and extended several times within Bell Labs. For example, [RefMan81] contains most of the common extensions to [K&R] that

---

[4] One exception to this principle is that portable C *does* assume the binary encoding of positive integers.

eventually show up in the System V Programmer's Guide [SVPG RefMan]. The extensions to [K&R] included such new features as `void` and `enum` types, structure assignments, and structure-valued functions.

Since C makes use of function calls for basic operations like string operations and I/O, the *standard library* associated with C is an essential aspect of programming in C. Unfortunately, the "standard library" has been historically even less standard than the language itself. Fortunately, the ANSI standard includes a specification for a standard library.

In addition to ANSI, other groups have involved themselves in the specification of standard libraries. Some, like AT&T's System V Interface Definition, form alternatives to ANSI's library. Others, like the manufacturers' consortium X/OPEN and the Open Software Foundation, seek to consolidate a variety of existing standards such as ANSI C into meta-standards for software development. See §9.1 on libraries.

1.3.1 Do standards yield portability?

Will the advent of the ANSI standard for C eliminate portability problems? If the standard achieves widespread acceptance, it will do much to enhance portability of C code, especially due to the standardization of the standard library. However, there remain numerous areas where the C language's behavior is unspecified, and numerous opportunities to write machine-dependent code even in ANSI C. Even in an ANSI environment there is benefit to following the portable C rules discussed in this book.

In the words of X/OPEN, "Whilst the C language provides the basis for applications portability, it is easy to write statements, using valid C constructs that are machine specific. Care has to be taken when writing programs that are intended to be portable across a range of systems."[5]

1.4 Why bother with portable programming?

Why not leave porting to the poor soul who someday may have to port your program? Why bother to think about many different environments when you want your program to work efficiently in *your* environment?

Portable style is intimately entwined with making your code maintainable. Just as the largest part of the lifetime (and expense) of a good piece of software is

---

[5] *X/OPEN Portability Guide*, Vol. 4, "Programming Languages," pp. 3.1-4.9, and Vol. 3 "XVS Supplementary Definitions: XVS Internationalisation," Elsevier Science Publishers B.V., Amsterdam, 1987.

spent in maintenance, coding for maintainability can lead to lifetime efficiencies of the code.

The obvious benefit of making the effort to use a portable programming style when you write a program is that over its lifetime, you can easily move your program to other environments. You are no longer stuck with a particular hardware or compiler vendor. One of the reasons people use C is precisely this benefit of *vendor independence*. Perhaps as your application grows in number of users, you want to move it from micros to mainframes. Perhaps you wrote your program for a workstation/UNIX environment and now want to tap the vast MS-DOS PC market, or vice versa. The more portable your code, the more easily you will be able to serve *new markets*. Your program, no longer tied to the environment for which you first wrote it, achieves a longer life, and a wider market.

1.4.1 Portability and program design

Although this book is devoted to teaching a series of rules for programming in portable C, it is possible to ignore all the rules and still have code that ports well. Just as the most important aspects of program optimization are language-independent, so too the most important aspects of portability transcend the C language. Well-structured code contributes to ease of porting. For example, early versions of UNIX were written in a highly nonportable dialect of C that was tied closely to the architecture of the PDP-11 computer. Nonetheless, UNIX achieved popularity as a "portable" operating system because the code was easier to port than that of previous operating systems. How? Because UNIX was written in a well-structured manner that confined most machine-dependent aspects to a small part of the code. The moral is that there is no substitute for well-designed, well-structured code.

1.4.2 Does portable C reduce efficiency?

Efforts at optimization make the most difference when optimizations are selectively applied to those parts of the code that are used the most. Since it is impossible to know in advance which parts those will be, it is best to code in a style that enhances portability and ease of maintenance, and then to apply selective optimizations later, after analyzing the performance of the code. Much coding style used in the name of "efficiency" has only the effect of making the code hard to read, or to port.

Since a program spends most of its lifetime in the "maintenance" phase (if it is any good), good programming style (emphasizing maintenance and portability) leads to "human efficiencies" in the maintenance of the code.

1.5 How to read this book

Chapters 2 and 6 contain background information on the C-World abstract machine. They provide a model for understanding C that is useful both for the study of portable code and for the enhanced understanding of C itself. However, the reader eager to pursue the details of portability can skip these chapters and proceed to Chapters 3, 4, 5, 7, and 8, which discuss the portability issues associated with the various data types. Chapter 9 concludes the book with general topics including the portable use of library calls, linkage issues, name spaces, and internationalization. An appendix contains a summary of all the rules for portable C.

CHAPTER 2

THE "C-WORLD" ABSTRACT MACHINE

This chapter introduces an *abstract machine* that allows the programmer to envision how a C program will run without referring to a specific environment. The machine provides a portable model of the execution of a C program. To find out what a given piece of C code will do in execution, the zealous programmer may look at the assembly code that a compiler generates, but that code is environment dependent. The operational model introduced here works as a kind of portable assembly code—a portable way to specify the execution of the program. The model is based on the [K&R] model, which is extended and made more precise.

The reader willing to consider this model will gain an improved understanding of how C works. The model can be useful also in contexts beyond the scope of this book. It is a helpful frame of reference for thinking about C when reading other C language books and documents, particularly for difficult documents like C reference manuals and the ANSI standard. The handling of pointers in the model is further elaborated in Chapter 6 and finds its greatest use in Chapter 7 on pointers.

The chapter concludes with a discussion of how the abstract model is realized in diverse environments through the representation of the value of data objects. Differences in the representation of values are one form of environment dependence that affects portability.

2.1 A model of C programs in execution

The *C-World* is a semantic model of the execution of a C program. The C-World model is an abstract machine, not based on the architecture of a particular machine or on any aspect of a particular environment. Understanding how a program will execute in the C-World enables you to program without depending on features of a particular environment.

The C-World model makes more precise the semantic model implicit in [K&R], adhering as much as possible to their concepts and terminology. Sometimes we have replaced existing concepts or terminology in order to generalize or simplify the model.

A C program models data processing activity. Data are represented by *data objects* and data manipulations by *operations*. The execution of a C program consists of a sequence of operations whose operands are data objects. We say that

15

the C-World models the execution of a C program. What happens? Data objects are created. Operators act on data objects, creating new data objects. Every C program can be viewed as a sequence of operations.[1]

2.2 Syntax and semantics

The C-World semantic model reveals what happens as a C program executes. This is different from a syntactic model which specifies the grammar of the language, that is, the way a correct program must look on the page.

A program can be syntactically valid yet semantically meaningless. For example, the statement

```
i;
```

is syntactically valid, yet it *does* nothing in execution. Such statements are not excluded from the syntax of C because often a statement is used for its side effects.

Much writing about C, including [K&R] and [ANSI], mixes syntactic and semantic categories freely. One of the purposes of the C-World model is to separate out the semantic concepts. Once the reader understands how that separation should be made, it is possible to return to the common practice of mixing semantic and syntactic language, now with greater understanding of what is really meant.

For example, data objects and data object attributes are semantic categories, while names and expressions are syntactic categories. It is common and convenient, though perhaps sloppy, to equate a data object (semantic category) with the identifier or expression that denotes it (syntactic category). For example, [K&R] state, "A character constant is a character enclosed in single quotes, as in `'x'`."[2] In the more careful language of the semantic model we would say, "A character constant is *denoted by an expression consisting of* a character in single quotes." While this may initially seem like a quibbling distinction, its value becomes apparent as we continue.

---

[1] In the words of [K&R], "Variables and constants are the basic *data objects* manipulated in a program. Declarations list the variables to be used, and state what type they have and perhaps what their initial values are. *Operators* specify what is to be done to them." Kernighan and Ritchie, *The C Programming Language*, p. 33. Emphasis ours.

[2] [K&R], p. 180.

2.3 Data objects and their attributes

A *data object* can be created as the result of a declaration in a C program, as the result of an operation, as the result of dynamic memory allocation, or by being mentioned as a literal constant in a C program.

A data object has a variety of attributes. Some of the attributes of a data object are *name, type, access permissions, value, address,* and *lifetime.*

A data object has a *name* if it is created by a declaration; the name is the identifier in the declaration. Not every data object has a name. For example, members of a structure or union are unnamed data objects. They must be referred to by expressions containing the `->` or the `.` operator.

An *expression* is a syntactic entity used to denote a data object. A name can be used as an expression to denote a data object with that name.

For example, in the program fragment

```
int i, j;

i = j + 3;
```

the following expressions each denote a data object: `j, 3, j + 3, i, i = j + 3`. Among them, `j` and `i` are name expressions; the others are not.

A data object's *type* specifies what kind of value to expect. A data object of type `int` has an integer value, an object of type `char *` has the address of a character as its value. Note that the type does not specify the representation of the value of the data object. The representation of the value depends upon the particular environment and is not part of the C-World.

In the C-World model, the data object, not the identifier, has a type. Thus, when [K&R] say "C bases the interpretation of an identifier upon two attributes of the identifier, its storage class and its type,"[3] the semantic model would rephrase the statement as "C bases the interpretation of a data object *denoted by an identifier* upon two attributes of *the data object as specified in the declaration of* the identifier."

Access permissions for a data object specify in what way its value can be accessed. *Read-only access* means the data object is a *constant*; its value cannot be changed. *Read/write access* means the data object is a *variable*; its value can be inspected and modified. Function objects have *execute-only access*. The value of a function is code that can neither be inspected nor changed; it can only be executed.[4]

---

[3] [K&R], p. 182.

[4] The semantic model uses the access permissions of a data object to generalize what [K&R] call constants and variables. One advantage of the terminology is that it permits the classification of functions as data objects with execute-only access permission. Being a constant or variable is now on a par with an attribute like data type.

The *address* and *lifetime* of a data object are discussed in Chapter 6.

Data objects can be nested. A composite object (except `union`) consists of an ordered collection of objects. The *value* of a composite object is the sequence of values of its member objects. Thus, the array

```
int dom[12] = {31, 28, 31, 30, 31, 30,
               31, 31, 30, 31, 30, 31};
```

is initialized to the value {31, 28, 31, 30, 31, 30, 31, 31, 30, 31, 30, 31}.

The attributes of a data object have portability problems which the C-World gives us a framework to discuss. For example, the set of types available, the number of characters of significance in a name, and the access permissions of string constants all vary between different dialects of C.

2.4 Pictorial representations

In a program, every declaration and expression refers to a data object. For instance, the declaration

```
int n;
```

causes a data object to be created. We picture the data object like this:

type:	int
expr:	n
name:	n
value:	unspecified
access permissions:	read/write

n

??

The C-World uses an oval to denote the data object to remove any suggestion of its implementation in storage locations (which are often pictured by a boxlike notation). The value of the variable object is shown inside the oval. The expression n which refers to the data object floats like a kite over the oval.

Similarly, the literal constant

3

appearing in a C program refers to a data object which we picture like this:

type: `int`
expr: 3
name: none
value: 3
access permissions: read only

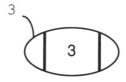

The data object has integer type but no name. The vertical bars inside the oval mean that the value is not modifiable. (The bars are meant to suggest that the value is "imprisoned.")

2.5 Operations

An *operator* operates on one or more data objects and yields as its *result* a data object. Hence, operations can be nested; the result of an operation can serve as operand in a subsequent operation.

Actually, the operands of some operators are not always data objects. The `sizeof` operator can be applied to a type, and the member selection operators . and -> take a (generic) member name as right hand operand.

The result of an operation is, without exception, either a newly created data object or a pre-existing data object. If it is a newly created data object, then the result is a short-lived constant data object.

An expression that specifies an operation denotes at the same time the object yielded by that operation. In fact, the only way to refer to a data object is through an expression. Thus, in the program fragment

```
int k, n = 2;

k = n + 3;
```

the expression n + 3 both specifies that an addition is to occur, and also refers to the short-lived constant data object that results from the addition.

The operation denoted by the expression n + 3 is pictured like this:

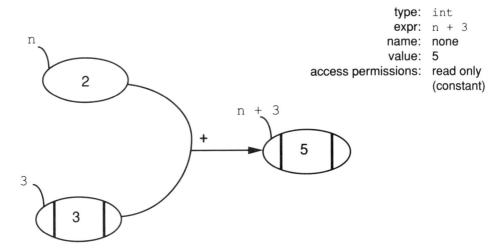

We say that n + 3 refers to a *constant* data object because it cannot be assigned a new value. We cannot say

```
n + 3 = 4;
```

The constant data object denoted by the expression n + 3 is created as the result of the addition operation and it ceases to exist immediately after it is used as operand for the next (=) operation.

One of the key aspects of the C-World model is the fact that an operation like n + 3 yields a data object rather than just a value. This fact greatly simplifies the model because it supplies a uniform, self-evident explanation for the nesting of operations. It also closely resembles the implementation, where intermediate evaluation results are often stored in registers.

An operator works on a data object and not on an attribute of a data object. Likewise, an operation yields a data object and not an attribute of a data object. Often, we talk somewhat sloppily about the execution of a C program. We say that an expression produces a value. What we mean is, that the expression refers to an operation that yields a short-lived constant data object with that value. That is, we often say, "if n is 2, then n + 3 is 5." What we mean is, "if we apply the + operator to the data objects denoted by the expressions n and 3, where the variable denoted by the expression n has the value 2, then the expression n + 3 denotes a short-lived constant data object with the value 5."[5]

---

[5] In this area, the semantic model is more precise than [K&R], which states, "Expressions combine variables and constants to produce new values." The result of an operation can serve as operand of another operator. Does that operator take a value or a data object as operand? To be consistent, one has to say that expressions combine variables and constants to produce new (or pre-existing) *data objects*. This formulation gives the model a pleasing simplicity.

Clearly, we *do* want to use shortcuts in our talk about C operations, without losing track of the full meaning. The explicitness of the model helps to bridge this gap.

Each operation places specific constraints on its operands, constraints that can be formulated in terms of the operands' attributes. For example, the multiplication operator restricts the type of its operands to arithmetic types. The assignment operator requires that the access permission of its left operand is read/write.

Many of the rules of portable C are formulated as additional constraints on the operands of an operator, beyond those specified in the language itself. These portability constraints help solve the portability problems of the attributes of the operands. For example,

- NUM7: *"The integer division operators (/ % /= %=) require non-negative operands,"* is a constraint on the *value* of the operands.

- STRING1: *"Don't modify string literals,"* is a constraint on the *access permissions* of operands.

Not all operations yield short-lived constant data objects. Some operations yield existing data objects. For example, in the code fragment

```
int n = 2;
int * p = &n;

while (*p > 0)
    ...
```

the expression *p refers to the existing data object whose name is n. The expression *p is a non-name expression for the data object whose name is n. It is often used when the name is not in scope. We picture the result of the operation *p as follows:

type: `int`
expr: `*p`
name: `n`
value: 2
access permissions: read/write

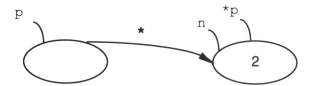

Exercise 2-1: Results of operations. Assume these declarations

```
int i = 1, j = 2;
int *p = &i;
```

Describe the data objects denoted by these expressions:

Expression	Type	Value	Name	Access permissions
i + 5				
i * 3 + j				
i = 10				
i = j = 19				
*p				
&i				
p				

☐

Solution to Exercise 2-1.

Expression	Type	Value	Name	Access permissions
i + 5	int	6	none	read-only
i * 3 + j	int	5	none	read-only
i = 10	int	10	none	read-only
i = j = 19	int	19	none	read-only
*p	int	19	i	read/write
&i	int *	address of i	none	read-only
p	int *	address of i	p	read/write

☐

2.5.1 Functions

In the C-World model, a function is a data object. Just as a structure is a data object composed of a series of other data objects, a function call is a composite operation formed from a sequence of other operations.

In the expression f(a, b), the function call operator () takes as its operands the name of the function, f, and its arguments, a and b. The data object resulting from the function call operation is the data object returned by the function.

Just as a structure can be a member of another structure, one function call operation can be an element of the series of operations that constitutes another function call operation. Thus, ultimately the execution of a C program can be reduced to a single operation: the function call operation `()` with the function `main` as operand.

2.6 Levels of encoding

When we move from the abstract machine of the C-World to the diverse environments of the real world, the differences in *representation* of data objects become a source of portability problems. The representation of a data object consists of its size, its byte ordering in storage, and its *encoding*. The value of a data object can be viewed at multiple levels of encoding. For example, the value of an `int` is a *number* on one level and a *bit pattern* at a lower level of encoding.

(The downward arrow ↓ means "is encoded by.") More precisely, the number has a binary encoding as a bit pattern. Operators view the value of their operands at a specific level of encoding. For example, an arithmetic operator such as +, *, -, /, >, <, etc., views its operands as numbers while a bitwise operator such as &, |, ^, ~, <<, >>, views its operands as a bit patterns.

A Boolean data object has one of two possible values: *true* or *false*. Since C has no separate data type to implement Boolean values, arithmetic or pointer types are used to represent Booleans. For example, a Boolean data object can be of type `int`; its truth value is encoded as a number, which in turn is encoded as a bit pattern.

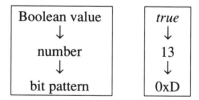

Here we have three levels of encoding. A Boolean operator views its operand as a Boolean value, not as number or a bit pattern. Boolean values can be used in expressions belonging to certain control flow constructs, e.g., `if` and `while` expressions, and as operands of logical operators, such as `&&`, `||`, and `!`.

Similarly, a data object of type `char` has a character value represented as an element of the codeset, which has an encoding as a number, which has an encoding as a bit pattern.

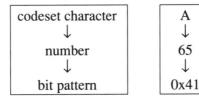

At the lowest level of encoding, bit patterns, or sequences of bits within bit patterns, may themselves represent sequences of numbers, enumerations, and Boolean values of various sizes. For example, a 1-bit field can be used as a flag (Boolean), and a small number of bits can be used to represent the state of a machine (enumeration) or a small counter (number). Sometimes bit patterns are used to match external layouts, such as the layout of a machine-language instruction, or to optimize storage space.

A sequence of bits that is part of the total bit pattern can use the same binary encoding as the hardware uses to implement non-negative numbers. After extraction, such a bit sequence can readily be used as the operand of an appropriate arithmetic operator. Using bit patterns to represent sequences of Boolean variables offers the advantage that it is possible to test for more than one condition at once. For example

```
#define READ  1
#define WRITE 2
#define EXEC  4

int perm;

if (perm & (READ|WRITE))
     ...
```

Note that the expression `perm & (READ|WRITE)` represents a bit pattern used as a Boolean value. This common technique in C uses the encoding of bit patterns to achieve a shorthand for the longer Boolean expression `perm & READ ||` `perm & WRITE`.

As the above example shows, a data object may be viewed at different levels of encoding depending on the context. For another example, consider the code fragment below:

```
int fcount = 0; /* counts # of invocations of f() */

int
f()
{
    ...
    fcount++;
}

int
g()
{
    if (fcount) /* if f() has ever been called */
        ...
}
```

The global variable `fcount` is used to count the number of invocations of function f. Each time `f` is called, `fcount` is incremented. In the expression `fcount++`, the increment operator `++` views `fcount` as a number. But in function `g`, to test if `f` has been called at all, we say

```
if (fcount)
```

where `if` views the value of `fcount` as a Boolean value.[6]

2.6.1 Who/what encodes?

The encoding of a value can be a function of the compiler on behalf of the target machine (number to bit pattern), of the C language (Boolean to number), or of the programmer (enumeration to number).

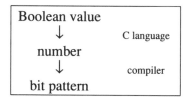
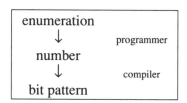

An example of the latter is the use of `int` to represent the days of the week. Sunday, Monday, ..., Saturday can be encoded by the programmer as the numbers 1, 2, ..., 7.

---

[6] We assume here that `fcount` is small enough that it will not wrap around to zero. Cf. §4.5

```
#define SUNDAY    1
#define MONDAY    2
...
#define SATURDAY 7
```

But the programmer is also free to make any other choice of seven unique numbers. The actual values used in the representation are irrelevant and could just as well have been 0 thru 6 or even −2 thru 4. We call such a representation of a series of values by integers an *enumeration*. Note that an enumeration can be represented by integers; it does not require the C type enum. §8.7 discusses the enum data type.

Enumerations are small sets of items with or without an order relationship. When an order relationship is defined, it is expressed through the standard ordering of integers. In the example shown above of the days of the week, a successor or predecessor operation can be implemented by adding or subtracting 1.

As an example of an enumeration *without* order, we could have

```
#define MASSACHUSETTS 1
#define CALIFORNIA    2
#define NEW_YORK      3
#define ARKANSAS      4
...
```

as a set of values for a variable declared

```
int state;
```

The values chosen for the different states are arbitrary. There is no meaningful ordering of these values.

As another example, in an ANSI or UNIX environment the different error types that the external variable errno can represent form an enumeration without order relationship. The values chosen to represent the errors are essentially arbitrary, without meaningful ordering. When we say

```
extern int errno;
...
if (errno)
    handle_error(errno);
```

errno acts as an enumeration of error types, but also as an implicit Boolean value. errno is "true" if it contains any error number. errno is "false" if it contains 0.

The encoding of the codeset characters into integers is a function of the codeset itself. Traditionally in C, the ASCII encoding has been the most common. However, implementations of C exist that use EBCDIC encodings, and with the spread of C to international applications, other codesets are coming into use. The order of characters within a codeset—when viewed as their underlying numeric representations—may differ between codesets. See Internationalization, §9.11.

2.6.2 Encoding of pointers

As with integers, the value of a pointer can be viewed at different levels of encoding. The value of a pointer is the address of a data object or the value of the null pointer. Just like a number, an address is encoded by the hardware as a bit pattern. (A C interpreter may use its own encoding for addresses, which differs from that of the hardware.)

Unlike the case with integers, C programmers usually do not operate on pointers at the bit pattern level of encoding. If they do, say to "realign" a pointer, the arithmetic operations must be carried out on a pointer cast to an integer. All such manipulations are non-portable.

A pointer can act as a Boolean value; any address of a data object represents the value *true* and the value of the null pointer represents the value *false*. Thus, a common C shorthand is

```
if (p)
```

to mean

```
if (p != 0)
```

Both versions are correct in portable C, and both should yield identical code when compiled. See Chapter 7 for more on pointers.

2.6.3 Encoding of numbers

Non-negative numbers of integral type are encoded by the hardware in a binary encoding which is hardware independent, except possibly for the number of leading zero bits. The encoding of negative numbers is, on the other hand, environment dependent. Machines have differing representations for negative numbers such as two's-complement, one's-complement, and sign-magnitude (though two's-complement is by far the most common). Also, machines differ in the number of bits associated with the various integral types, which means a different encoding of negative numbers. For example, given two machines with two's-complement arithmetic, if one has 16 bit integers and the other has 36 bit integers, then their representations of −1 are 0xFFFF and 0xFFFFFFFFFF, respectively.[7]

The expression 0 denotes an integer constant whose value viewed as a number is zero and whose bit pattern value consists of all zeros. On a one's-complement machine, a bit pattern of all ones also represents the number value 0 (usually called negative zero). Whenever we mention the number 0, we will assume the value encoded by all zero bits and not any other encoding.

Unlike the integral types, the floating point types have no portable encoding on the bit pattern level. The encoding of floating point types is hardware dependent. IEEE standard 754 provides a convention for Binary Floating Point arithmetic, but at this writing and in the foreseeable future, it is far from universal adoption, since it involves major hardware changes.

---

[7] See §4.6.7.

CHAPTER 3
PORTABLE USE OF FUNCTIONS

A C program is written as a series of functions. The improper declaration and use of functions are frequent sources of portability problems. The rules for the portable use of functions are so important that they are the first rules discussed in this book. The rules for functions are more than just stylistic conventions; they help enforce, across functions, the other rules that will follow for arithmetic and pointer types.

Portability problems with functions can be reduced by using ANSI prototypes,[1] which, of course, can only work in an ANSI environment. The ANSI innovation of prototypes is so helpful—for portability and for assuring program correctness—that we recommend their use, despite compatibility problems with non-ANSI environments. This chapter explains the value of prototypes for portability and suggests ways to incorporate prototypes while still remaining compatible with non-ANSI environments.

We start with an example. File **create_node.c** contains a function that allocates nodes of a dynamic data structure. Can you find any nonportable constructs in this file?

```
struct node {
    ...
};
typedef struct node NODE;

NODE *
create_node()
{
    return (NODE *)malloc(sizeof(NODE));
}
```

This example is similar to the example using **strcat** in Chapter 1. All C compilers will assume that an undeclared function returns an `int`. In the example above, **malloc** is used without previous declaration, so the compiler assumes it returns an `int`.

```
return (NODE *)malloc(sizeof (NODE));
```

---

[1] See the `setbuf` example in §3.2.2.

The code should work on machines where `int` and `char *` are the same size
(such as the VAX), but will fail on machines where `int` and `char *` are different sizes (such as Intel 80286 under the "large model").

The program-checking tool **lint** can detect this error in two ways. **lint** might
complain

```
test.c(12): warning: illegal combination of pointer and inte
ger, op CAST
malloc value used inconsistently  llib-lc(59) :: test.c(12)
```

These messages result from **lint**'s observation that we have implicitly declared
malloc as a function returning an `int`. The first message from **lint** notes that
casting the `int` returned by **malloc** to a pointer type (`NODE *`) is suspect. The
second message stems from a contradiction between the way we have implicitly
declared **malloc** and the way it is declared in **lint**'s standard library specification
file (which states that **malloc** returns a `char *`).

In an ANSI C environment if you included the standard header file **stdlib.h**,
which contains a *prototype* for **malloc**, then you wouldn't have to declare **malloc**
in this file. ANSI function prototypes are declarations that show not only the
return type of the function, but also the number and types of the arguments of the
function. Function prototypes allow the compiler to do much of the type checking formerly relegated to **lint**, ensuring safer C code.

You can take a similar approach in a non-ANSI environment, writing your
own **stdlib.h**, which would contain the line

```
extern char *malloc();
```

The declaration of **malloc** in **stdlib.h** is a *nondefining* declaration. A *defining*
declaration, or *definition*, of a function contains the code of the function as well
as its type.

A portable version of the program, in an ANSI *or* non-ANSI environment, is
then

```
#include <stdlib.h>

struct node {
    ...
};
typedef struct node NODE;

NODE *
create_node()
{
    return (NODE *)malloc(sizeof(NODE));
}
```

3.1 Header files and prototypes

We generalize the above observations into a rule:

FUNC1: *Declare every function in a header file.*

Header files should contain nondefining declarations for all functions you use. These will not conflict with subsequent definitions of the functions that you will put in source files. (Actually, we exclude functions of file scope from this rule, i.e., functions defined with the storage class `static`. See §9.3.5.)

For standard library functions, we recommend you use the appropriate header files specified in [ANSI]. If you are not in an ANSI environment, write your own project-wide version of the ANSI header files. ANSI header files are supposed to be "idempotent," that is, includable multiple times. There is a simple trick to achieve idempotence. Suppose you are writing your own version of ANSI's **string.h**. Then write

```
#ifndef STRING_H
#define STRING_H
... (here put the contents of the file)
#endif
```

For your own functions and for system calls in your local environment, we recommend defining one or more header files. The header files should be compatible with both ANSI and non-ANSI environments. That is, in an ANSI environment, the header file should contain prototypes for your functions, while in a non-ANSI environment, the header file should contain external declarations for your functions. This can be achieved either by using explicit `#ifdefs` to determine the environment, or by using the macro `P_` shown below.

We illustrate the use of header files by creating **example.h**, which contains declarations appropriate for the examples in this chapter and Chapter 1.

```
struct node {
    ...
};
typedef struct node NODE;

#ifdef __STDC__   /* ANSI C */
extern void prVersion(void);
extern NODE *create_node(void);
#else             /* non-ANSI */
extern void prVersion();
extern NODE *create_node();
#endif
```

The use of `void` for the prototype's argument list is ANSI's way of saying that the function takes no arguments.

We could write **example.h** using the macro `P_` as follows:

```
struct node {
    ...
};
typedef struct node NODE;

extern void prVersion P_((void));
extern NODE *create_node P_((void));
```

where `P_` is defined in the header file **environ.h** as

```
#ifdef __STDC__
#define P_(A) A
#else   /* non-ANSI */
#define P_(A)   ()
#endif
```

3.1.1 Modularization

The next example clearly does not follow Rule FUNC1; it uses a different level of *modularization* than we recommend. Why would it cause portability problems?

```
typedef ... BIGNODE;
typedef ... SMALLNODE;

BIGNODE *
alloc_bignode()
{
    extern char *malloc();

    return (BIGNODE *)malloc(sizeof(BIGNODE));
}

SMALLNODE *
alloc_smallnode()
{
    return (SMALLNODE *)malloc(sizeof(SMALLNODE));
}
```

The example does not follow Rule FUNC1 because **malloc** is declared inside a block rather than in a header file.

```
BIGNODE *
alloc_bignode()
{
    extern char * malloc();

    return (BIGNODE *)malloc(sizeof(BIGNODE));
}

SMALLNODE *
alloc_smallnode()
{
    return (SMALLNODE *)malloc(sizeof(SMALLNODE));
}
```

Compilers will differ in their handling of this code, depending on whether the lexical scope of the **malloc** declaration is to the end of the file or the end of the block. ([K&R] is ambiguous here; ANSI C specifies to the end of the block.)

For those compilers that treat the declaration of **malloc** in `alloc_bignode` as being of file scope, its declaration would apply, as desired, inside `alloc_smallnode`. For other compilers that treat the declaration of **malloc** in `alloc_bignode` as being local to `alloc_bignode`, the second appearance of **malloc** would be treated, by default, as a function returning an `int`.

The best solution is simply to follow Rule FUNC1 and declare the function **malloc** in a header file as in the previous example.

```
#include <stdlib.h>

BIGNODE *
alloc_bignode()
{
    return (BIGNODE *)malloc(sizeof(BIGNODE));
}

SMALLNODE *
alloc_smallnode()
{
    return (SMALLNODE *)malloc(sizeof(SMALLNODE));
}
```

The example just shown illustrates the issue of modularization—the question of how to divide up code into logical units ("modules"). The C language allows a number of different approaches; unlike Ada, Modula, or C++, it lacks formal facilities for specifying modules of code. Nonetheless, it is desirable in C to think in terms of modules that are self-contained and have a simple interface to the outside world.

C offers a choice of what entity to designate as a module: a function or external data object, a file, or a set of files. In practice, for most applications a set of files is the right size for a module. Small programs may consist of a single module.

Let us then define a module as a set of source files (. c files) together with a single associated header file (a .h file). We can designate two parts to the module: the *public* part, or *specification*, and the *private* part, or *implementation*. The specification of a module is contained in its header file; the implementation of a module is in its source files (and may also include macros defined in the header file). Each source file of the module should include the module's header file. The header file should contain declarations for all functions, types, and data objects of program scope found in the source files of the module, in accordance with Rule FUNC1. Any source file outside the module that wishes to use the public facilities of the module must include the module's header file.

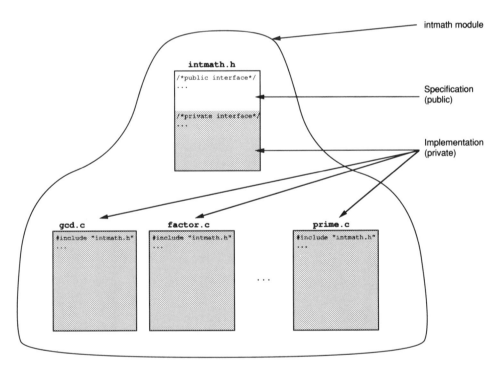

The header file should *not* contain any defining declarations (declarations that allocate storage). C does not provide a formal facility for designating which of the declarations are public (accessible to other modules) and which are private to the module. That is left to the documentation (manual pages, etc.) and could be indicated by comments in the header file.

The public part of the header file of a module specifies how other modules can interact with it. For example, suppose a module consists of a table and a set of functions that manipulate the table (add entries, delete entries, change entries, etc.). The header file should contain a structure definition for an element of the table, an external declaration for the table, and declarations for the functions that manipulate the table. The designer of the module may choose to designate as public in the header file only the functions that manipulate the table. These functions then become the only way that other modules should access the table. Or, the designer may choose to designate the table itself as a public data object in the header file, thus making the table available directly to the manipulations of other modules.

This suggested format for module design is an ideal based on the data abstraction facilities of more recent programming languages. In reality, much C code may not achieve the clean module boundaries suggested by this design. Nonetheless, as long as Rule FUNC1 is followed, portability will be enhanced. Since C permits but does not readily facilitate the modularization necessary for data abstraction, the programmer must be firmly committed to this discipline of programming in order to keep the boundaries of a module well-defined. What happens more commonly is that a module becomes an arbitrary collection of related functions, and all source files end up including all header files.[2]

A good example of modularization is the way ANSI has divided its standard library functions into modules, each module with its own header file. The header **stdio.h** is the specification for the I/O library; **string.h** is the specification for the string handling library, and so on. Data structures like the I/O buffers in **stdio.h** are private—hidden from other modules—they should only be accessed through the functions in the **stdio** module.

3.2 Function definition and function call

The diagram below shows a suggested style for the declaration, definition, and use of functions. The basic idea is that the header file contains both an ANSI prototype and a pre-ANSI external declaration for the function, while the source file contains the function definition in pre-ANSI format only. The declaration of

---

[2] For a good introduction to data abstraction, see Bjarne Stroustrup, "What is Object-Oriented Programming?", *IEEE Software*, May 1988, pp. 10-20..

function `gcd` in the header file **intmath.h** follows Rule FUNC1, and will prevent
the type of portability problem just seen in the `create_node` example.

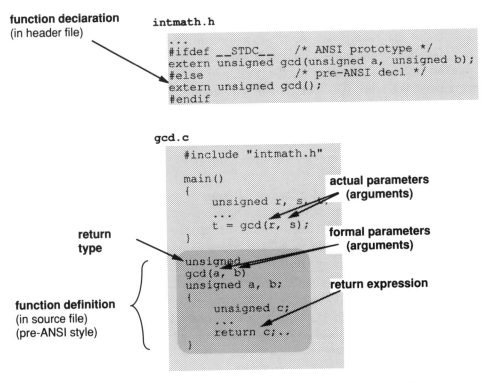

The arguments provided on a function call are called the *actual parameters*
of the function. The arguments that appear in the definition of the function itself
are its *formal parameters*.

A *return expression* is the optional expression following the keyword
`return`. A function can have many return statements, hence many return
expressions. The *return type* is the type specified in the function definition. The
return expression is converted to the return type, as if by assignment. Only a
function of return type `void` should have no return expression.[3]

3.2.1 Function definition: ANSI vs non-ANSI

The ANSI prototype syntax for function declarations can also be used in function
definitions. The ANSI format for defining `gcd` would be

---

[3] See §3.2.2.

```
unsigned
gcd(unsigned a, unsigned b)
{
    unsigned c;
    ...
    return c;
}
```

The advantage of the ANSI definition syntax is that, as with prototype declarations, the compiler can check the type and number of the actual parameters on subsequent calls to the function, eliminating a common source of errors in C. More than that, the presence, in scope, of a function prototype *coerces* conversions of the actual parameters to the types of the formal parameters.

The obvious disadvantage of the new syntax for function definition is that it is not portable to pre-ANSI compilers. Fortunately, ANSI compilers will accept old style function definitions.

Although ANSI C diverges from non-ANSI C in its style of function declarations, we would like to be able to accommodate ANSI-style declarations because ANSI prototypes enhance compile-time checking and portability. Rule FUNC1 mandates header files containing function declarations for all functions. Since header files are generally hidden from the programmer's view, it is not a problem to use #ifdefs or macros to accommodate both ANSI and pre-ANSI declaration styles, as shown in §3.2.

For function *definitions* we recommend using only the pre-ANSI style. This style is portable to both pre-ANSI and ANSI compilers, yet we do not lose the power of the ANSI prototype, since we have put a prototype in the header file.

By using only the pre-ANSI function definition style, we keep the source files free from the messiness of #ifdefs, in accord with Rule PORT3: *Identify, isolate, and parameterize environment-dependent code and definitions in separate source or header files.*[4]

---

[4] Otherwise, every function definition in your source files would look something like this:

```
#ifdef __STDC__
void errexit(int errno, char *errmsg)
#else
void
errexit(errno, errmsg)
int errno;
char *errmsg;
#endif
{
    ...
}
```

surely not a desirable format.

Moreover, undoubtedly someone will develop an automated tool for converting function definitions from ANSI to non-ANSI style and vice versa.

3.2.2 Rules for function definition and function call

We can now specify some of the important rules for the portable use of functions.

FUNC2: *The actual and formal parameters of a function should have the same types.*

This rule actually follows from the general principal PORT1: *Be explicit.* It is an instance of the use of "strict typing" in portable C. The way to use this rule is to cast the actual parameters of the function call so they have the same types as the corresponding formal parameters in the function definition.

Since non-ANSI C compilers have no way to check or coerce type agreement between formal and actual parameters, lack of type agreement is a frequent source of errors and portability problems. Prototypes permit ANSI compilers to coerce the actual parameters to the types of the formal parameters. Rule FUNC2 assures that function calls will behave the same way in non-ANSI and ANSI environments.[5]

When we say that the actual and formal parameters of a function should have the same types, we mean their types as they appear in the C program, *before* any default argument promotions. Thus, if the formal parameter has type `char`, then the actual parameter should have type `char`. We treat `char` constants like `'a'` as having type `char`.

FUNC3: *The number of actual and formal parameters of a function must match.*

Don't leave out trailing actual parameters of a function call, even if they will not be used by the function. For functions that require a variable number of arguments, use the **stdarg** mechanism discussed in §3.3.

FUNC4: *The type of a return expression should be the same as the return type of the function.*

The C language itself will enforce this rule by an implicit assignment from the

---

[5] This is so, even though ANSI environments with prototypes do not use the default argument promotions. In non-ANSI C, and for ANSI C functions without prototypes, actual parameters passed to a function are subject to the *default argument promotions.* Under most circumstances, these promotions are not noticed by the programmer, but in certain cases it is important to understand what the default argument promotions are.

The default argument promotions include the *integral promotions* and the *floating point promotions.* The integral promotions cause actual parameters of type `char` and `short` to be widened to `int`, and actual parameters of type `unsigned char` and `unsigned short` to be widened to either `int` or `unsigned`, depending on the compiler and the machine. (See §4.6.5.) The floating point promotions cause actual parameters of type `float` to be widened to `double`.

In ANSI C default argument promotions do *not* occur if there is a function prototype present that fully specifies the type of all arguments.

return expression to a data object with the return type.[6] By requiring an explicit cast in case of a type mismatch, Rule FUNC4 focuses your attention on the cast and on the constraints of portable C on casts. Consider the following examples, which illustrate these rules.

In the following example we wish to turn off buffering for a file designated by `fp`. The conventional way to do this using the standard library is by calling `setbuf` with a null pointer.

```
#include <stdio.h>
FILE *fp;
...
/* turn off buffering */
setbuf(fp, 0);
```

The example violates Rule FUNC2 since the second actual parameter in the function call, 0, is of type `int`, while the second formal parameter of `setbuf` is of type `char *`.

```
setbuf(fp, 0);
```

The code will work on machines where `int` and `char *` are the same size, such as the Sun 3, but will fail on machines where they are not the same size, such as the Unisys 1100.

The code will work successfully in all ANSI environments, since the header file **stdio.h** contains a prototype for `setbuf` that coerces a conversion of 0 to type `void *`, the generic pointer type in ANSI C.

To make the code work in all environments, including non-ANSI, apply Rule FUNC2 to get

```
setbuf(fp, (char *)0);
```

This example and others are discussed in greater detail in §7.3.

The next example also violates one of the rules just stated. Where is the portability problem?

---

[6] However, in the case of two different pointer types, C may not perform an implicit conversion. This could lead to nonportability. See §7.5.

```
#include <stdio.h>

#define MAXQUIET    1000
#define EPART1   10
#define EPART2   1011

/*
 * errexit -- print an optional error msg and exit
 * Note: if errno is less than MAXQUIET, don't print
 *         an errmsg
 */
void
errexit(errno, errmsg)
int errno;
char *errmsg;
{
    if (errno > MAXQUIET)
        puts(errmsg);
    exit(errno);
}

main()
{
    ... /* part 1 of program */
    if (...)
        errexit(EPART1);
    ... /* part 2 of program */
    if (...)
        errexit(EPART2, "Problem in part 2");
}
```

The problem is that `errexit` is called with differing numbers of actual parameters, in violation of Rule FUNC3.

```
if (...)
    errexit(EPART1);
```

Even if a trailing parameter is not needed, it is not portable to leave it out! This code will work in many environments, but in others it will fail. **lint** will diagnose this problem. ANSI-conforming compilers may also detect it.

The solution is straightforward: always use the number and type of actual parameters that match the number and type of the formal parameters, even if the trailing parameters are unused dummy placeholders.

```
if (...)
    errexit(EPART1, "");
```

This code will pass **lint** and will pass an ANSI compiler.

In addition to the important rules already discussed, there are two more rules that will improve the style and portability of your use of functions.

FUNC5: *Define every function with an explicit return type.*

Use `void` return type for functions that don't return a value. Use `int` return type explicitly for functions that return an `int`. (Even though `int` is the default return type, it is better to be explicit, as it clarifies your intentions.)

C programmers often don't bother to declare an explicit return type for functions that return an `int` and for functions that do not return a value. Rule FUNC5 suggests that it is better not to rely on this default of the C language. Thus, it would be a violation of Rule FUNC5 to define the function `errexit` as

```
errexit(errno, errmsg)
int errno;
char *errmsg;
{
    ...
```

Rule FUNC5 suggests a programming style in which all function return types are made explicit. This style helps to avoid problems like the one just seen with **malloc,** by sensitizing the programmer to the return type of each function. It also makes **lint** more helpful in diagnosing problems with returned values of functions; **lint**—or the compiler—could warn when you are attempting to return an expression from a function that is declared as returning `void`, or when you have a simple

```
return;
```

statement—or no return statement at all—in a function declared as returning an `int`.

Rule FUNC5 recommends the use of `void` return type for functions that do not return a value. But what if your compiler does not support `void`? [K&R] does not mention `void`; `void` arrived on the scene in [RefMan81] and is supported by most recent C compilers and by [ANSI], [SVPG RefMan], [X/OPEN], and [K&R2]. If your compiler has no `void`, there is a simple workaround. In your **environ.h**

```
typedef int void;
```[7]

---

[7] If you use the typedef, **lint** will still complain about such uses as

```
(void)strcat(s, t);
```

lint will also complain about `void` functions having no return value.

ANSI C also introduces the new type `void *`. The above typedef will not always work properly to implement `void *`. In any case, we recommend avoiding the type `void *` in portable C. The type `void` is a helpful innovation in the language, and possible to emulate in older environments that don't have it. However, `void *` does not add much to the language and is hard to emulate on non-ANSI systems; we recommend you use `char *` instead, except in code that is intended for ANSI environments only. One reason to avoid use of `void *` in portable C is that non-ANSI compilers that support `void` will be confused by `void *`. In such environments you will have to typedef `void` as `char` or `int`, thus losing the benefit of the `void` type. See §7.5.

Since not all compilers accept structures or unions as function arguments or return types, and since a similar effect can be achieved by using pointers to structures or unions, Rule FUNC6 excludes structures and unions as function arguments or return types in portable C.

FUNC6: *Don't use structures or unions for argument types or return types.*

Using pointers may at times be less elegant, but could be more efficient.

Most compilers implement structure or union return types in such a way that the function in question becomes non-reentrant. If such a function is called both from the base program, synchronously, and from a signal handler, asynchronously, the structure or union return value can get garbled. This is another reason to follow Rule FUNC6.

There are two other reasons to follow Rule FUNC6. If you cast a structure-valued function to `void`, and `void` is typedef'd as above to `int`, then the compiler will complain. Also, the `?:` operator and the comma operator have trouble with structure operands in some compilers.

There may be occasions when it is appropriate to break Rule FUNC6, for example, when the ease of using structure-valued functions outweighs any portability loss. For example, to do arithmetic on complex numbers, the code

```
complex a, b, c;

c = times(a, plus(b, c));
```

uses structure-valued functions and structure parameters. To write the same code using pointers would be more complicated.

3.3 Functions with a variable number of arguments

How would you write a function with the following specification?

```
/*
 *   maxn(nitems, f1, f2, ...)
 *       returns the max of its floating point args
 *   PARAMS
 *       nitems   int      # of floating point args that follow
 *       f1, ... float     args of which we take the max
 *   RETURNS
 *                float    the max
 *   NOTE
 *       if nitems is 0, print errmsg,
 *                       return FLT_MIN
 */
```

3.3.1 The ANSI interface: stdarg macros

The ANSI C standard library contains a **stdarg** interface that provides a portable way to implement `maxn`.

It is not portable to make assumptions about the manner in which actual parameters are passed to a function. For example, the arguments may be pushed on the stack in various orders, or (some) may be passed in registers. Hence, it is not portable to write a function with many formal parameters that you call with fewer actual parameters. In order to write a function, such as `maxn` or **printf**, that can take a variable number of arguments, it is necessary to use a library interface called **stdarg**. **stdarg** is a set of macros (and possibly functions) that are called from within the function definition of a function that is to take a variable number of arguments.

stdarg is part of the ANSI standard library and is also provided with the standard library of some non-ANSI compilers. If your compiler does not provide a **stdarg** interface, you can write your own macro implementations. The *implementation* of **stdarg** will differ from environment to environment, but the *specification* of the macros, and thus their use, is portable to all environments.

Unfortunately, the ANSI specification of **stdarg** differs slightly from the UNIX specification (on which it is based), which is called **varargs**. We will show how to write code to accommodate either version of the macros.

A function that employs the **stdarg** macros must determine the number and type of its arguments *from the arguments themselves*. Two common strategies are the following.

- The first argument contains a format string that specifies the number and type of all the following arguments. **printf** and **scanf** follow this model.

- The type of all the arguments is specified by convention in advance, but the number of arguments is determined by having the last argument be 0 or a null pointer. The UNIX system call **execl** follows this model.

When writing a **stdarg**-style function of a variable number of arguments, it is handy sometimes to be able to call a **printf**-like function that can use the **stdarg** syntax for specifying a variable argument list. Fortunately, ANSI and SVID provide **vptrinf**, which can take **stdarg**-style arguments. UNIX System V provides **vprintf** in its standard library as well.

Note the following features of the **stdarg** interface:

- You must include the header file **stdarg.h**.

- The function definition uses standard ANSI prototype syntax to show it has a variable number of formal parameters. That is, after declaring each fixed parameter, three dots (. . .) show that a variable number of arguments follow. In a non-ANSI environment, you need only declare the fixed parameters and leave out the three dots.

- There must be at least one fixed argument of fixed type.

- va_start takes the name of the last fixed argument as its second parameter. That argument may not be a register type, nor a type that is widened by the default argument promotions. (e.g., not a char, nor a float).

The following example illustrates the use of the **stdarg** macros to build a function definition for a function with a variable number of arguments.

```
#include <stdarg.h>

return_type          /* return type of the function f */
f(arg1, ...)         /* at least 1 fixed argument */
{
    va_list argp;    /* points to next arg to be processed */
                     /* argp can be passed as arg */
                     /* to another function */
    va_start(argp, arg1);   /* sets up argp to point to */
                            /* the 1st arg after arg1 */

    ...
```

```
    /* for each argument to be processed:
     * arg_type is the type of the actual parameter after
     *    the default argument promotions   (see notes below).
     * va_arg    obtains the argument,
     * n         should be same type as the actual parameter
     */
    n = va_arg(argp, arg_type);
    ...
    va_end(argp);    /* cleans up */
}
```

The type of `arg_type` is the type of the actual parameter after the default argument promotions (Cf. §3.2.2). The default argument promotions are not suppressed by the presence of a prototype, since the three dots in the prototype cannot predict the types of the arguments. For example, the prototype

```
    int fprintf(FILE *fp, const char *format, ...);
```

does not allow the compiler to predict the types of the third or subsequent parameters, which are therefore subject to the default argument promotions.

Hence, if the actual parameter is

- narrower than `int`, `arg_type` should be `int`

- `float`, `arg_type` should be `double`

The routine `va_arg` must be implemented as a macro because it takes a type as an argument, which is impossible for a function. Many implementations of **stdarg** implement all the **stdarg** routines as macros.

Following is the file **maxn.c** which contains the definition of `maxn` using the **stdarg** interface.

```
#include <stdarg.h>
#include <float.h>       /* has the value of FLT_MIN */
/*
 *   maxn(nitems,f1,f2,...)
 *        returns the max of its floating point args
 *   PARAMS
 *        nitems  int      # of floating point args that follow
 *        f1, ... float    args of which we take the max
 *   RETURNS
 *                float    the max
 *   NOTE
 *        if nitems is 0, print errmsg, return FLT_MIN
 */
```

```
float
maxn(int nitems, ...)
{
    va_list ap;
    float max, f;
    int i;

    if (nitems == 0)
    {
        printf("maxn: nitems error\n");
        return FLT_MIN;
    }


    va_start(ap, nitems);

    /* peel off 1st float to start max */
    max = va_arg(ap, double);

    for (i = 1; i < nitems; i++)
    {
        f = va_arg(ap, double);
        max = (max > f ? max : f);
    }
    va_end(ap);

    return max;
}
```

As we have defined it, maxn can be called with any number of arguments, as long as they conform to the conventions we have established. Any file in which you use maxn should include a header file—in this case we call it **util.h**—which contains a declaration of maxn. To demonstrate, we have a test file **main.c**.
    In **util.h**:

```
#ifdef __STDC__
  ...
extern float maxn(int nitems,...);
#else
  ...
extern float maxn();
#endif
```

In **main.c**:

```
#include <util.h>

main()
{
    printf("maxn(4, 1., 2., -1., 3.)=%f\n",
            maxn(4, 1., 2., -1., 3.));
    printf("maxn(0)=%f\n", maxn(0));
    printf("maxn(2, -10.1, -200.22)=%f\n",
            maxn(2, -10.1, -200.22));
}
```

The output produced on a M68000-based machine running UNIX is

```
maxn(4, 1., 2., -1., 3.)=3.000000
maxn: nitems error
maxn(0)=0.000000
maxn(2, -10.1, -200.22)=-10.099999
```

(The roundoff error in the last line is due to the imprecision of floating point arithmetic, not to **stdarg**).

Note that if we used the type `float` as an argument to `va_arg`, we would not get the correct results, since `float` actual parameters are passed as `double`s to functions, by the default argument promotions. If we had said

```
f = va_arg(ap, float);
```

the result (on the same M68000 machine) would be

```
maxn(4, 1., 2., -1., 3.)=2.000000
maxn: nitems error
maxn(0)=0.000000
maxn(2, -10.1, -200.22)=0.000000
```

3.3.2 UNIX-style varargs

Many non-ANSI systems, including UNIX environments, have a different macro interface called **varargs**, which has the same purpose as **stdarg**. The **varargs** interface is slightly different from the **stdarg** interface. Note that, unlike **stdarg**, a **varargs** function needs no fixed parameters; the model shown here does not declare any fixed parameters.

```
return_type            /* return type of the function f */
f(va_alist) /* va_alist: the parameter list */
va_dcl         /* va_dcl: declares va_alist. Note: no ; */
{
    va_list argp;    /* points to next arg to be processed */
             /* argp can be passed as arg */
             /* to another function */

    va_start(argp); /* sets up argp to point to 1st arg */
    ...
    /* for each argument to be processed:
     * arg_type is the type of the actual parameter after
     *   the default argument promotions  (see notes below).
     * va_arg   obtains the argument,
     * n        should be same type as the actual parameter
     */
    n = va_arg(argp, arg_type);
    ...
    va_end(argp);    /* cleans up */
}
```

Here is how maxn looks using the **varargs** interface. We highlight the differences from the **stdarg** version.

```
#include <varargs.h>
#include <float.h>       /* def of FLT_MIN */
/*
 *  maxn(nitems, f1, f2, ...)
 *     returns the max of its floating point args
 *  PARAMS
 *     nitems  int     # of floating point args that follow
 *     f1, ... float   args of which we take the max
 *  RETURNS
 *             float   the max
 *  NOTE
 *     if nitems is 0, print errmsg, return FLT_MIN
 */
/*VARARGS*/
float
maxn(va_alist)
va_dcl
{
    va_list ap;
    register int nitems, i;
    float max, f;
```

```
    va_start(ap);
    nitems = va_arg(ap, int);
    if (nitems == 0)
    {
        printf("maxn: nitems error\n");
        va_end(ap);
        return FLT_MIN;
    }

    /* peel off 1st float to start max */
    max = va_arg(ap, double);
    for (i = 1; i < nitems; i++)
    {
        f = va_arg(ap, double);
        max = (max > f ? max : f);
    }
    va_end(ap);

    return max;
}
```

The comment /*VARARGS*/ is for **lint**. /*VARARGS*/ tells **lint** that this is a **varargs** function and therefore disables checking for the number and type of arguments.

Note that the first time va_arg is called, it is called with type int, since the first parameter to max is an int. All subsequent calls to va_arg are with type double, since all subsequent arguments are of type float, and they are widened to double by the default argument promotions.

3.3.3 Portable approaches to stdarg

Given the differences between **varargs** and **stdarg**, neither of which may exist on some systems, we present a portable approach to the coding of functions with a variable number of arguments.

1. If your local environment lacks one, write a **stdarg.h** file. This is not as hard as it may sound. An example that works on many machines appears at the end of this section. A program in §8.3.2 can help you figure out the alignment requirements for automatic variables in your environment. This approach coincides nicely with our general principle to follow the ANSI interface whenever it is practical to do so. Then,

2. Write the function definition in both ANSI and non-ANSI style, using #ifdefs to delineate both versions.

Generally, we like to avoid the ugliness of #ifdefs in source files. But in this case, it is not clear if an ANSI compiler would tolerate a pre-ANSI definition for a **stdarg**-style function, even with a prototype declaration in scope. So to be conservative, we put in both styles.

The following version of maxn works in either an ANSI or non-ANSI environment, once you've provided a **stdarg.h** file.

```
#include <stdarg.h>
#include <float.h>        /* has the value of FLT_MIN */
/*
 *   maxn(nitems, f1, f2, ...)
 *       returns the max of its floating point args
 *   PARAMS
 *       nitems  int      # of floating point args that follow
 *       f1, ... float    args of which we take the max
 *   RETURNS
 *               float    the max
 *   NOTE
 *       if nitems is 0, print errmsg, return FLT_MIN
 */


float
#ifdef __STDC__
maxn(int nitems, ...)
#else
maxn(nitems) int nitems;
#endif
{
    va_list ap;
    float max, f;

    if (nitems == 0)
    {
        printf("maxn: nitems error\n");
        return FLT_MIN;
    }

    va_start(ap, nitems);

    /* peel off 1st float to start max */
    max = va_arg(ap, double);
```

```
    for (i = 1; i < nitems; i++)
    {
        f = va_arg(ap, double);
        max = (max > f ? max : f);
    }
    va_end(ap);

    return max;
}
```

Lest you think that the **stdarg** macros are long and complicated, we list here a typical set of **stdarg** definitions as they would appear in **stdarg.h**. These definitions would work on a 68000 machine, an 80286, or a VAX, and do not require an ANSI compiler.

```
typedef char *va_list;
# define va_start(ap, parm)  (ap = (char *)&(parm) \
                                  + sizeof(parm))
# define va_arg(ap, type)    (((type *)(ap += \
                                  sizeof(type)))[-1])
# define va_end(ap)
```

Note that in this implementation, va_end does nothing. It is nonetheless important to include it in your code—the environments that need va_end to clean up will get very confused without it.

It is not our purpose here to explain these macros, since their implementation is environment-dependent, but it is an interesting exercise for the reader to figure out how the macros work.

Exercise 3-1: stdarg. Write a function cat with the following specification.

```
char *
cat(destination, source1, source2, ..., sourcen, (char *)0);
char *destination, *source1, *source2, ..., *sourcen;
```

- cat concatenates the strings pointed to by source1, source2, ..., sourcen, putting the result in destination. It is a generalization of **strcat**; in copying the strings, null terminators will be removed from all strings except sourcen.

- The number of arguments is indicated by the presence of (char *)0 as the last argument.

- `cat` puts the resulting string in `destination`, which is assumed to have enough room.

- `cat` returns `destination`.

□

Solution to Exercise 3-1.

```
#include <stdarg.h>
/*
 *  Concatenate strings.
 *  cat(destination, source1, source2, ..., sourcen,
 *                                      (char *)0);
 *  PARAMS:  destination      ptr to area to hold result
 *           source1, source2  ptrs to strings
 *  RETURNS: destination.
 *  NOTE:    destination is assumed big enough to hold
 *           concatenated string.  no error checking done.
 */
/*VARARGS*/
char *
#ifdef __STDC__
cat(char *dest, . . .)
#else
cat(dest) char *dest;
#endif
{
    va_list ap;
    register char *d, *s;

    d = dest;
    va_start(ap, dest);
    for (s = va_arg(ap, char *); s != (char *)0;
        s = va_arg(ap, char *))
    {
        while (*d++ = *s++)
            ;
        d--;            /* write over the '\0' delimiter */
    }
    return dest;
}
```

□

3.4 Function pointers

Function pointers, i.e. pointers to functions, can be the operands of only a few operators. Pointer arithmetic or relational comparison on function pointers is not allowed. Strict typing conventions should be applied to function pointers. In particular, function pointers should not be mixed with pointers to other data types. For that reason, we discuss function pointers here and not in Chapter 7 on pointers.

Function pointers of the same type can be operands of the assignment (=) and equality operators (==, !=), and the two rightmost operands of the conditional operator (? :). For example

```
int (*fp)(), f(), n;

if (fp != f)
    fp = f;
```

A function pointer—just like any other pointer—can serve as a Boolean variable, as in

```
    . . .
if (fp)      /* if fp is a non-null pointer */
    (*fp)(n);
```

The code is equivalent to the more explicit

```
if (fp != (int(*)())0)
    (*fp)(n);
```

We have specified that only function pointers of the *same* type should be operands of the operators listed above. Similarly with rules FUNC2 and FUNC4, when passing a function pointer as an argument or returning it as a function value. But what constitutes the "same" type? The function's return type is part of the type of a function pointer. In ANSI, the parameter types also form part of the type of a function pointer. This can lead to problems in porting non-ANSI code to ANSI environments, if you want to use prototype-style function declarations.

## CHAPTER 4

PORTABLE USE OF ARITHMETIC DATA TYPES

C's arithmetic data types consist of *integral types* with different ranges and *floating-point types* with different ranges and precisions. The most important principle guiding the portable use of arithmetic data types is that the value of a data object must not exceed the *portable range* of the data object's type. The portable range of a type is the set of values that data objects of that type can contain in *all* reasonable environments.

Portable use of arithmetic data types can be tricky because the implicit conversions on operands of an operator differ among different C dialects and environments. The rules introduced in this chapter will help you avoid unexpected conversions, and will help you avoid overflow.

This chapter begins by recalling the different uses for arithmetic data types since the rules depend in part on the way the data types are used by the programmer. We review the history of arithmetic data types in C, and specify the subset of types that can be used portably. We then show two examples that illustrate the kinds of pitfalls that can harm the portability of programs using arithmetic data types. The chapter presents a set of rules for the portable use of arithmetic data types viewed as numbers. Since the rules depend on the concept of portable range, the portable range of each type is explained in detail. We illustrate the rules with a series of examples. Then a similar set of rules is presented for the portable use of arithmetic data types viewed as bit patterns. We discuss how to choose the right data types for different arithmetic purposes, including the "parameterization" of data types. We show the implications for data portability of the different ways integers are stored in memory. The chapter concludes with an examination of problems involved in the use of floating point numbers.

4.1 Uses of integral types

The constraints on the portable use of arithmetic data types are based on the semantics of their use, that is, what the data objects represent. To explain clearly the constraints that apply to operators on arithmetic data types, we must first distinguish the different purposes for which arithmetic data types are used in C.

As seen in §2.6, integral types in C can be used for a number of different purposes: to represent numbers (of course), but also to represent enumerations, bit patterns, and Boolean values. It is possible to use a variable of integral type for several of these purposes in succession.

For the purposes of the rules on integral types, the main distinction is between integral types used to represent *numbers* and integral types used to represent *bit patterns*. Numbers may in turn represent enumerations or Boolean values. Similarly, bit patterns may represent sequences of numbers, enumerations, and Boolean values of various sizes. We label the rules as follows: the rules for numbers are NUM1 to NUM7; the rules for bit patterns are BIT1 to BIT7; the rules for Boolean values are BOOL1 and BOOL2; the rule for floating point numbers is FLOAT1.

4.2 Arithmetic data types in C and portable C

4.2.1 A short history of arithmetic data types in C

The integral types that appear in [K&R] are `long`, `unsigned`, `int`, `short`, and `char`. Type `char` appears among the integral types because it can be used to store small integers. The collection of arithmetic types has expanded since the definition of C in [K&R]; most compilers now support unsigned versions of all the integral types: `unsigned char`, `unsigned short`, and `unsigned long`. (The type `unsigned int` is the same as `unsigned`.) The newer unsigned types first appeared in a Reference Manual internal to Bell Laboratories, [RefMan81], and now appear in all C "standards" documents, such as [SVPG RefMan], [X/OPEN], [ANSI], and [K&R2].

In addition to these widespread types, ANSI C introduces some new types: `signed char` and `long double`. ANSI C also allows `signed` to modify all existing integral types (`long`, `int`, `short`) without changing their meaning.[1] The new type `signed char` is intended to provide a character that is signed, whether or not `char` is a signed type in a given implementation. The new type `long double` implements extended-precision floating point arithmetic, if the hardware supports it. Otherwise, `long double` is the same as `double`.

4.2.2 Arithmetic data types in portable C

Which arithmetic types can portable C programs use? Portable C includes the original [K&R] types: `long`, `unsigned`, `int`, `short`, and `char`, as well as the newer unsigned types found in many compilers: `unsigned long`,

---

[1] An exception is bit-fields. The ANSI modifier `signed` may change the meaning of `int` in a bit-field, since in that context the signedness of `int` is environment dependent.

unsigned short, and unsigned char. We include the newer unsigned types in portable C despite their lack of universality because they are useful and they are widespread. Machines that lack these types can parameterize them in **environ.h** as follows:

```
typedef long      ulong; /* or unsigned, depending on
                          * machine & application */
typedef unsigned ushort;
typedef unsigned uchar; /* or char, if machine's
                        * characters are unsigned */
```

You could then use the types ulong, ushort, and uchar in place of the missing types in your environment.[2]

4.3 Pitfalls

Before we introduce the rules and a formal discussion of portable ranges, let's look at two examples of nonportable code involving integers. These examples demonstrate some of the problems that the rules will help you avoid.

Will the example below execute do_n_bigger or do_m_bigger?

```
/* Ambiguous comparison */
unsigned n = 32;
long m = -4;

if (n > m)
    do_n_bigger();
else
    do_m_bigger();
```

The behavior of this program fragment depends on which compiler you use because dialects of C differ in the "usual arithmetic conversions" that they perform. Look at the line

```
if (n > m)
```

In [K&R], the unsigned variable n is promoted to long. Since n's value remains unchanged at 32, the program performs the intuitive do_n_bigger.

In [SVPG RefMan], n and m both promote to unsigned long. If long is 32 bits on the machine, then m will have the value

---

[2] This is an imperfect solution since typedef'ing an unsigned as uchar may break code that expects sizeof(uchar) to be 1. Also, typedef'ing long as ulong may cause problems since their ranges may not be the same.

$$2^{32} - 4 = 2147483648 - 4 = 2147483644$$

Thus, the program performs `do_m_bigger`. This is probably not what the programmer intended!

[ANSI] follows [K&R] if `long` can represent all the values of an `unsigned`, e.g., on a machine with 16-bit `int`s; otherwise, [ANSI] follows [SVPG RefMan], e.g., on a machine with 32-bit `int`s.

The portable C version of this example appears in §4.6.5.

In the next example, we wish to put the program to sleep for 24 hours, using the UNIX library function **sleep**. What are the nonportable constructs here?

```
/* Sleep for a day */
#define DAY 86400    /* # seconds in day */
extern unsigned sleep();
...
sleep(DAY);
```

By its nature, this example has limited portability since it can only be ported to UNIX systems or others with a **sleep** function; **sleep** is not part of the ANSI standard C library. But even assuming a UNIX environment, this code will work on some machines yet fail on others.

We pass 86,400 seconds as the actual parameter to **sleep**, yet **sleep** expects an `unsigned` argument. In an environment with 32-bit `int`s, this is not a problem, since the constant `86400` is understood by the compiler to be of type `int`, and for positive numbers, the representation as `int` or `unsigned` is the same. But in an environment with 16-bit `int`s, the compiler will interpret `86400` as a `long` constant. In that case the **sleep** function will not receive the number that was passed; it will receive only 16 bits of it.

The nasty part of this portability problem is that it is a *silent*—but dangerous—problem. The code will compile and run without complaint in most environments. But in a 16-bit environment, it will produce incorrect results.[3] One reassurance is that **lint** can detect this problem.

The code violates function Rule FUNC2: *The actual and formal parameters of a function should have the same types.* But even if we cast explicitly

```
sleep((unsigned)DAY);
```

there would still be a problem, because 86,400 exceeds the portable range of

---

[3] If you were using an ANSI compiler and had included the prototype

```
unsigned sleep(unsigned);
```

then the compiler might at least warn you that the constant 86400 would be truncated.

`unsigned`. Unfortunately, there is no easy way to make such code portable, other than to do two half-day sleeps. You cannot portably cast 86,400 to `unsigned`. The ambiguity is in the library function **sleep** itself, which specifies an `unsigned` formal parameter, a type whose range of values varies greatly between environments. This problem afflicts many standard library functions.

4.4 Principles for the portable use of numbers

The basic principles that govern the portable use of numbers are contained in rules NUM1 and NUM2. Rule NUM1 stresses the importance of the portable range of a type. Rule NUM2 constrains the conversion from one arithmetic type to another.

NUM1: *The value of a data object of arithmetic type must lie within the portable range of that type.*

Rule NUM1 states a general principle concerning the value of data objects, but how do they get their values? Presumably by initialization, assignment, or as the result of other operations. We shall look at rules constraining arithmetic operations in portable C. The first is Rule NUM2 which constrains conversions from one arithmetic type to another.

NUM2: *A value to be converted must lie within the portable range of the type converted to.*

For example, the assignment

```
char d;

d = 256;
```

causes d to get the value 0 in machines with 8-bit bytes. This assignment is allowed by NUM1 since 0 is within the portable range of `char`, but it is prohibited by the more stringent requirements of Rule NUM2, since 256 lies outside the portable range of `char`.

As a result of NUM2, negative numbers should not be converted to unsigned types. Thus, the initialization

```
unsigned k = -1;
```

is not allowed in portable C.

4.5 Portable range

We have stressed the importance of the portable range of a type; now it is time to look more closely at just what the portable range is. Unfortunately for portability, C's definition of the range of values for integral data types is vague and machine-dependent. The [K&R] specification of C leaves the definition of these types largely to the compiler implementer: "The intent is that `short` and `long` should provide different lengths of integers where practical; `int` will normally reflect the most 'natural' size for a particular machine...each compiler is free to interpret `short` and `long` as appropriate for its own hardware. About all you should count on is that `short` is no longer than `long`."[4] One would like to be able to count on more than that, as in, say PL/1, where you can specify `FIXED BINARY(15)`—the number of bits of precision in the integer—or in Pascal, where you can specify the range of certain data types explicitly.

The size in bytes of the various arithmetic types is environment dependent. The size of a byte in bits is also environment dependent. Therefore, the range of values representable by each of the integral types is environment dependent. The range and precision of floating point types is also environment dependent.

4.5.1 Portable storage sizes of integral data types

Since the size in bytes of a type limits its range of values, in order to determine the portable range of various types, we first examine their portable sizes in bytes and bits. The *portable size* is the minimum size of the data type in all reasonable environments.

Portable storage size of integral types (Unsigned types have the same size as the corresponding signed types.)		
type	`sizeof`(type) in bytes	bitlength (# bits to store)
char	1	≥ 8
short	≥ 2	≥ 16
int	≥ 2	≥ 16
long	≥ 4	≥ 32

We can always assert the following comparisons of the number of bytes of storage taken up by the various integer data types, in any environment.

---

[4] [K&R], p. 34.

```
sizeof(char) < sizeof(short) ≤ sizeof(int) ≤ sizeof(long)
```

Note that the above inequalities tell us only about the number of bytes of storage and not about the portable range of values of the different data types.

4.5.2 Portable ranges of arithmetic data types

The *portable range* of a data type, shown in the following table, is the intersection of the ranges of values that can be found on all but the most deviant machines. A given machine may have a greater range of values for a particular data type than the portable range, but no reasonable machine should have a smaller range than the portable range. These ranges accord with the minimal limits defined for ANSI C's **limits.h** file. Note that the lower end of the portable range for signed types is defined to include one's-complement machines.

We use a Pascal-like notation for the portable range of a type. [a..b] means $\{x: a \le x \le b\}$, that is, all numbers between a and b, inclusive. For integers used as bit patterns, the analogous concept is the portable bit pattern length of a type, discussed in §4.7.

The type `char` can be either signed or unsigned in C, depending on the hardware and software environment. On machines where `char` is signed, its numeric range is at least $[-127..127]$. On machines where `char` is unsigned, its numeric range is at least $[0..255]$. Thus, the portable numeric range of `char` is the intersection of those two ranges: $[0..127]$. Since a `char` promotes to a signed type, `int`, in C, we classify `char` among the signed types, but with non-negative values only.

Portable range of integral types		
Signed types		
type	portable range	
`char`	$0 \le n < 2^7$	$[0..127]$
`short`	$\lvert n \rvert < 2^{15}$	$[-32,767..32,767]$
`int`	$\lvert n \rvert < 2^{15}$	$[-32,767..32,767]$
`long`	$\lvert n \rvert < 2^{31}$	$[-2,147,483,647..2,147,483,647]$
Unsigned types		
`unsigned char`	$0 \le n < 2^8$	$[0..255]$
`unsigned short`	$0 \le n < 2^{16}$	$[0..65,535]$
`unsigned`	$0 \le n < 2^{16}$	$[0..65,535]$
`unsigned long`	$0 \le n < 2^{32}$	$[0..4,294,967,295]$

Floating point data types			
type	maximum positive value	minimum positive value	decimal digits of precision
`float`	10^{37}	10^{-37}	6
`double`	10^{37}	10^{-37}	10

We can also picture the portable ranges of arithmetic types graphically. Note that the graph shown here is nowhere near being drawn to scale because of the huge disparities in the portable ranges.

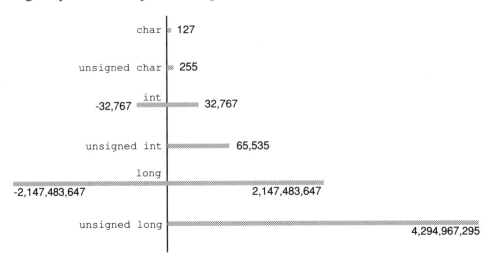

Portable ranges of arithmetic types

4.6 Rules for numbers

4.6.1 Overflow

Rule NUM1 stated that the value of an arithmetic data object must lie within its portable range. But it is possible for an integral operation to wrap around due to overflow, yielding a value within the portable range. Rule NUM1 is not enough to prevent this possibility. Just as Rule NUM2 restricts assignment to prevent wraparound, so Rule NUM3 restricts arithmetic operations.

NUM3: *Arithmetic operations must not overflow the portable range of the resulting type.*

Rule NUM3 is a constraint on the operators that could overflow: $+$ $-$ $*$ $+=$ $-=$ $*=$ $++$ $--$. By *overflow*, we mean exceeding the upper or lower end of the portable range. There are two reasons for avoiding overflow.

- Not all machines behave the same way on overflow. C guarantees that unsigned types wrap around silently, i.e., all unsigned integer operations are modulo $2^{\text{size of the integer in bits}}$. But for signed integral types, it is possible that overflow could raise an exception. Much C code assumes that on overflow the value will quietly wrap around, but this is not a portable assumption. Moreover, floating point types usually *do* raise an exception on overflow.

- Even if the machine *does* quietly wrap around on integer overflow (and most do), overflow is still not portable because it will occur at different points on different machines due to differences in the size of integral types in bits. Only if values remain within the portable range of the integral type can nonportable overflow be avoided.[5]

What is the "resulting type" of an operation, referred to in NUM3? We have seen that different compilers determine the resulting type differently. Portable C defines a "portable resulting type" for use in this rule. The portable resulting type of an operation will be defined in Rule NUM4.

To verify that your code satisfies the NUM rules on overflow, it suffices to use the following method of desk-checking an arithmetic operation:

---

[5] In certain cases we do not care if different machines wrap around at different points. For example, suppose we wish to generate ID numbers to identify certain objects in use. These objects may be retired from use and their IDs reused. The function `newid` returns a new ID that is not in use; it calls a Boolean function `inUse` to determine if an ID is still in use.

```
unsigned
newid()
{
    static unsigned id = 0; /* last id given out */

    while (inUse(++id))
        ;
    return id;
}
```

Function `newid` will behave differently on different machines; it will wrap around to zero at different points depending on the size in bits of type `unsigned`. Nonetheless, it provides the desired functionality on all machines: it returns a new, unused ID number; hence we can view it as portable. (We assume it is impossible for all ID numbers to be in use at once.)

1. Figure out the "portable resulting type" of the operation, using the following rule NUM4.

2. Make sure the result of the operation lies within the portable range of that portable resulting type.

3. Make sure that the operation does not overflow in *your* environment.

Sometimes, it is impossible to assure yourself in advance that overflow will not occur; in such cases it is necessary to check for overflow at runtime. (See §4.6.4).

4.6.2 "Resulting type" defined

Rule NUM4 provides the definition of the "portable resulting type" of an arithmetic operation.

NUM4: *In portable C we view a binary operator as if it promotes the operand of "smaller" type to the type of the operand of "larger" type, where "smaller" and "larger" are defined by the following two hierarchies:*

```
char, short, int, long, float, double
```

and

```
unsigned char, unsigned short, unsigned,
unsigned long.
```

In portable C we view unary operators as if they perform no implicit conversions; thus we view the type of the result as the same as the type of the operand.

We view the "portable resulting type" of a binary operator as the larger of the two operand types in the above hierarchies.

Although `double` and `float` are larger in range than `long`, a loss of precision may occur in going from an integral type to a floating point type.

In a given environment, the compiler's actual default arithmetic conversions may differ from the way they are viewed in portable C. It suffices that by programming *as if* these conversions occur, and adhering to the other rules in this chapter, you can achieve portable code.

4.6.3 Desk checking for overflow

The following examples illustrate how to desk-check for overflow using the NUM rules. The first example calculates the average temperature for a year in degrees Fahrenheit. Is the following code portable? Desk-check each operation for possible overflow.

```
/* average temperature for year */
#define DAYS_IN_YR   365

int sum;
int temperature[DAYS_IN_YR]; /* in degrees F */
float average;
int i;

for (i = 0; i < DAYS_IN_YR; i++)
    sum += temperature[i];
average = (float)sum / DAYS_IN_YR;
```

The only possible problem in applying Rule NUM3 here is the running total in sum. Let's estimate that the highest average temperature in the world is around 100°F. Then the highest possible value for sum is roughly 365*100 = 36500. Since this could overflow the portable range of int (which is [−32767..32767]), we should change the declaration of sum to make it a long. (We can't use unsigned since sum could be negative.)

```
/* average temperature for year */

long sum;
...
```

The next example provides another opportunity for desk-checking to make sure Rule NUM3 is followed.

```
/* assignment of long to short */

short s;
long g;

...
g %= 100;
s = (short)g;
```

We cast g explicitly to type short, even though it would be converted implicitly by assignment. This style of coding helps draw our attention to the type conversions involved.

```
s = (short)g;
```

The cast makes us careful to apply Rule NUM2 to assure ourselves that g is in the portable range of short: [−32767..32767]. Since we know by the previous statement

```
g %= 100;
```

that g must be in the range [−99..99], Rule NUM2 is easily satisfied here. There is no portability problem.

C compilers are free to rearrange the order of evaluation of subexpressions involving operators that are both commutative and associative, even in the presence of explicit parentheses. That is, in expressions containing several consecutive additions or multiplications, C can ignore parentheses.[6] Thus,

```
int a, b, c, d;

d = a + (b + c);
```

could be evaluated by a compiler as if it were written

```
d = (c + a) + b;
```

Fortunately, it is not necessary to desk-check for overflow on each possible permutation of the order of such subexpressions; one check will suffice. This is because portable C is willing to assume silent wraparound on overflow. If an operation silently wraps around and then wraps back again to the normal range, we consider it as if no overflow had occurred. We can generalize this observation to any subexpression overflow: if the overall expression does not overflow, we do not need to worry about subexpression overflow. For example, consider a possible implementation of `atoi`, a standard library function that converts strings of digits to integers.

```
/* atoi(s)     takes a string and converts it to int.
 * PARAMETERS  s    the string to be converted
 * RETURNS     int  the binary value
 * note        We assume the string contains only
 *             characters in the range '0' to '9'.
 *             We assume the string contains a number
 *             within the portable range of int.
 *             We assume s is not NULL.
 */
```

---

[6] ANSI changes this rule of C, allowing parentheses to coerce evaluation ordering as in other languages such as Fortran. However, portable C must follow the non-ANSI convention in this matter.

```
int
atoi(s)
char s[];
{
    int n = 0;

    while (*s != '\0')
    {
        n = 10 * n + *s - '0';
        s++;
    }
}
```

In the expression

```
n = 10 * n + *s - '0';
```

the + operation may overflow (for example if s is "32767" on a 16-bit machine), yet as long as the result of the entire expression fits in an int, there is no problem.

4.6.4 Runtime checking for overflow

Sometimes desk-checking cannot suffice to detect possible overflow, for instance when data are dependent on input. We can detect overflow at runtime in the addition of two positive integers by checking if the result is less than one of the operands, i.e., checking if wraparound has occurred. Unsigned types are the best types to use for code that detects runtime overflow, since they are guaranteed to wrap around without raising an exception.

The following example applies runtime checking while adding numbers input by the user. The example assumes only positive numbers are input.

```
/* add numbers input by user */
#include <stdio.h>
unsigned total;
int n;

total = 0;
while (scanf("%d", &n) == 1)
{
    total += (unsigned)n;
    if (total < (unsigned)n)
        handle_overflow();
}
```

In the example, overflow will occur at different points on different machines, so in one sense the behavior of the program will differ between environments. But that may not matter; the important thing is that we are able to detect and deal with overflow when it occurs.

The portable range, as shown earlier in this chapter, defines the portable maximum value of a type, i.e., the largest value that can fit in a data object of that type on *all* reasonable machines. It is also possible to define a macro that gives, in *each* environment, the maximum value of a type *in that environment*. For example, the following macros define environment-dependent maxima for types `unsigned` and `int` using the names specified by ANSI.

```
#define UINT_MAX    ((unsigned)(~0))
#define INT_MAX     ((int)(UINT_MAX >> 1))
```

On a given machine, `UINT_MAX` may be greater than the maximum of the portable range of an `unsigned`.

These definitions demonstrate the difference between a portable *specification* and a portable *implementation* of a macro. The specification "`UINT_MAX` is the maximum value of an `unsigned int`" is portable to all environments, though the implementation of `UINT_MAX` may be a `#define` to a different constant on each machine. The definitions shown here are interesting as examples of portable implementations of the `UINT_MAX` and `INT_MAX` macros. The definitions rely on the binary encoding of numbers at the bit pattern level, and on two's-complement representation.

We can now show an alternate way to perform a runtime check for overflow in cases where you wish to use signed arithmetic but are concerned about machines that may trap on integer overflow. This method avoids any possible overflow by testing before actually performing the addition.

```
/* add numbers input by user */
#include <stdio.h>
int total;
int n;

total = 0;
while (scanf("%d", &n) == 1)
{
    if (total > INT_MAX - n)
        handle_overflow();
    else
        total += n;
}
```

Note that in the above version, as in the earlier version, `total` may overflow the portable range of type `int` on some machines. Although this technically violates Rule NUM1, and will reach overflow at different points on different machines, the code is portable in that it correctly handles overflow in all environments.

4.6.5 Signed and unsigned types

Having seen some examples of the application of the NUM rules, we return for a closer look at the issue of the "resulting type" of an operation. The careful reader may have realized that our set of rules is not yet complete. One problem in following Rule NUM3 is that the "resulting type" of an arithmetic operation is not always portably defined, even by Rule NUM4. We need a new rule, NUM5, to eliminate the cases where ambiguities could arise.

NUM5: *Don't mix signed and unsigned types in operations on numbers.*

You can, however, freely mix all signed types with each other, including floating point types. Similarly, you can mix all unsigned types with each other.

As we saw in the `do_n_bigger` example, the "usual arithmetic conversions" are not as "usual" as one would like: the major existing dialects of C disagree on the promotion of unsigned types. The basic division is between *value preserving* promotions, espoused by ANSI C, and *unsignedness preserving* promotions, espoused by [SVPG RefMan].

- Value-preserving promotions attempt to promote a type to the smallest type large enough to hold its values in a given implementation; thus, `unsigned short` can be promoted to `int` in some environments, `unsigned int` in others.

- Unsignedness-preserving promotions attempt to promote unsigned types to larger unsigned types; thus, `unsigned short` is always promoted to `unsigned int`.[7]

If you adhere to Rule NUM5, you can ignore all these differences.

We say an operation is *signed* if its operands are signed types (after the usual arithmetic conversions). We say an operation is *unsigned* if its operands are unsigned types (after the usual arithmetic conversions). The purpose of Rule NUM5 is to make the programmer think carefully about the effects of mixing unsigned and signed data types. There are several reasons for being careful about the sign of operations.

---

[7] See [ANSI Rat], Section 3.2.1.1, "Characters and integers," p. 34.

1. As seen in the `do_n_bigger` example, mixing signed and unsigned operands can lead to unintuitive results with the comparison operators (<, >, <=, >=). If a negative number is "promoted" to an unsigned type in the course of the usual arithmetic conversions, the results will be undesirable.

2. In calculating overflow, one must know the type of the result of an operation. That type may not be portably defined. For example, in the fragment

```
unsigned u;
long b;
unsigned long total;

u = 5;
b = 2147483647;
total = u + b;
```

is there overflow? In [ANSI] and [K&R], u + b has type `long`; its value overflows the portable range of `long`. In [SVPGRefMan], u and b are converted to type `unsigned long`, and u + b has type `unsigned long`; its value does not overflow the portable range of an `unsigned long`.

To make the code portable, follow Rule NUM5 to decide whether we want an unsigned or signed addition. In this case, assuming that b would not have negative values, an unsigned operation would make the code portable:

```
total = u + (unsigned long)b;
```

We are now ready to rewrite the `do_n_bigger` example in portable C. Following Rule NUM5, we must decide if the comparison operation > is to be a signed or an unsigned operation. Since one of the operands, m, can have a negative value, we assume that > is a signed operation.

```
/* Ambiguous comparison */
unsigned n = 32;
long m = -4;

if ((long)n > m)
    do_n_bigger();
else
    do_m_bigger();
```

The portable version of the code casts n to `long` so that both operands of > are signed types. This will work as long as we know in advance that the value of n will not be greater than the maximum value of a `long` (on a 32-bit machine, an `unsigned` could hold larger values than a `long`). If n might have a greater value than the maximum value of a `long`, the code must be more complicated. (Exercise: how would you code in such a case?)

4.6.6 Assignment

Style suggestion: *Both operands of an assignment (=) should have the same type.*

Thus, the right-hand operand should be cast explicitly to the type of the left-hand operand.

Being explicit about the cast involved in an assignment forces the programmer to be aware of the conversion involved, and the necessity to apply Rule NUM2: *"A value to be converted must lie within the portable range of the type converted to."*

The following fragment shows how to apply the style suggestion:

```
float fahr, celsius;

celsius = (float)((5.0 / 9.0) * (fahr - 32.0));
```

The expression `((5.0 / 9.0) * (fahr - 32.0))` has type `double` since the constants have type `double`. The cast to `float`, while implicit in the assignment, is made explicit here. By writing the cast explicitly, the programmer reminds the reader of the code that precision is being lost in this operation.

4.6.7 Representation of negative numbers

Despite Rule PORT2: *"Avoid relying on the representation of values,"* it can sometimes be helpful to understand the different ways signed integers are represented in hardware. There are three standard representations: two's-complement, one's-complement, and sign-magnitude. We will ignore sign-magnitude representation since it is rare. Portable C assumes two's-complement representation, although you can port to one's-complement machines with some effort.

Two's-complement is by far the most common representation, and C is prejudiced in its favor. For example, when negative numbers are converted to unsigned types, they are stored in two's-complement form, regardless of the underlying architecture.

In two's-complement representation, a negative number is indicated by a 1 in the high order bit, called the *sign bit*. To represent a negative number in the range $[-2^{n-1}..-1]$, where n is the *bitlength*—the number of bits in the representation of the integral type—simply add 2^n to the number.

It is helpful to picture two's-complement arithmetic on the face of a clock. For simplicity, let's take an unlikely bitlength of 3 bits (n=3). Actually, this would be the bitlength for a bit-field declared

```
typedef struct {
    int number : 3;
} TEENY;
```

Then the unsigned numbers we can represent are in the range [0..7]. We can view the two's-complement representation as:

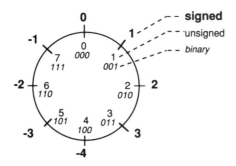

Two's complement
bitlength n=3

Note that the binary pattern of all ones (all bits set) represents -1, and that the range of negative numbers exceeds the range of positive numbers by 1. Given a bit pattern with the high bit set, we can figure out its two's-complement representation by subtracting from 8 (2^3). That is, given a bit pattern with the high bit set, we can figure out the number it represents as follows: let x be the interpretation of the bit pattern as an unsigned integer. Then its signed interpretation is $-(2^3-x)$ or $x-8$.

Following is the two's-complement representation for a more typical example, n=16.

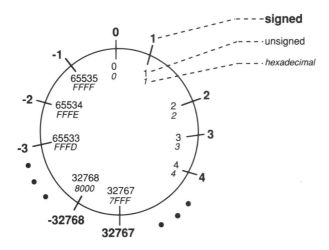

Two's complement
bitlength n=16

One's-complement representation is rarer, but is found, for example, on Unisys Univac machines. A negative number is indicated by a 1 in the high order bit. Negative numbers are represented by taking the bitwise complement of the absolute value of the number. Thus, if k is an integer in the range $[-2^{n-1}..2^{n-1}]$, where n is the bitlength of the type, $-k$ and $\tilde{}k$ have the same representation. Following is a picture of one's-complement arithmetic for n=3.

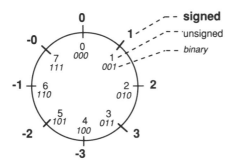

One's complement
bitlength n=3

Note that the binary pattern of all ones (all bits set) represents -0. Thus, there are two representations of zero in one's-complement arithmetic. They should compare as equal. Following is the one's-complement representation for n=16:

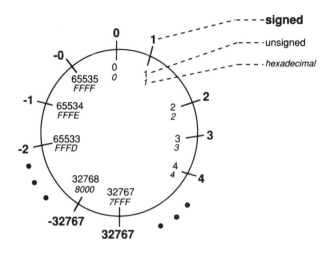

One's complement
bitlength n=16

One's-complement machines can be difficult targets for porting C code, especially in their handling of bit patterns. We therefore generally exclude them from the universe of C portability because one's-complement arithmetic causes so many portability problems for C that it would be difficult to formulate simple, reasonable rules for portable C if one's-complement machines had to be included. The C language is biased toward two's-complement machines and produces difficult issues on other architectures. For example, suppose we have a one's-complement machine with 16-bit `int`s. Then in the fragment

```
unsigned a;

if (a & 0177776)
    . . .
```

if the compiler treats `0177776` as type `int`, then by the usual arithmetic conversions, it is converted to `unsigned`, and its value changes to `0177777`.[8] Surely this is an unexpected result!

---

[8] The number 0177776 has the value −1. By [K&R], negative values, when converted to unsigned type, are stored in two's-complement representation. Hence its value changes to 0177777. However, existing implementations of C on one's-complement machines solve the problem by simply ignoring this specification and do not store the value in two's-complement representation.

4.6.8 Constants

In portable C, we view all integer constants as having type `int` or `long`; we view character constants as if they have type `char`, and floating point constants as having type `double`.

For each value in the relevant portable range of an arithmetic type, there should be at least one way to specify an integer constant with that value. A cast may be necessary to give the constant its desired type.

ANSI-conforming compilers treat integer constants differently than non-ANSI compilers. For example, in an environment like the IBM PC with 16-bit `int`s, the constant `0x8000` is treated as an `int` with value −32,768 by non-ANSI compilers, and as an `unsigned` with value 32,768 by ANSI compilers.

ANSI also allows a constant to be suffixed by `u`, `ul`, or `f` (or `U`, `UL`, or `F`) to explicitly indicate various unsigned types or `float`, but this syntax is not portable to non-ANSI compilers.[9]

You can avoid the problem of dialect differences in the handling of constants by following rules NUM1 and NUM6. By Rule NUM1, each constant must lie within the portable range of its type. Rule NUM6 tells how to write long constants.

NUM6: *Number constants of type* `long` *should be written with an* L *suffixed to the decimal, octal, or hexadecimal format.*

For example, the constant `120000` violates Rule NUM1. It may be an `int` in your environment, but it is not within the portable range of `int`. To write it as a `long`, following Rule NUM6, write `120000L`.

Constants of type `int`, `long`, and `double` can be written directly in portable C. Other signed or unsigned type constants must be specified by applying an appropriate cast to an `int`, `long`, or `double` constant, meanwhile observing

---

[9] Non-ANSI compilers use the following rule for unsuffixed constants:

- A decimal constant is of type `int` unless it won't fit in an `int`; then it is of type `long`.

- An octal or hexadecimal constant is of type `int` unless it won't fit in an `unsigned`; then it is of type `long`.

ANSI-conforming compilers use the following rule for unsuffixed constants:

- A decimal constant has the first type in the following list into which it can fit: `int`, `long`, `unsigned long`.

- An octal or hexadecimal constant has the first type in the following list into which it can fit: `int`, `unsigned`, `long`, `unsigned long`.

rules NUM1 and NUM2. Thus, the unsigned constant with value 60,000 should be written `(unsigned)60000L`.

It would be nice to encapsulate the cast in a parameterized constant like

```
#define MAX_VALUE    (unsigned)60000L
```

However, it is probably not a good idea to put the cast in the parameterized constant because not all compilers allow casts in initializers. Thus, it is more portable to write

```
#define MAX_VALUE    60000L
```

and cast `MAX_VALUE` explicitly when using it.

That way you can avoid casting when using `MAX_VALUE` as an initializer.

C does not actually have negative constants. A negative number is treated as an expression consisting of the unary minus operator followed by a positive constant. The positive constant is subject to all our NUM rules.

Exercise 4-1: Writing portable constants. Following is a list of constants. Determine if each one is portable or not, according to rules NUM1, NUM2, and NUM6.

```
-32768
0x8000
(long)0x8000
0x8000L
(unsigned)32768L
32000
(short)32000
(short)0x7d00
(char)127
(char)128
60000L
0L
2147483648L
(unsigned long)2147483648L
```

☐

Solution to Exercise 4-1.

`-32768`   nonportable. `32768` lies outside the portable range of `int`.

`0x8000`   nonportable. Lies outside the portable range of `int`. Note this constant may have the same value as the previous example, viz., on a machine with 16-bit integers. Or, it may have the value +32,768.

`(long) 0x8000` nonportable. Casting to `long` won't change the fact that this is a negative number on machines with 16-bit integers. Doesn't follow Rule NUM6.

`0x8000L` portable. Within the portable range of a `long`. Note here that suffixing an L works, while casting to `long` does not.

`(unsigned) 32768L` portable. `32768` is within the portable range of `long`, but not within the portable range of `int`. Thus, the format shown here with L is preferable to writing `(unsigned) 32768`.

`32000` portable. Within the portable range of `int`.

`(short) 32000` portable. Within the portable range of `short`.

`(short) 0x7d00` portable. Same value as previous, using hexadecimal representation.

`(char) 127` portable. Within the portable range of `char`.

`(char) 128` nonportable. Outside the portable range of `char`. On machines where `char` is a signed type, this value may sign-extend.

`60000L` portable. Within the portable range of a `long`.

`0L` portable. Within the portable range of a `long`.

`2147483648L` nonportable. Outside the portable range of a `long`.

`(unsigned long) 2147483648L` portable. Strictly speaking, 2,147,483,648 is outside the portable range of a `long` and thus violates NUM1. However, we make an exception for `unsigned longs`, since this is the only way to write such a constant.

□

Here is a longer example illustrating the use of Rule NUM6.

```
main()
{
    f(40000);
    ...
}
```

```
int
f(n)
int n;
{
    . . .
}
```

This code violates Rule NUM6. It will work on machines with 32-bit `int`s, but will fail on machines with 16-bit `int`s. To make the code portable, first, following NUM6, change `main` so the call to `f` reads

```
f(40000L);
```

This change should sensitize the programmer to the fact that now Rule FUNC2, *"The actual and formal parameters of a function should have the same types,"* is violated. Then, following Rule FUNC2, change the function definition of `f`, so it takes a `long` argument.

```
int
f(n)
long n;
{
    . . .
}
```

What if `f` is a library function that you cannot change, as in the **sleep** example in §4.3.

Then there is no simple fix for portability. You have three choices:

1. Exclude 16-bit machines from your universe of portability.

2. Rewrite your application so you don't need to use values outside the portable range of the parameters of the standard library functions.

3. Use your own library function instead of **sleep**.

4.6.9 Division

NUM7: *The integer division operators (/ % /= %=) require non-negative operands.*

Integer division is not well defined on negative numbers because the direction of truncation is not specified in C. For example, is $-9/5$ equal to -2 or -1? The answer depends on the implementation, so the expression is nonportable. One alternative is to use or emulate the ANSI library function `div`, which performs integer division with a well-specified direction of truncation.

4.7 Integral types as bit patterns

The main portability problems that arise from using integral data types as bit patterns are due to unexpected sign extension and to exceeding the portable bitlength of a type. The BIT rules presented in this section will help you avoid these problems. The rules also prevent nonportable shifting and nonportable bit pattern constants.

4.7.1 Portable bitlength of types

For each bit pattern you use in C, you must consider its *bitlength*, the number of significant bits in the pattern. For example, you might define a bit pattern that represents the ownership permissions of a file. Suppose you allow read, write, and execute permissions for three different groups of users. Then you need a bit pattern with bitlength 9 to represent the permissions of the file. In choosing a type to represent the permissions, you must choose a type whose portable bit length is at least 9. Thus, `char` would not suffice. We summarize these ideas in Rule BIT1.

BIT1: *The bitlength of a bit pattern represented by a data object of integral type must not exceed the portable bitlength of its type.*

For example, a bit pattern of bitlength 13 or 16 can be represented by an `int`; a bit pattern of bitlength 17 requires a `long`. We repeat here the portable bitlengths of the integral types from §4.5.1.

Portable bitlength of integral types used as bit patterns	
type	portable bitlength for bit patterns
`char` `unsigned char`	≥8
`short` `unsigned short`	≥16
`int` `unsigned`	≥16
`long` `unsigned long`	≥32

Note that from the point of view of a bit pattern, the signedness of its type is irrelevant to its bitlength. Signedness is essentially irrelevant when using integers as bit patterns. However, signedness does play a role in sign extension, so we need to be aware of it.

4.7.2 Sign extension

Sign extension occurs when a data object of signed integral data type is converted to a wider integral data type, regardless of whether the wider type is signed or not. The sign bit (high order bit) is repeated to fill in all the new high-order bits in the wider type. Thus, for example, on a machine with 16-bit `shorts` and 32-bit `longs`, the assignments

```
short s = 0xA000, t = 0x6000;
unsigned long j, k;

j = (unsigned long)s;
k = (unsigned long)t;
```

will cause the variable `j` to have the value 0xFFFFA000, and `k` to have the value 0x6000. For `j`, the sign bit 1 of `s` is used to pad out the new 16 high order bits, while for `k`, the sign bit 0 of `t` is used to pad out the 16 high order bits. The reason for sign extension is simple: it preserves the numeric value in both one's and two's-complement notation. Thus, assuming two's complement notation, both `j` and `s` have the value $-24,576$, while both `k` and `t` have the value 24,576.

Sign extension occurs when widening a signed type, but not when widening an unsigned type. While sign extension is "natural" for numbers, it can create unintended effects for bit patterns. Consider the following code written for a VAX, which has 32-bit `ints`.

```
#define PERMA     0x00001      /* permission for group A */
#define PERMB     0x00002      /* permission for group B */
...
#define PERMP     0x08000      /* permission for group P */
#define PERMQ     0x10000      /* permission for group Q */
...
long permissions;     /* bit sequence of Boolean
                       * values, bitlength is 17 */
permissions = PERMQ;
if (permissions & PERMP)
     allow_p();       /* permit group P to use object */
```

This code fails dangerously on a machine with 16-bit `ints`. When such a machine evaluates `permissions & PERMP`, it promotes the integer constant 0x8000 to the long constant 0xFFFF8000. Hence, `allow_p` would be executed! (This problem would not occur on an ANSI compiler, since 0x8000 is treated as an `unsigned` constant and hence not sign extended when promoted to `long`.)

The simplest way to make the code portable is to change all the constants to long constants, since bitlength 17 won't fit in an `int`.

```
#define PERMA    0x00001L    /* permission for group A */
#define PERMB    0x00002L    /* permission for group B */
...
#define PERMP    0x08000L    /* permission for group P */
#define PERMQ    0x10000L    /* permission for group Q */
```

4.7.3 Bit pattern rules

To avoid the problems of unexpected sign extension, follow the BIT rules.

BIT2: *Signed and unsigned integral types can represent bit patterns, and can be mixed in expressions, though unsigned types are preferable. We view a binary bitwise operator as if it promotes the operand of "smaller" type to the type of the operand of "larger" type, where "smaller" and "larger" are defined by the following hierarchy:*

```
char
```
or `unsigned char`,
```
   short
```
or `unsigned short`,
```
   int
```
or `unsigned int`,
```
   long
```
or `unsigned long`

For bit patterns, signed and unsigned types are essentially the same, but we need to be careful in combining them. The purest solution is to use only unsigned types to represent bit patterns. If you can do so, you will not encounter unexpected sign extension. However, in real life, you must often deal with externally defined structures or constants that are defined as signed types. When mixing types, consider rules BIT3 and BIT4.

BIT3: *Beware of bit patterns of bitlength 8 or 16.*

Rule BIT3 is our least prescriptive rule because there are no simple solutions to the problem. If you use signed types for bit patterns of bitlength 8 or 16, and the highest bit is set, you will encounter sign extension. To handle the problem, you must mask the result.

For example, suppose you have defined a function `f` as

```
int
f(lb)
long lb;
{
    ...
```

where f takes a long bit pattern as its argument. If you write

```
int bits;

bits = 0xF000;
f((long)bits);
```

you will get sign extension on a machine with 16-bit ints. Better to mask first and say

```
f(bits & 0xffffL);
```

4.7.4 Bit pattern constants

Rule BIT4 for bit pattern constants is similar to Rule NUM6 for number constants.

BIT4: *Append an* L *to bit pattern constants of bitlength greater than 16. Where possible, cast constants to unsigned types. Use octal or hexadecimal formats for bit pattern constants—don't use decimal format.*

We avoid decimal format because it is machine dependent whether certain constants are negative, while in octal or hexadecimal format we can write all constants as positive numbers.

Because our bit pattern constants are preferably prefixed by a cast to an unsigned type, there can be problems in using them in places where constant expressions are needed, e.g. initializers, case labels, etc. In such cases, it may be necessary to use signed constants, being careful to avoid situations of sign extension by following BIT3.

4.7.5 Shifting

Shift and mask operations have two purposes in C.

- We shift and mask bit patterns in order to be able to extract certain subsets of their bits.

- Since non-negative integers have a portable bit pattern encoding, we can use shifts and masks on non-negative numbers to efficiently implement multiplication and division by powers of two.[10] For example, we can say

  x >> 7 instead of x / 128

---

[10] Right shifting does *not* work as a portable shortcut for division on negative operands. Why?

x << 2 instead of x * 4

x & 0x1F instead of x % 32

There are two rules constraining the use of shift operators. The first constrains the size of the shift. The second rule deals with right shifting on signed quantities.

BIT5: *For the shift operators (<< >> <<= >>=), if the type of the left operand is in the left column, then the right operand should be in the range specified by the right column.*

Left Operand	Right Operand
char unsigned char	[0..7]
short unsigned short int unsigned	[0..15]
long unsigned long	[0..31]

That is, the right operand of the shift operator cannot be negative, nor can it equal or exceed the portable bitlength of the left operand.

Rule BIT6 concerns right shifts on signed operands. When the left operand of the right shift operator >> is a signed type, C permits the shift to be implemented as an arithmetic shift operation (fill vacated bits with original sign bit) or a logical shift (fill vacated bits with zeros). The choice is left to the compiler implementer. Rule BIT6 offers two ways to avoid this source of nonportability.

BIT6: *For >> with a left operand of signed type, either*

- *Mask the result to the desired number of bits, or*

- *Cast the left operand to the appropriate unsigned type.*

When the left-hand operand of >> is an unsigned type, C mandates a logical shift. Thus, casting to an unsigned type yields uniform behavior.

For example, instead of

```
long m;
...
m >>= 3;
```

we should say, following Rule BIT6,

```
unsigned long m;
...
m >>= 3;
```

or if your environment lacks `unsigned long`,

```
#define MASK3 0x1FFFFFFFL /* assuming 32-bit long */
long m;
...
m = (m >> 3) & MASK3;
```

`MASK3` should be defined in **environ.h**, where it can be changed according to the size of `long`.

Exercise 4-2: Macro for bit pattern constants. Write a macro `BITS(n, m)` that yields an integer constant with only bits n through m turned on; the rest of its bits should be 0. We number the bits of an integer 0, 1, 2, ... (bitlength of the integer) − 1, in order of increasing significance. That is,

$$0 \leq n \leq m < \text{BITSPERINT}$$

Your solution should obey all the BIT rules.

Solution to Exercise 4-2. One possible solution is the following:

```
#define BITS(n, m)   (~(~0 << (m) << 1)&(~0 << (n)))
```

Note that we say `~0 << (m) << 1` rather than `~0 << ((m)+1)` because the latter formulation might violate Rule BIT5. □

4.8 Bit-fields vs integer bit patterns

Bit patterns can be represented in C using integers or using bit-fields in a structure. Although bit-fields in a structure, like `enums`, offer some nice features, they have portability problems. Since all the functionality of bit-fields can be reproduced more portably using integer bit patterns, we recommend using the latter.

4.8.1 Advantages of bit-fields

Bit-fields offer a fully formed integral data type of a size smaller than the standard integral types. It is more readable to assign a value to a bit-field, or to do arithmetic on a bit-field, than to do the corresponding operation on a bit pattern inside an integral type, since the latter often involves masking.

For example, suppose we use a bit-field to hold an enumeration of different machine language instruction codes:

```
struct instruction {
    unsigned i_type:     2;
    unsigned i_opcode:   3;
    unsigned i_operand1: 3;
    ...
} instruction;

#define ADD       1
#define INV       2
#define SUBTRACT  3
...
```

To assign a particular value to the opcode, we could use a simple assignment statement:

```
instruction.i_opcode = SUBTRACT;
```

To perform an equivalent assignment using a bit pattern stored in an integer would require shifting and masking:

```
#define TYPE_MASK     0xC000
#define OPCODE_MASK   0x3800
#define OPCODE_OFFSET 13

unsigned short instruction;
    ...
instruction &= ~OPCODE_MASK;    /* clear opcode */
instruction |= (SUBTRACT << OPCODE_OFFSET);
```

4.8.2 Advantages of integer bit patterns

Efficiency can be served by using integer bit patterns, since more than one Boolean operation can be performed at once. For example,

```
#define READ   (unsigned)0x1
#define WRITE  (unsigned)0x2
#define EXEC   (unsigned)0x4

unsigned perm;
...
if (perm & (READ|WRITE|EXEC))
    ...
```

tests both the read flag, the write flag, and the exec flag at once. (Note that (READ|WRITE|EXEC) is a constant flag that may be computed at compile time.) If written using bit-fields, it would have to be written

```
struct perm {
    unsigned read: 1;
    unsigned write:1;
    unsigned exec: 1;
} perm;

...

if (perm.read || perm.write || perm.exec)
    ...
```

which is less efficient.

4.8.3 Portability problems of bit-fields

Despite the greater clarity of bit-field operations in some instances, bit-fields have a number of portability problems:

1. The maximum number of bits in a bit-field varies between implementations. According to [K&R], the maximum size of a bit-field is constrained by the size of a "word" in bits. Hence, it is nonportable to declare bit-fields with more than 16 bits.

2. The types allowed for bit-fields are implementation-defined. The type `unsigned` is the most portable type to use, as in the example of `struct instruction` just shown. Although `int` is allowed as the type of a bit-field in most compilers, the bit-field may nonetheless be treated as an unsigned number if the compiler implementer chooses. That is, the signedness of bit-fields is unspecified.[11]

3. Bit-fields are often used to represent layouts, as in the example above of a machine language instruction. The problem is that the layout of bit-fields within an integer is implementation-defined. Some compilers fill integers from low significance to high significance bits with bit-fields. Some compilers fill integers in the opposite direction. Moreover, in many implementations, padding is inserted in the structure to keep each bit-field within a word boundary. Since word boundaries vary between environments, the padding between bit-fields is environment-dependent. Thus, it is impossible to keep the analogy of a bit-field with an external layout in a portable way.

---

[11] [K&R],[ANSI]

This problem does not exist when using integers to represent bit patterns, since the layout of bits in the binary representation of a number is portably defined. (However, the layout of bytes is not; see §4.11.1.)

Because the layout of bit-fields is not portably defined, never mix bit-field representations with integral bit pattern representations for the same data. Such code is always environment-dependent. For example, some people put a bit-field in a union and then manipulate the fields as bit patterns for "efficiency."

```
union u {
    struct perm {
        unsigned u_read:  1;
        unsigned u_write: 1;
        unsigned u_exec:  1;
    } u_p;
    unsigned char u_perm_bits;
} perm;

perm.u_p.u_read = perm.u_p.u_write =
perm.u_p.u_exec = 0;
...
if (perm.u_perm_bits & 03)
    do_read_write();
```

The above code is nonportable. A union should never be used to view bit-fields as a bit pattern, because such code relies on an ordering of the bit-fields within the integer, which may vary between machines.

4. The above portability problems are also significant for data portability: sending the bit-fields between different machines. Because of the differences shown above, it is difficult to use bit-fields for communications between machines of diverse architecture.

4.8.4 The rule

We summarize the foregoing discussion in a simple rule for portable C.

BIT7: *Use integral types, instead of bit-field structure members, to represent bit patterns.*

4.9 Booleans

Any integral or pointer type can be used to represent Boolean values. In C, there are really two kinds of Boolean values:

- Boolean values that result from a Boolean operation (`&&` `||` `!`), a comparison operation (`>` `<` `>=` `<=`), or an equality operation (`==` `!=`) are the integers 1 (which encodes the Boolean value *true*) or 0 (which encodes the Boolean value *false*). These values can also be assigned to a Boolean variable.

- *Any* integral or pointer value can be viewed as a Boolean value, in which case a non-zero integer (or non-null pointer) encodes the value *true*, while zero (or the null pointer) encodes the value *false*.

Booleans are used as the operands of the Boolean operators `!`, `&&`, `||`, and the first operand of `?:`. They are also used in the conditional statements, `if ()`, `while ()`, `do...()`, and `for (;;)`. They are used as the operands of the assignment operator `=` and the equality operators `==` and `!=`. They can be passed as function arguments and used as the return value of a function.

BOOL1: *Any integer or pointer type can be used as a Boolean, but floating point types cannot.*

Floating point types are excluded from use as Booleans because small floating point numbers can be zero in one environment and non-zero in another. Also, floating point zero may not be all-bits zero (*false*) in some environments.

BOOL2: *For the Boolean operators (`&&` and `||`), pointer and integral operands can be mixed.*

Unlike other operators, for which pointers and integers other than 0 cannot portably be mixed, the Boolean operators `&&` and `||` can mix pointer and integral operands. For example

```
char *p;
char ready_to_go;
...
if ((p = malloc(BUFSIZ)) && ready_to_go)
    go_ahead(p);
```

The following example of nonportable code follows closely the nonportable model shown in the [SVID] on the manual page for **getopt**. The example reads the arguments on the command line, and if the −m or −p flag is set on the command line, arranges for appropriate processing.

```
main(argc, argv)
int argc;
char *argv[];
{
    int option;
    char mflag; /* true if -m on command line */
    char pflag; /* true if -p on command line */

    while ((option = getopt(argc, argv, "mp")) != EOF)
        switch ((char)option)
        {
        case 'm':
            mflag++;
            break;
        case 'p':
            pflag++;
            break;
        case '?':
            fprintf(stderr, "usage: %s [-m] [-p]\n",
                    argv[0]);
        }
    if (mflag)
        do_mprocess();
    if (pflag)
        do_pprocess();
}
```

The example is nonportable for two reasons.

- First, the Boolean variables `mflag` and `pflag` are not initialized. The code assumes that by default they will be initialized to *false*, but that is not a portable assumption for automatic variables.[12]

- Second, the code uses the common C-ism `mflag++` to set the value of `mflag` to *true*. This practice arose because on the PDP-11, incrementing an integer is faster than assigning it a value. But surely this is a misplaced optimization, especially in startup code, which is executed only once.[13] What

---

[12] See [K&R], p.37.

[13] On a typical RISC chip, assignment may be faster and more compact than incrementing if the target is in memory. In no case is the assignment slower on a RISC.

we wish to do is assign the value *true* to `mflag`; the ++ operator here is confusing to the reader. Moreover, at least in theory, using ++ could cause wraparound to zero, which would unintentionally yield the wrong result. We therefore recommend against this practice.

To make the example portable, initialize the Boolean variables properly, and assign them values using = rather than ++. You may prefer to define TRUE and FALSE in your file **environ.h**.

```
#define TRUE    1
#define FALSE   0

main(argc, argv)
int argc;
char *argv[];
{
    int option;
    char mflag = FALSE;    /* -m option set */
    char pflag = FALSE;    /* -p option set */

    while ((option = getopt(argc, argv, "mp"))
            != EOF)
        switch (option)
        {
        case 'm':
            mflag = TRUE;
            break;
        case 'p':
            pflag = TRUE;
            break;
        case '?':
            fprintf(stderr, "usage: %s [-m] [-p]\n",
                    argv[0]);
        }
    if (mflag)
        do_mprocess();
    if (pflag)
        do_pprocess();
}
```

We have said that integers can be used to encode Boolean values. The integers that encode Booleans can be viewed as numbers or as bit patterns. A bit pattern of all zeros represents *false*; any other bit pattern represents *true*. Consider the following example.

```
unsigned flags = 0xFFFF;     /* a bit pattern */
...
if (flags)        /* if any flags are set */
    do_flag_routines();
```

The problem is that on a one's-complement machine with 16-bit integers, the
value 0xFFFF evaluates to zero, so flags would be *false*! This example illustrates another problem of doing bit operations in a one's-complement environment. For this reason we generally exclude one's-complement machines from the
universe of portability.

4.10 Choosing the right arithmetic data type

Choosing the right integral data type for a variable can enhance the portability of
a program. Conversely, one of the most frequent areas that need fixing when you
are called upon to port someone else's program is the choice of integral data
types.

When choosing an integral data type, in addition to considering the portable
range of that type, you must also determine whether your concern is space
efficiency or time efficiency. Typically, int is used for time efficiency, while
short is used for space efficiency. (Both have the same portable range.)

4.10.1 Time efficiency vs space efficiency

The integral type most natural to the hardware is int. Use int if your concern
is for time-efficiency of operations and if the range of values you need for the
variable falls within the portable range [−32767..32767].

Type int is frequently the choice for looping variables, for example,

```
register int n;

for (n = 0; n < max; n++)
    do_something();
```

Use short or char if you wish to make sure that the variable uses a small
amount of storage. You must make sure that, if you are using the variable to hold
numbers, they fall within the portable range [−32767..32767] for short or
[0..127] for char. If you are using the variable to hold bit patterns, you can use
the range [0..65535] for (unsigned) short or [0..255] for (unsigned)
char.

Type short or char is a common choice for variables used in a large array
or array of structures, as in

```
struct msg {
    short           msg_size;
    unsigned char msg_flags;
    unsigned char msg_perms;
    char            *msg_data;
} messages[MAX_MSGS];
```

Note that the urgency of space efficiency depends on the size of the address space. In a small address space machine like the PDP11/70, or the IBM PC under the "small model" of linkage, space efficiency is crucial because the address space limitation forms a hard wall preventing execution if the program is too big. On large address space machines like the VAX, there is practically no way to run out of space in the program; in such an environment, "space efficiency" becomes a matter of time efficiency in terms of page-faults and resource utilization. Even in a large address space machine, an array with `shorts` can provide *locality of reference*, which results in fewer hardware cache "misses" and fewer page faults, and hence greater time efficiency.

Space efficiency is also of concern for data to be stored in files or sent over a communication line.

4.10.2 Integral types for greater range

Use `long` if the variable may exceed the range $[-32,767..32,767]$ but will not exceed the range $[-2,147,483,647..2,147,483,647]$.

What if your variable may exceed the range of `long`, but you still need the precision of an integral type? There are algorithms for arbitrary-precision integral arithmetic that can be implemented in C using ASCII strings or linked lists of integers. The routines for arbitrary-precision arithmetic are beyond the scope of this book.

The unsigned types can be used to squeeze twice as large a number into the same space as the corresponding signed types, provided the number is never negative.

4.10.3 Type parameterization

The `typedef` facility in C allows you to define your own types, which we call *parameterized types*. Sometimes you may use a parameterized type merely to give a special name to a particular use of a type, even though the underlying type will never change. For example, you may wish to make the definition

```
typedef int BOOL;    /* Boolean type */
```

The main use of such a parameterization is to make your code more readable. For example, the declaration

```
BOOL
is_ready()
{
    ...
```

more clearly shows the reader that the function `is_ready` returns a Boolean value than if we had declared `is_ready` with a return type of `int`.

Another use of parameterized types is to insulate the program from changes in the underlying data type. Those changes may be due to differences between environments, or due to changes in the application itself. Unfortunately, C does not provide the full support for the parameterization of types found in later languages such as Ada or C++, which allow overloading of operators to give them special meanings for new types. As a result, people coding with parameterized types tend to have in mind the underlying type; it is rare that the underlying type can be changed without requiring changes to the code itself.

Nonetheless, because the ranges of C's arithmetic types vary from machine to machine, one can achieve some degree of machine independence by using parameterized types. Parameterized types are defined either by the requirements of a particular application or by some abstract criteria that are not application specific.

You can define your own *application-specific types*, which can then be implemented using an underlying C type. For example, suppose you are writing a financial application that involves the price of stocks. You could make the application-specific definition

```
typedef unsigned PRICE; /* in 1/8ths of a dollar */
```

Then any variables involving price would use the application-specific type

```
PRICE selling_price;
```

Since, as we saw above, we can assume that an `unsigned` has a maximum value of at least 65535, then the maximum value of a variable of type `PRICE` is $8191⅛, which ought to suffice for all stocks. But suppose that due to a booming market, some stocks exceed $8191⅛, then it may be necessary to change the `typedef` of `PRICE`.

You could also parameterize types based on general considerations, for example,

```
typedef char   INT8;       /* at least 8 bits */
typedef int    INT16_TIME; /* time-efficient type */
typedef short  INT16_SPACE;/* space-efficient type */
typedef long   INT32;      /* at least 32 bits */
```

This parameterization is an attempt to define a machine-independent set of types that yields more specific range information than C's own set of integer data types. The problem with such a parameterization is that, as already mentioned, C lacks the facilities to fully carry through the invention of a new type, so the use of parameterized types inevitably ends up making assumptions about which types actually underlie the parameterized types.

One problem in the use of a parameterized type is that we don't know what its portable range is, hence we don't know when it overflows. We also don't know what type results from mixing the parameterized type with other types in operations. We don't know whether the underlying type is signed or unsigned. These problems make the enforcement of our arithmetic portability rules difficult.

4.11 Data portability

One of the most common problems in shipping data between diverse computers, either by file transfer or by network communication, is that computer environments differ in the way they represent arithmetic data types. The differences in the representation of floating point types are generally so great that it is impossible to exchange binary floating point data between diverse environments, though the problem may be reduced if the environments all adhere to IEEE floating point standard 754. The differences in the representation of integral types are usually more manageable. They amount to different byte orderings of the integers.

Achieving data portability is not as easily done as achieving program portability. To write portable programs, follow the rules of this book. To get your data to port to a different environment often requires an *ad hoc* solution based on the particular computers involved. This chapter explains the byte order problem for integral types and suggests some techniques you can use for achieving data portability with integral types. §8.3 contains further suggestions on achieving data portability using structures.

4.11.1 Byte order of integral types

The following example shows a way to take a number modulo 256. Why is it nonportable?

```
/* efficient way to mod by 256 */
long g;

g = *(unsigned char *)&g;
```

The example is nonportable for two reasons. First, it assumes that an unsigned char is 8 bits long. Portable C only assumes that a char is *at least* 8 bits long. Second, even assuming 8 bit chars, it confuses byte order in memory with the significance of the bytes. This code would work on "little-endian" machines, machines for which the low address byte of an integer is its least significant byte, like the Intel 80386 and VAX. It would fail on "big-endian" machines, machines for which the low address byte of an integer is its high significance byte, like the Motorola 68030.[14]

```
g = *(unsigned char *)&g;
```

To make the example portable, we mask the variable g with BMASK to get the least significant 8 bits of g.

```
#define BMASK    0xFF
...
g = g & BMASK;
```

This code relies on the fact that n mod 2^k is the same as n & ($2^k - 1$).

A similar example is the following simplified **cat** program, which copies standard input to standard output:

```
int c;

while ((c = getchar()) != EOF)
        fwrite((char *)&c, 1, 1, stdout);
```

The code confuses the *low address byte* of c, which it writes out, with the *least significant byte* of c, which is where **getchar** places the integer it has read in. See §5.3.1. A portable version is

```
int c;

while ((c = getchar()) != EOF)
        putchar(c);
```

---

[14] The colloquial terms "little-endian" and "big-endian" come from Jonathan Swift's *Gulliver's Travels*. Swift invented the terms to refer to the egg-eating habits of two different groups of people. Each group was so committed to its convention for cracking eggs, that they started a war over this "religious" difference. Computer scientists are equally religious in their commitment to little- or big-endian-ness as the "natural order" for computer architecture.

The macro **putchar** writes out the character value stored in the least significant portion of an int.

Portable C assumes that integers are represented using a binary encoding. However, the layout of the bytes in storage can differ from machine to machine. Some machines are "big-endian," others "little-endian," a few are neither.

The difference in storage layouts is made clearer by the following diagram in which i_0 represents the least significant byte of an integer.

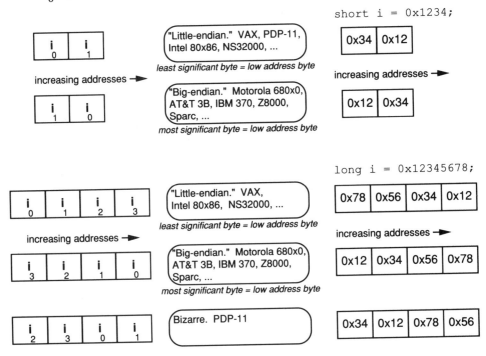

Note that for the 80x86 and PDP-11, long is not a "native" data type (supported in machine's instruction set). Arithmetic on longs must be emulated by the compiler.

4.11.2 Byte order and data portability

The differing storage orders for the bytes of an integer can lead to portability problems in code which depends on the byte order of a particular environment. To avoid such problems, do not assume a particular layout of bytes in an integer. Distinguish clearly between the least significant byte of an integer[15]

---

[15] Our definition of BYTEMASK assumes 8 bit bytes. For a more portable definition, see §5.3.2.

```
#define BYTEMASK 0xFF
/* least significant byte: */
#define LSB(n) ((n) & BYTEMASK)
```

and the low address byte of an integer

```
/* low address byte: */
#define LAB(n) (*(unsigned char *)&(n))
```

Differing storage orders for the bytes of an integer can cause "data portability" problems when transmitting data between different kinds of machines. Communication between heterogeneous computer environments requires a solution to the data portability problem engendered by diverse byte-orderings of integers.

- One solution is to do all communications in ASCII, and never send binary data. (See §8.3.)

- Another, less appealing, solution is to write custom translation routines at the receiving end to twiddle the bytes of the received integers.

- A third solution is to fix a "canonical" byte ordering (say, that of your most common machine environment), and then use a function to encode each integer into canonical form, and another function to decode an integer from canonical form. Such functions are available in BSD Unix; for example, htons (host to network short) and ntohl (network to host long).

Exercise 4-3: Canonical byte ordering for data portability. Suppose for this exercise that we wish to achieve data portability among several machines, all of which satisfy the following:

1. a long is 32 bits

2. a char is 8 bits

3. 2's complement arithmetic

Write a function

```
long
to_can(n)
long n;
```

that will take a long integer n and return a 4 byte pseudo "long" that is in fact encoded in a canonical byte ordering (say, "little-endian").
    Write a corresponding function

```
long
from_can(n)
long n;
```

that takes a pseudo "long" integer in canonical byte ordering, and converts it to
the ordering of this machine's environment. □

Solution to Exercise 4-3.

```
/* macro: GETBYTE: returns a byte of a long
 * params:
 *  g -- a long integer
 *  n -- 0, 1, 2, or 3. The byte #.
 *       0 is least significant byte,
 *       3 is most significant byte.
 * returns: the desired byte
 */
#define GETBYTE(n, k)    ((n) >> 8*(k) & 0xff)

/*
 * to_can: convert a long to a "canonical"
 * pseudo-long in "little-endian" byte-ordering
 * (least significant byte is low address byte).
 */
long
to_can(n)
long n;
{
    union {
        long canl;    /* canonical pseudo-long */
        char canc[4]; /* view as bytes */
    } u;

    u.canc[0] = GETBYTE(n, 0);
    u.canc[1] = GETBYTE(n, 1);
    u.canc[2] = GETBYTE(n, 2);
    u.canc[3] = GETBYTE(n, 3);
    return u.canl;
}
```

```
/* macro: PUTBYTE: make a long from a byte
 *                  filling other bytes with 0
 * params: b -- a character
 *         n -- 0, 1, 2, or 3. The byte # in result
 * returns: the desired long
 */
#define PUTBYTE(n, k)    (((n) & 0xffL) << (8*(k)))

/*
 * from_can: convert a "canonical" pseudo-long
 *   in "little-endian" byte ordering
 *   to a real long for this machine
 */
long
from_can(n)
long n;
{
    union {
        long canl;        /* canonical pseudo-long */
        char canc[4];     /* view as bytes */
    } u;

    u.canl = n;
    return  PUTBYTE(u.canc[0], 0) |
            PUTBYTE(u.canc[1], 1) |
            PUTBYTE(u.canc[2], 2) |
            PUTBYTE(u.canc[3], 3);
}
```

□

4.12 Floating point data types

Portable C supports float and double as floating point data types. Which
type you use is determined by your need for space efficiency as opposed to your
need for precision. Pre-ANSI C compilers, following [K&R], perform all arithmetic in double precision no matter which type you use for storage. ANSI C
changes the [K&R] rules and specifies single precision operations on float
operands.[16] Floating point arithmetic can produce varying results on different
machines due to lack of standardization. The IEEE Floating Point standard 754 is

---

[16] Some pre-ANSI compilers have a switch that turns on this feature as an option.

an attempt to overcome this problem. However, it remains far from universal implementation.

Beware that the mathematical libraries commonly available with C compilers have been shown to produce erroneous results in many environments.[17] For serious scientific or mathematical computations, unfortunately we must recommend you carefully test the accuracy of the mathematical libraries, or use FORTRAN.

There is no standard response to floating point overflow conditions. In System V UNIX, a signal SIGFPE occurs upon floating point overflow. By contrast, in BSD UNIX, no signal is generated, but an external error variable is set upon floating point over/underflow. The IEEE 754 standard causes no signal to occur upon over/underflow, but special reserved values for the result, such as "infinity" or "not-a-number," make clear that over/underflow has occurred.[18] Microsoft C on the PC follows the IEEE standard, and also posts an error value in the global variable `errno`.

The initialization of floating point numbers is analogous to the initialization of pointers. Floating point 0.0 may not be "all bits zero" on some machines. However, the compiler and loader may initialize variables to "all bits 0"; **calloc** certainly does. (ANSI C says static and external floating point variables are initialized to 0.0, but this may be difficult to implement.)

Hence, the following rule.

FLOAT1: *Explicitly initialize all floating point variables.*

Don't rely on default initialization, even for static and external variables.

Conversions involving floating point numbers are left partly undefined in C so the compiler implementer can follow the hardware's arithmetic.

Negative floating point numbers, when converted to integer, may truncate upwards or downwards, depending on the environment.

Integers and floating point literals like `1.3`, when converted to `float` or `double`, will have different values in different environments due to rounding, since they may not be exactly representable as a binary fraction times a power of 2. (Not every decimal fraction can be exactly represented as a binary fraction.) For example,

---

[17] [Spaf&Flas] observe that among the UNIX environments they tested for scientific function libraries, "the only versions of the math libraries producing consistently good results in our tests were those running on the AT&T machines, and they performed poorly in two of the power tests."

[18] [Spaf&Flas], p. 53.

```
main()
{
    double d;
    float f;

    f = d = 123.456;
    printf("d=%f, f=%f\n",d,f);
}
```

prints the following on a 68000-based machine:

```
d=123.456000, f=123.455994
```

Similarly, doubles, when converted to floats, will have different values in different environments, due to rounding, since a double value may not be exactly representable as a float value. In such a case, the direction of rounding is left unspecified in [ANSI], even though [K&R] specifies the direction based on that of the PDP11.

## CHAPTER 5

PORTABLE USE OF CHARACTERS

5.1 Three uses of `char`

We can distinguish three basic uses for the data types `char` and `unsigned char` in C—as a character, a byte, and a small integer. In the following discussion, mention of `char` includes `unsigned char` as well.

- *Codeset character.* A `char` can represent a *character* in the codeset. In many environments this means an ASCII character, though other codesets can be used. The character is encoded as an integer by the codeset encoding.

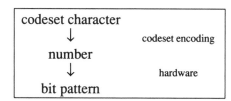 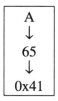

ASCII characters are always positive when viewed as numbers, since they occupy only seven bits. The same assurance cannot be made about all codesets; some codesets use the high order bit, so their characters may be "negative" when viewed as numbers.[1]

- *Smallest unit of addressable storage, smallest unit of copying.* A `char` can represent a *byte* of storage. This is the minimal atomic unit used for copying data from place to place in storage or between storage and other devices. When used as a byte for copying, we have no concern about the value of a `char`'s bit pattern or even its bitlength. The byte is merely a token to be used for moving data from one place to another. Hence, we need not worry about the portable range of `char` when used as a byte.

---

[1] While [K&R] guarantees that codeset characters are nonnegative, [ANSI]—which is more concerned with international codesets—guarantees only that codeset characters belonging to the standard English alphabet, digits, and certain special characters are nonnegative. However, codeset characters that do not belong to those groups, such as letters outside the English alphabet, may be negative when viewed as numbers.

- *Small integer*. We have already encountered `char` as a small integral type in Chapter 4. In its role as integral type, a `char` can be used for all the purposes of an integral type: small number, small bit pattern, enumeration, and Boolean value.

It is possible to parameterize `char` as a variety of `typedef`'d types according to the typology of uses just given, for example

```
typedef char          CHAR;   /* codeset character */
typedef unsigned char BYTE;   /* unit of storage */
typedef char          TINY;   /* small number */
typedef unsigned char CBITS;  /* small bit pattern */
```

One problem with this parameterization is that a `char` is often used for several of these purposes in turn.

5.2 Using `char` as integer: the signedness of `char`

The main portability problem in using `char`s as integers is that the signedness of type `char` is unspecified in C. Depending on the hardware and the choice made by the compiler implementer, `char`s can be signed or unsigned. Hence, the sign extension of `char`s when promoted to integers varies between environments. `char` is a signed type on Intel 80x86, DEC VAX, Motorola 680x0, and Sun Sparc series. `char` is an unsigned type on the IBM 370, NS32000, and AT&T 3B series.

Type `unsigned char` is always unsigned, whether or not type `char` is. Similarly, type `signed char`, an innovation of ANSI C, is always signed, whether or not type `char` is.

Does sign extension occur when converting a `char` to an `int`? The result depends on whether type `char` is signed or unsigned in the environment. As we saw in §4.7.2, only signed types sign-extend when converted to wider types. If type `char` is unsigned in the environment, then when promoted to `int`, it retains its same (non-negative) numeric value and hence is padded with 0's in the most significant byte(s); that is, it does not sign-extend. If `char` is signed in the environment and contains a negative number, then when promoted to `int`, in order to retain the same numeric value, it must be padded with 1's in the most significant byte(s); that is, it sign extends.

The following nonportable example prints different results in different environments.

```
/* store bit pattern in char,
 * then print its value
 */
main()
{
    char c = '\300';
    unsigned char d = '\300';

    printf("c=%d=0%o,  d=%d=0%o,\n",c,c,d,d);
    printf("(short)c=%d=0%o, (long)c=%ld=0%lo,\n",
           (short)c,(short)c,(long)c,(long)c);
    printf("(short)d=%d=0%o, (long)d=%ld=0%lo,\n",
           (short)d,(short)d,(long)d,(long)d);
}
```

In an environment where chars are signed, c has the value -64.[2] So (short)c must have the value -64, which is 0177700_8 (assuming it is 16 bits). And (long)c has the value 037777777700_8 (assuming it is 32 bits).

In an environment where chars are unsigned, c has the value 192. So (short)c and (long)c must have the value 192, which is 0300_8 on a 16-bit machine and 0300_8 on a 32-bit machine.

What would the example print on a machine with signed chars and 16 bit ints? Here is the output on an 80386 machine:

```
c=-64=0177700, d=192=0300,
(short)c=-64=0177700, (long)c=-64=037777777700,
(short)c=192=0300, (long)c=192=0300,
```

Sign extension upon conversion Machine for which char is signed	
variable	binary representation
c	‖11100‖0000
(short)c	‖1111‖1111‖11100‖0000
(long)c	‖1111‖1111‖1111‖1111‖1111‖1111‖11100‖0000

What would the example print on a machine with unsigned chars? Here is the output on a 3B2 machine

---

[2] You can calculate c's decimal value using two's-complement arithmetic. Subtract $2^8 - 0300_8$, and get 64.

```
c=192=0300, d=192=0300,
(short)c=192=0300, (long)c=192=0300,
(short)c=192=0300, (long)c=192=0300,
```

No sign extension upon conversion Machine for which `char` is unsigned	
variable	binary representation
c	||1100|0000
(short)c	|0000|0000||1100|0000
(long)c	|0000|0000|0000|0000|0000|0000||1100|0000

The code in the example is obviously not portable. It violates Rule BIT2 as well as BIT3. A more portable version would be

```
unsigned char c = 0300;
unsigned char d = 0300;
```

Using `unsigned char` as the type of c and d assures that sign extension will not take place when they are converted to `short`s or `long`s.

5.3 Using `char` as byte of storage

A `char` is used to represent both the smallest addressable unit of memory and to represent the smallest data unit of I/O. In portable C, we make the assumption that a `char` coincides with a byte, or in other words, `sizeof(char)` equals 1.[3]

The size of a byte in bits is environment dependent. Consider the copying of a chunk of memory containing an array of structures to another place in memory. Typically, the copy is accomplished by moving each of the chunk's bytes separately. Even though individual bytes may differ in size or value from one environment to the next, the move itself is portable. Note that even the number of bytes in the chunk of memory is environment dependent.

5.3.1 getchar

In most applications, I/O is performed on a record basis (**fread**, **fwrite**) or line basis (**fgets**, **fputs**). However, at the lowest level, the C library provides routines for byte-at-a-time I/O (**fgetc**, **fputc**, **getchar**, **putchar**). The specifications of the **fgetc** family are awkward; the functions are often used nonportably as a result.

---

[3] [ANSI] makes this assumption an explicit requirement. (Section 3.3.3.4)

The following program reads standard input and copies it to standard output. The example contains a common portability error. Why is the code nonportable?

```
/* copy standard input to standard output */
#include <stdio.h>

main()
{
    char c;

    while ((c = getchar()) != EOF)
        putchar(c);
}
```

The code as written will work only if char is a signed type and the standard input contains only ASCII characters. The problem lies in the declaration of c as type char.

`char` c;

Though it may seem unintuitive, **getchar** returns an int. The only way **getchar** can signal end-of-file is by returning a value that could not possibly be a legitimate char. Since a byte from the standard input could contain any bit pattern (if the standard input is a non-ASCII file, say a binary file), in order for **getchar** to return a distinguished value at the end of file, it is necessary for **getchar** to be able to return a value outside the range that a byte can hold.

Hence, **getchar** returns an int in which the input character occupies the least significant byte and the more significant bytes are filled with zeros. The value of EOF is by convention -1, an integer with all bits set (in two's-complement machines).[4] Two typical return values for **getchar** on a machine with 32 bit ints and 8 bit bytes are pictured below.

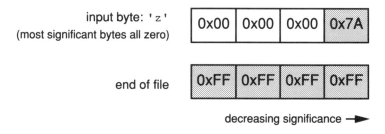

input byte: 'z'
(most significant bytes all zero)

| 0x00 | 0x00 | 0x00 | 0x7A |

end of file

| 0xFF | 0xFF | 0xFF | 0xFF |

decreasing significance ➡

values returned by getchar

---

[4] ANSI guarantees only that EOF is a negative number. The explanation given here would work as well for any negative number.

Now, consider what happens in the **getchar** example above if the environment treats `char` as a signed type and the input byte is `'\377'`. The variable `c` gets the numeric value -1, which is promoted to `int` for comparison with `EOF`, which also has value -1. So the program detects a false end of file.

On the other hand, suppose the environment treats `char` as an unsigned type. Then, when `EOF` is encountered, `c` will get the value `'\377'` (a byte with all bits set), which has value 255. When comparing `c` with `EOF`, the result of `(c = getchar())` is promoted to `int`, still with the value 255, which does not equal -1. Hence, the code will *never* detect end of file.

To make the code portable, declare c to be of type `int`, which is the return type of **getchar**.

```
/* copy standard input to standard output */
#include <stdio.h>

main()
{
    int c;

    while ((c = getchar()) != EOF)
        putchar(c);
}
```

Now there is no confusion between the byte `'\377'` and the value -1 returned by **getchar** on end of file.

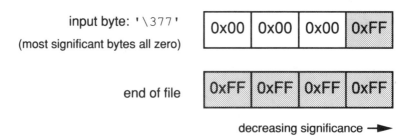

input byte: `'\377'`
(most significant bytes all zero)

| 0x00 | 0x00 | 0x00 | 0xFF |

end of file

| 0xFF | 0xFF | 0xFF | 0xFF |

decreasing significance ➡

The moral of the story is:

CHAR1: *The* **getchar** *family of routines,* **getchar***,* **getc***, and* **fgetc***, all return an* `int`*; use an* `int` *variable to store the return value of any of them.*

5.3.2 The ctype routines

Similarly, the **ctype** routines[5], isalpha, isdigit, tolower, etc., take an
int—not a char—as their parameter. But, for portability, that int must be in
the range that is returned by **getchar**, namely, either −1 or the value of a character padded with zero bits. Otherwise unwanted results may occur.[6] To assure that
the character falls within the desired range, you can define macro CTOI, which
converts from char to int. CTOI may be implemented in three possible ways,
depending on the environment. One way to implement CTOI is to define it as a
cast to unsigned char followed by a cast to int. This prevents sign extension when widening to int.

Consider the following example which reads in a line of characters from file
infile and converts the lower case ones in place to upper case.

```
#include "environ.h"
#include <stdio.h>

main()
{
    char buf[BUFSIZ];
    int  nbytes, *p;
    FILE *infile
    ...
    if (fgets(buf, sizeof(buf), infile) == (char *)0)
        errexit();
    for (p = buf; *p != '\0'; p++)
        *p = toupper(*p);
    ...
}
```

For ordinary English alphabet text, sign extension will not occur in the line

```
    *p = toupper(*p);
```

However, if the character *p is not a codeset character, or is not in the English
language codeset, it could sign extend, resulting in a value outside the domain of
toupper. Hence, it is more portable to write

```
    *p = toupper(CTOI(*p));
```

---

[5] We call them "routines" because although they are usually implemented as macros, they may be implemented
as functions.

[6] The SVID says that the **ctype** routines **isalpha**, **isdigit**, etc., are defined only on values for which **isascii** is true
(i.e., values in the range [0..127]). But this constraint is not portable to non-ASCII codesets, and is not
mentioned in [ANSI]. Fortunately, practical experience shows that in existing implementations it is safe to pass
any character value widened with zeros to the **ctype** routines.

The purpose of using CTOI to convert *p to type int is to avoid unwanted sign extension. We can define CTOI in **environ.h** as

```
#define CTOI(c)    ((int)(unsigned char)(c))
```

If unsigned char is not an available type in your environment, or if its implementation is "broken,"[7] you can define CTOI by

```
#define BYTEMASK (~(~0 << CHAR_BIT))
#define CTOI(c)    ((c) & BYTEMASK)
```

where CHAR_BIT is the number of bits in a char, a macro defined in ANSI's **limits.h** file, or in your own version of **limits.h**. In this version, buf[i] will be converted to an int by the usual arithmetic conversions. That int may have a negative value, but when masked with BYTEMASK, the most significant bytes will all be zero.

In environments where char is an unsigned type, it suffices to define CTOI as a null macro

```
#define CTOI(c) (c)
```

since there is no worry about sign extension in such environments.

We can state our observation as a rule

CHAR2: *Use an* int *whose value is representable as an* unsigned char *or* EOF *as the argument to the* **ctype** *routines.*

5.4 Using **char** as byte and as codeset character

We recommend the use of single-quoted constants such as 'a', '\n', 'Z' to represent char constants when using the char as a byte or codeset character. Although such constants actually have type int, we treat them in portable C as if they have type char. There is actually no harm in doing so, since (char)'x' is equivalent to 'x' for all practical purposes. When using chars as small integers, use integer constants according to Rules NUM1, BIT3, and BIT4.

---

[7] Unfortunately, there are some substandard C compilers where the definition

```
#define CTOI(c) ((int)(unsigned char)(c))
```

will fail to prevent sign extension.
  Another solution is to declare buf as

```
unsigned char buf[BUFSIZE];
```

and avoid CTOI entirely.

CHAR3: *Use single-quoted constants for codeset characters and bytes. In port-*
        able C, a single-quoted constant is treated as if it has type char.
        Where possible, use character representation rather than octal
        representation for single-quoted constants.

Thus, it is more portable to use `'\r'` than `'\015'` to represent a carriage
return, since the latter form is strictly an ASCII representation. If you must use
octal forms for characters such as "escape" or "bell," it is best to parameterize
them in a header file. Parameterization will enhance readability and will avoid
dependence on a particular codeset. For example, using the ASCII encodings[8]

```
#define BELL      '\7'
#define ESC       '\33'
#define CNTRLBYTE '\200'
```

Unfortunately, you cannot use these symbolic names inside string constants;
there you must write out the escape sequence. For example

```
fprintf(stderr, "\7Warning. Program is ending!\n");
```

When using `char`s as small integers, it is fine to mix them in operations with
other signed integral types. Not so with `char`s used as bytes or codeset characters. If you want to compare a `char` for equality with an `int`—say an int
returned by **getchar**—you must either expand the `char` to an `int` using the
CTOI macro shown in §5.3.2, or cast the `int` to `char`. Thus the following code
is nonportable:

```
#define CNTRLBYTE '\200'
...
int c;

while ((c = getchar()) != EOF) {
    if (c == CNTRLBYTE)
        do_cntrl();
```

The code compares the integer `c` with the `char` constant CNTRLBYTE.
(Remember that by Rule CHAR3, we view `'\200'` as having type `char`.) On a
machine with signed characters, `do_cntrl` would never be executed.
CNTRLBYTE would sign extend when converted to `int`; thus it would never
match any value returned by **getchar**.

---

[8] ANSI introduces `'\a'` ("alert") for the bell character, but this sequence is not portable to pre-ANSI compilers.

CHAR4: *Don't compare bytes or codeset characters with* ints. *Rather, when using the* == *or* != *operators, make sure both operands are* ints *or both are* chars.

We can now write a portable version of the above code:

```
#define CNTRLBYTE '\200'
...
int c;

while ((c = getchar()) != EOF) {
    if ((char)c == CNTRLBYTE) /* byte comparison */
        do_cntrl();
```

or equivalently,

```
while ((c = getchar()) != EOF) {
    if (c == CTOI(CNTRLBYTE)) /* byte comparison */
        do_cntrl();
```

The next example is not portable because it assumes that the alphabet maps to a set of contiguous numbers in the codeset representation. That assumption is true for the ASCII codeset, but not necessarily for other codesets. (The assumption of contiguity is portable for the digits, however.)

```
int c;

/* process upper case letters & digits */
while ((c = getchar()) != EOF)
{
    if ((c >= 'A' && c<= 'Z') ||
        (c >= '0' && c <= '9'))
        process(c);
}
```

The portable resolution is to use the library functions defined in **ctype.h**. The use of the **ctype** routines enhances both portability *and* efficiency, since the **ctype** routines are typically implemented efficiently using a simple table lookup.

The **ctype** routines also offer greater potential compatibility with alternate character sets used for internationalized programming. (See §9.11.)

```
#include <ctype.h>
...
int c;

/* process upper case letters & numbers */
while ((c = getchar()) != EOF)
{
    if (isupper(c) || isdigit(c))
        process(c);
}
```

We summarize the foregoing observations in Rule CHAR5.

CHAR5: *Don't apply arithmetic, relational comparison, or bitwise operators to codeset characters or bytes. Use* **ctype** *macros where possible.*

5.5 Mixed use of chars

The following example mixes the use of char as an input byte and as a small number used to index into an array. In the example, we read in a buffer of bytes from file infile, and wish to increment a frequency count of the different kinds of bytes found in the file. What is nonportable in this example?

```
/* frequency count of input bytes */
#include <stdio.h>

extern void profile();
long frequency[256];

main()
{
    char buf[BUFSIZ];
    int  nbytes;
    FILE *infile;
    ...
    if ((nbytes = fread(buf, 1, sizeof(buf),
                         infile)) == 0)
        errexit();
    profile(buf, nbytes);
    ...
}
```

```
void
profile(buf, count)
char *buf;
int count;
{
    char *p;

    for(p = buf; p < buf + count; p++)
        frequency[*p]++;
}
```

This example uses type `char` in two different ways at once. Pointer p traverses the buffer, inspecting bytes that have been read in from `infile`. In this sense, *p is a byte, a unit of I/O from the outside world. But *p is also used as an index into array `frequency`. In this role, *p is a number, the number whose encoding is the bit pattern value of the byte.

The code is nonportable because *p may exceed the portable range of `char`, thus violating Rule NUM1: *The value of a data object of arithmetic type must lie within the portable range of that type.* If the file `infile` contains any non-ASCII characters, *p may have values that overflow the portable range of `char`, which is [0..127]. On machines where `char` is a signed type, this means is that *p may be a negative number; when used as an index into the array `frequency`, it may refer to a data object that lies before the array in storage. (This violates Rule PTR5 in §7.6.)

```
void
profile(buf, count)
char *buf;
int count;
{
    char *p;

    for(p = buf; p < buf + count; p++)
        frequency[*p]++;
}
```

The best way to make the example portable is to use the macro `CTOI`, introduced in §5.3.2, to convert from input byte to integer.

```
void
profile(buf, count)
char *buf;
int count;
{
    char *p;

    for(p = buf; p < buf + count; p++)
        frequency[CTOI(*p)]++;
}
```

You can make the code portable without using CTOI by declaring buf as an array of unsigned chars, and p as a pointer to unsigned char. The code would then look like this

```
/* frequency count of input bytes */
#include <stdio.h>

extern void profile();
long frequency[256];

main()
{
    unsigned char    buf[BUFSIZ];
    int              nbytes;
    FILE             *infile;
    ...
    if ((nbytes = fread((char *)buf, 1, sizeof(buf),
                        infile)) == 0)
        errexit();
    profile(buf, nbytes);
    ...
}

void
profile(buf, count)
unsigned char *buf;
int count;
{
    char *p;

    for(p = buf; p < buf + count; p++)
        frequency[*p]++;
}
```

## CHAPTER 6

THE C-WORLD MODEL: POINTERS

Before discussing the portable use of pointers, we need to clarify the use of pointers in the C-World model. This chapter continues the description of the C-World model begun in Chapter 2. Much of the "payoff" of the model comes in the clarity it yields in understanding pointers. The terminology introduced in this chapter will be used to formulate pointer portability rules in Chapter 7.

In this chapter, the C-World attribute of *addressability* is elaborated and contrasted with *modifiability*. The chapter explains the C-World's underlying "grid of `chars`"—the abstract machine's analogue to storage locations in memory. The chapter defines *primary* and *nonprimary* data objects and explains how a data object is *associated* with a primary data object. The association with a primary data object will be essential in determining whether pointer operations are portable.

Finally, this chapter makes precise the *lifetime* of a data object, since pointers must point only to live data objects.

6.1 Modifiable and addressable data objects

The C-World model eliminates the use of the syntactic term *lvalue*. Informally, an lvalue is an expression that can appear on the left side of an assignment (=) operator. It also refers to an expression that can be the operand of the address (&) operator. These two definitions of lvalue do not always coincide; for example, a register variable can be assigned to, but not pointed to. The ANSI C standard further muddles the definition of lvalue by adding "modifiable lvalues."

The C-World semantic model avoids the term lvalue entirely. Instead, the C-World distinguishes two semantic properties of data objects, modifiability and addressability, which together roughly correspond to the notion of lvalue. There is, however, no inherent relationship between addressability and modifiability of data objects.[1]

---

[1] [K&R] state, "An *object* is a manipulatable region of storage; an *lvalue* is an expression referring to an object." A "data object" in the C-World model is a higher level entity than the "object" of [K&R] and [ANSI]. A data object has attributes, while an object is simply a region of storage. In [K&R] and [ANSI], there are really three layers of discussion:

6.1.1 Modifiability

A data object with read/write access permission is called *modifiable*. The value of a modifiable data object can change over time. A modifiable data object is also called a variable. A nonmodifiable data object is called a constant. Any expression that refers to a modifiable data object can appear on the left-hand side of an assignment (=) operator.

Constants can be literal constants that appear in the source code such as `6.05`. They can also be short-lived data objects that appear as the result of evaluating expressions such as `i+j`, or `a` where `a` is the name of an array. An expression denoting an array `a` is interpreted as denoting a short-lived constant pointer to the first element of the array (`a[0]`) in most contexts. The only contexts where such an expression stands for the array itself are `sizeof(a)` and—in ANSI C—`&a`.

Similarly, a *name* expression denoting a function is interpreted as referring to a pointer to the function, except in the context of a function call. The only other context where such an expression stands for the function itself is—in ANSI C—the expression `&f`.[2]

We can summarize the facts on constant and variable data objects as follows. All data objects are modifiable, *except*:

- literal constants—numeric or character constants that appear in the C program (e.g., `315`, `3.07`, `'q'`)

- short-lived constants resulting from operations (e.g., `n+5`, `x*i`, `-j`)

- short-lived constant pointers denoted by array or function expressions (e.g., given the code

---

```
the syntactic layer
the data object layer
the object layer
```

In most writing about C, the syntactic and data object layers are frequently collapsed, as when speaking of the value of an expression. By introducing access permissions and addressability to the data object layer, the C-World eliminates the need for an object layer. Thus the C-World has two layers of discussion:

```
the syntactic layer
the data object layer
```

In speaking about the C-World model, we strive to distinguish the two layers, though at times it is more convenient to collapse them here as well.

[2] Another way to think of these expressions is to assert that they always refer to the entire array or function, but that in most contexts, they are implicitly cast to a pointer type before being used.

```
int a[5], b[3][4], f(), (*fp)();
...
if (fp == f)
    a[1] = (*f)(a, b[0]);
```

the expressions a, b[0], and f denote pointer data objects that are not modifiable.[3] The expressions fp and a[1] denote modifiable data objects. The expressions a, fp, and f are name expressions, while b[0] and a[1] are nonname expressions.)

- string constants (e.g., "Enter your answer:\t")
  Portable C treats string constants as nonmodifiable although in many environments, they are actually modifiable. See §8.6.

- const data objects in ANSI C

- functions (e.g., in the expression f(a), the expression f refers to a function data object, which is not modifiable)

6.1.2 Addressability

A data object is *addressable* if a pointer can point to it. A function is an addressable data object, even though it is not modifiable. Similarly, in ANSI C, a pointer can point to a const data object, even though it is not modifiable. Aside from these two examples, no constant data objects are addressable.

Some data objects can be pointed to even though the & operator should not portably be applied to expressions referring to them. For example, if we declare an array

```
char a[5];
```

it is not portable practice to use the expression &a.[4] Nonetheless, it *is* possible to portably define a pointer that points to the array a. A pointer to a would have the type "pointer to an array of 5 characters." If we declare

```
char (*p)[5];
```

and say p = (char (*)[5])a, then p points to the array a. So too does the pointer denoted by the expression (char (*)[5])a. Hence, the array named a

---

[3] Note that the expression b[0] refers to an array of 4 integers. That is, b[0] has type int [4]. However, in the context in which it appears in the code fragment above, like most expressions denoting arrays, it acts as a pointer to the first element of the array it refers to; thus, it has type int *.

[4] [ANSI] treats &a as a pointer to the entire array a (a pointer of type char (*)[5]). Some compilers treat &a as a pointer to the first element of a (a pointer of type char *). Some compilers disallow &a. Hence, &a is not a portable expression.

is addressable. Note that `sizeof(*p)` is 5. The pointer p is *not* the same as a pointer to the first element of a, for which a shorthand notation is simply a.

Similarly, we say that any function f is addressable, though it is not portable practice to write `&f`. (The expression f, when not followed by a function call `()`, suffices as a pointer to the function f.)

All data objects are addressable, *except*:

- register variables

- literal constants—numerical or character constants that appear in the C source code (e.g., `315`, `3.07`, `'q'`)[5]

- short-lived constants resulting from operations (e.g., `n+5`, `x*i`)

- short-lived constant pointers denoted by array or function expressions

- bit-fields

Exercise 6-1: Modifiability and Addressability. Given the declarations that appear in the first column of the following table, for each of the expressions in the second column,

— decide whether it refers to a modifiable data object.

— decide whether it refers to an addressable data object.

Declaration & Initialization	Expression	Modifiable	Addressable
`short s;`	`s`		
`register int ri;`	`ri`		
`int f();`	`f`		
	`3`		
`const int yd = 365;`	`yd`		
`int ia[10];`	`ia`		
	`"Total ="`		
`int i, j;`	`i + j`		
	`i++`		

(table continued on next page)

---

[5] A literal constant like `315` has no address in the C-World. In fact, it may be implemented as an immediate constant in an instruction and hence really have no address in data memory. Even if it is stored at a data memory address in a given implementation, that address is considered undefined in C.

Declaration & Initialization	Expression	Modifiable	Addressable
int *p = &i;	*p		
	*p++		
	p++		

struct {
    unsigned b:3;
    unsigned d:4;
} bf;
	bf.b		

char *np; np = malloc((unsigned)5);	np[2]		

☐

Solution to Exercise 6-1.

Declaration & Initialization	Expression	Modifiable	Addressable	See Note
short s;	s	√	√	
register int ri;	ri	√	no	
int f();	f	no	??	1
	3	no	no	
const int yd = 365;	yd	no	√	2
int ia[10];	ia	??	??	3
	"Total ="	no	??	4
int i, j;	i + j	no	no	
	i++	no	no	5
int *p = &i;	*p	√	√	6
	*p++	√	√	7
	p++	no	no	8

struct {
    unsigned b:3;
    unsigned d:4;
} bf;
	bf.b	√	no	

char *np; np = malloc((unsigned)5);	np[2]	√	√	

Notes on the answers

1. The type of f appearing in an expression depends on the context in which it appears.

- E.g., `f(s)`. If `f` is followed by a left parenthesis (function call), `f` denotes a function object, which is not modifiable but is addressable. This is also the case in ANSI C for f in the expression `&f`.

- E.g., `if (f == g)`. In any context other than a function call, `f` refers to a constant pointer (to the function `f`), which is not modifiable and not addressable. This is true even for the expression `(f)(s)`.

2. Note that `const` is a keyword in ANSI C only. It is not part of portable C.

3. Once again, the answer depends on the context in which the expression `ia` appears. In most contexts `ia` denotes a constant pointer to the array `ia`. The pointer is not modifiable and not addressable. In the context of `sizeof(ia)` or, in ANSI, in the context of `&ia`, `ia` denotes the array itself, which is modifiable and addressable.

4. Since `"Total ="` is an expression that refers to a character array, we treat it similarly to the previous example `ia`. In most contexts, the appearance of the literal `"Total ="` denotes a short-lived constant pointer to the first character (T) in the string. The constant pointer is not modifiable and not addressable.

   In the context of `sizeof("Total =")` the string literal `"Total ="` refers to the array of characters itself. Is this array modifiable? [K&R] says yes; [ANSI] says it's undefined; portable C says treat it as not modifiable. Is it addressable? Yes.

5. `i++` is a short-lived constant data object, resulting from the `++` operator applied to `i`. Hence, it is neither modifiable nor addressable.

6. `*p` is an expression that refers to the variable named `i`. Hence, it is modifiable and addressable.

7. `*p++` is the same as `*(p++)`, which also refers to the variable named `i`. Hence it is modifiable and addressable.

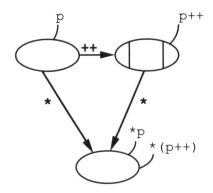

8. p++ is like i++, a short-lived constant data object, resulting from the ++ operator applied to p. Hence, it is neither modifiable nor addressable. (The side effect of incrementing p occurs *after* this expression is evaluated, and does not appear in the picture.)

□

6.2 Primary data objects

The C-World model divides addressable data objects into *primary* and *nonprimary* data objects. Roughly speaking, a primary data object is an addressable data object that is not part of a larger data object. Formally, primary data objects consist of the following:

- Named data objects declared explicitly. For example,

```
struct {
    int s_strsize;
    char s_c[MAXSTR];
} string, st[10];
```

declares two primary data objects, one named string, the other named st.

- Character arrays resulting from the occurrence of double quoted strings, for example, "Total = ".

- Character arrays resulting from calls to the library functions **malloc**, **calloc**, and **realloc**. These data objects are sometimes called heap objects or dynamically allocated objects.

Intuitively, the purpose of distinguishing primary from nonprimary data objects is to require that pointer arithmetic and relational comparisons of pointers should stay within the same primary data object; it is nonportable to perform arithmetic on a pointer that results in a pointer to a different primary data object, or to relationally compare pointers that point within different primary data objects.[6] We will make these notions more precise in the next chapter.

Nonprimary data objects are addressable data objects that are not primary. That is, they are referenced by expressions that involve the operators ., ->, [], and often *. The * (indirection) operator can yield a primary or a nonprimary data object. For example, given the declarations

---

[6] The relational *comparison* operators are <, >, <=, >=. Note that it *is* permissible to compare pointers to different primary data objects using the *equality* operators == or !=.

```
struct circle {
    float c_x;
    float c_y;
    float c_radius;
} c;
struct circle * cp = (struct circle *)&c.c_x;
```

the expressions `*cp` and `*&c.c_x` refer to a nonprimary data objects, while `*&c` refers to a primary data object.

In the C-World model, there is no relation assumed between the storage locations of primary data objects. By definition, primary data objects do not overlap other primary data objects in storage space. Typically, nonprimary data objects overlap primary data objects, and can also overlap each other.

6.2.1 Associated primary data object

Every addressable data object is *associated* with a primary data object. Intuitively, a data object is associated with a primary data object if it is derived from the primary data object by a series of operations. The reason for specifying such an association is that it allows us in the next chapter to state constraints on certain pointer operations in a way that is environment independent.

How is the association defined?

1. A primary data object is associated with itself.

2. If structure `s` is associated with a primary data object, then so is `s.m`, where `m` is a member of `s`.

3. If `p` points to a data object associated with a primary data object, then so is

    - the object pointed to by `p + i` (or `p - i`, `p++`, `p--`, `++p`, `--p`), where `i` is an integer

    - the object pointed to by (*pointer-type*) `p`

    - the object `p->m`, where `m` is a member of `*p`.

6.3 Real and imaginary data objects

The C-World model divides addressable data objects into *real* and *imaginary* data objects. An imaginary data object is a data object that does not lie entirely inside its associated primary data object. A real data object lies entirely inside its associated primary data object. Clearly, all primary data objects are real.

A pointer in the C-World can legitimately point to an imaginary data object. For example, if we declare

```
int k[4];
```

then k+4 points to an imaginary data object of type int that lies just beyond k.

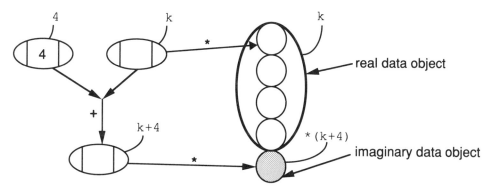

In the example above, the imaginary data object k[4] lies entirely outside the primary data object k. It is also possible for an imaginary data object to lie partly inside and partly outside its associated primary data object. Only the part of an imaginary data object that lies inside the associated primary data object occupies storage space. An imaginary structure can have real and imaginary members:

Since at least part of an imaginary object has no storage space, it cannot have a value in the C-World. Though a pointer can point to an imaginary data object, it is not permissible in the C-World to access the value of the imaginary object to which the pointer points. It is, however, permissible to access any real part of an imaginary data object.

Exercise 6-2: Associated primary data object. Given the following code

```
struct a {
    int a_i[5];
    char a_c[10];
} a[3], *ap, *bp;

char *p, *q;

ap = &a[1];
p = &(ap->a_c[5]);
q = &a[0].a_c[15];
```

What is the primary data object associated with the data object referred to by each of these expressions?

```
a                       a[1]                    &a[1]
ap                      *ap                     ap->a_c
(ap->a_c) + 5           ap->a_c[5]              p
*p                      (struct a *)p           *(struct a *)p
a[50]                   q                       *q
```

☐

Solution to Exercise 6-2.

		Associated primary data object
expression	name of associated primary data object	comment
a	a	a is already a primary data object.
a[1]	a	
&a[1]	none	&a[1] does not denote an addressable data object, hence there is no associated primary data object.
ap	ap	
*ap	a	*ap is already a primary data object.
ap->a_c	a	
(ap->a_c) + 5	none	(ap->a_c) + 5 denotes a short-lived constant, not an addressable data object, hence there is no associated primary data object.
ap->a_c[5]	a	
p	p	
*p	a	
(struct a *)p	none	(struct a *)p denotes a short-lived constant, not an addressable data object, hence there is no associated primary data object.
*(struct a *)p	a	*(struct a *)p is a partly "imaginary" data object which is nonetheless associated with a.
a[50]	a	a[50] is an "imaginary" data object which is nonetheless associated with a.
q	q	
*q	a	*q is an "maginary" data object which is nonetheless associated with a.

☐

6.4 Grid of chars

In the C-World abstract machine, every addressable data object coincides in storage with an array of chars. We picture a data object as laid out on a "grid" of chars.

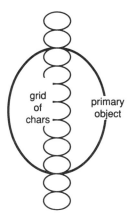

Whenever we picture the grid of chars level of the C-World, the picture becomes environment-specific, since in order to show the layout of various types on the grid, it is necessary to make environment-specific assumptions. However, the general assertions we make about the C-World are *not* environment-specific: for instance, the existence of the grid of chars is independent of the environment; only the number of grid chars that coincide with a data object depends on the environment.

Every addressable data object occupies an integral number of grid chars. In the C-World, the sizeof operator applied to an addressable data object yields the number of grid chars that lie inside it.

The grid array does not appear explicitly in a C program, but it can be accessed by casting a pointer to a data object to type char *. The C-World assumes that the compiler must be able to perform (or simulate) byte addressing.

6.4.1 Arrays, pointer arithmetic, and the grid of chars

Adding one to a pointer that points to an array element yields a pointer to the next element of the array. Adding two yields a pointer to the element following the next element, and so on. Likewise, subtracting one yields a pointer to the preceding element.

By this definition of pointer arithmetic, array elements are addressable (nonprimary) data objects. In particular, the characters of the grid array are addressable. The grid and its characters are nonprimary objects.

The first element of an array-type data object coincides with the first grid `char` of the data object. The same is true for the first member of a structure-type data object. That is, there is no "padding" at the beginning of an array or structure.[7]

For two consecutive array elements, the last grid `char` in the first element and the first grid `char` in the second element are consecutive grid `char`s. That is, there are no holes, no padding `char`s between array elements.[8]

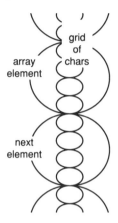

This fact allows us to extend the definition of pointer arithmetic beyond array elements. Suppose we have a pointer `p` to *any* data object. In the C-World, adding one yields a pointer to an imaginary data object of the same type immediately following `*p`. That is, the first grid `char` in the data object pointed to by `p+1` follows the last grid `char` in the data object pointed to by `p`.

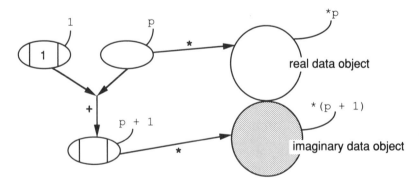

---

[7] See Rule PTR4 in Chapter 7.

[8] However, if the array is an array of structures, then each element of the array may contain padding chars. A structure can contain padding characters at its end (after all its members) to assure that it will be aligned on the proper boundaries when repeated in an array.

This definition of pointer arithmetic allows us to view any data object as embedded in an array of data objects of the same type. We can, therefore, view data as an array even though it is not declared as an array. For example, suppose we wish to dynamically allocate an array of 10 structures and initialize them. We can say

```
struct big *bp;
int i;

bp = (struct big *)malloc(sizeof(struct big)*10);
if (bp == (char *)0)
    errexit(NO_ROOM);
for (i = 0; i < 10; i++)
    big_init(&bp[i]);    /* initialize "array" elements */
```

What we are doing in the expression &bp[i] is pointer arithmetic on a nonde-clared array of structures that we impose on the underlying grid of chars allocated by **malloc**.

In the C-World, we cannot rely on the representation of pointers as integers in order to define pointer arithmetic. Instead, we define pointer arithmetic in terms of arrays through the simple definitions above. The C-World definition of pointer arithmetic allows for greater generality and simplicity, and covers environments such as segmented architectures and interpreters, where pointer arithmetic may not be easily interpreted in terms of integer arithmetic.

6.4.2 Structures and the grid of chars

A structure may have padding between its members or after all its members. The padding is always an integral number of grid chars.[9] The members of a structure are nonprimary data objects.

Suppose we want to initialize a structure to all bits zero without writing out initializations for each member. We can utilize the underlying grid of chars.

```
struct s {
    ...
} s;
char *p;

/* initialize structure to all bits 0 */
for (p = (char *)&s; p < (char *)&s + sizeof(s); p++)
    *p = '\0';
```

---

[9] This is so except in the case of bit-fields. See §4.8.

The code sets all the `chars` of the grid array that coincides with structure `s` to zero, including the `chars` that coincide with padding between the members of `s`. The code is portable, even though the size of `s` and the layout of padding characters inside `s` may differ between environments.

6.5 Lifetime of a data object

Look at the following program. Can you find anything nonportable in the code?

```
/* print a number whose address is
 * returned by a function
 */

extern int *f();

main()
{
    printf("the result of f is %d\n", *f());
}

int *
f()
{
    int k = 100;
    ...
    return &k;
}
```

The code above works in some environments, but it is not portable. The problem is that when **printf** in `main` de-references the pointer returned by `f`, that pointer is no longer pointing at a *live* data object.

During its *lifetime*, a data object is called *live*. In the C-World, every data object has a lifetime. The lifetime of a data object begins when the data object comes into being and ends when the data object disappears. A *dangling pointer* is a pointer that points to a data object that is no longer live. Although dangling pointers may work by chance in some environment, *don't use dangling pointers*.

The lifetime of a data object is shown in the following table.

Lifetime of a data object	
Data object	Lifetime
static, external	from beginning of program execution to the end of program execution
automatic, register	from entry into the block ({ }) in which it is declared, until leaving that block
formal parameter	from the time of invocation of the function in which it is declared to the time it returns
temporary constant resulting from an operation	from the time it is created as the result of the operation to the time it is first used
heap object (result of **malloc**, etc.)	from the time of allocation (**malloc**) to the time of deallocation (**free**), i.e., programmer-controlled

In the next chapter we will assume all pointer references are to live data objects.

CHAPTER 7
PORTABLE USE OF POINTERS

The ease of use of pointers in C gives it an advantage over languages with more limited pointers, like Pascal, or with no pointers at all, like FORTRAN. Yet the ease of use of pointers in C can also lead to code that is highly machine-dependent. In portable C, we wish to retain as much of the power of pointers as possible without sacrificing portability of code.

In this chapter you will learn a set of rules that will enable you to program portably using pointers. Since pointer manipulation is central to the C language, this chapter must touch on a number of related subjects, including alignment of data objects and padding in structures. This chapter relies on the C-World terminology developed in Chapter 6.

We begin by categorizing the uses for pointers in C, both C-specific uses and general programming uses. We then proceed through each operator that takes pointer operands, giving rules that constrain the use of those operators for portable C. We start with a discussion of cast operations: both pointer/integer and pointer/pointer. The discussion of pointer/integer conversions emphasizes the proper use of the null pointer. The discussion of conversions between pointers of different types necessitates a digression on the alignment restrictions of machines and the alignment policies of compilers. We then show rules and examples for the other operators that affect pointers, notably those used for pointer arithmetic and pointer comparison.

The rules in this chapter constrain the use of pointers but do not specify how to use the data objects that are pointed to. It is possible to point to data objects that may not be copied or used.

7.1 Uses of pointers in C

C uses pointers for C-specific purposes as well as for their universal role in the implementation of dynamic data structures. The C-specific uses for pointers are simulation of call-by-reference, accessing array elements, and *type punning*—viewing storage in a way other than the way it is declared.

- *Simulate call-by-reference.* In C, all actual parameters (arguments) are passed "by value" to the called function, meaning that the called function receives only a copy of the actual parameters and cannot change the value of any of the actual parameters. The only way a called function can alter the value of a variable in the calling function is for the calling function to pass a pointer to that variable as the actual parameter. Thus, pointers are used to simulate "call by reference," or Fortran-style argument-passing.

In early dialects of C such as [K&R], the *only* way to pass a structure to a called function is to use a pointer to that structure as an actual parameter to the function call. Even in more recent dialects, which allow the passing of entire structures as actual parameters, it is more portable, and more efficient, to retain the practice of passing only pointers to structures.

Note that when we pass a pointer as an actual parameter, if the data object is "live" at the time of the function call, then it will be live during the execution of the called function.[1] Thus this use of pointers is unlikely to cause dangling pointers.

The same cannot be said in the other direction. As we have seen in §6.5, if a called function passes back a pointer to a data object that is live during the execution of the called function, it is not necessarily live upon return to the calling function.

- *Access array elements.* The subscript (`[]`) operator in C is really a *pseudo-subscript* operator; it does not require an array name as an operand. It can be used on any two operands as long as one evaluates to a pointer and the other evaluates to an integer. For any pointer p and integer i, p[i] is defined to mean $*(p + i)$. Thus array access is really defined in terms of pointer arithmetic. If we declare

```
long b[10];
```

then b[5] means $*(b + 5)$. Since b, appearing in an expression, acts as a pointer to the first element of the array, b + 5 is a pointer to the sixth element of the array. Although it is not very useful to do so, the `[]` operator can even be used commutatively; i.e., we could say 5[b] instead of b[5].

We say that `[]` is a pseudo-subscript operator since it is defined in terms of other operators (`*` and `+`). Moreover, the subscript operator `[]` does not require that the subscript refer to a valid element of the array. Thus the expressions b[-10], b[5], b[100] are all syntactically correct C expressions. So are p[-10], p[5], p[100], for any arbitrary pointer p. But which of these expressions are allowable in portable C? To answer the question for any subscript operation, translate it to its equivalent operations in terms of indirection (`*`) and pointer arithmetic (`+`). The constraints on `[]` are the same as the pointer arithmetic constraints on +, discussed in §7.6.

---

[1] This is so unless it is a heap object deallocated during the called function.

- *Type punning.* This is one of the most powerful uses of pointers in C, and the use most likely to be nonportable. Nonetheless, by following the rules stated in §7.5.3 for pointer conversion, it is possible to use pointers portably for this purpose.

Of course, C also uses pointers for their universal role in the implementation of linked data structures: lists, trees, etc. This use of pointers is the least likely to cause portability problems. However, it must be remembered that on some machines, not all pointers have the same size, and some pointer conversions may entail value changes. Thus the rules in this chapter on pointer conversions and comparisons with the null pointer must be followed.

7.2 Rules for portable operations on pointers

We will consider rules constraining the portable use of each of the operators that apply to pointer operands. All these rules are in addition to the constraints imposed by the C language itself.

Some of the rules have the caveat that the constraint must apply "independent of environment." This means you must reassure yourself that not only have you followed the constraints on your machine, but that the constraints must also hold in other possible environments. That is, you cannot rely on the size in bytes or the layout in bytes of data objects.

Of course, some operations on pointers are inherently nonportable. For instance, in a device driver you may want to assign a constant integer value to a pointer. This value will be machine-dependent in any case.

The general portability rules for functions, FUNC2 and FUNC4, should be followed rigorously where pointers are involved. In the early days of C (including early versions of the UNIX operating system written in C), much code assumed that pointers of all types and integers could be freely interchanged without even bothering to cast them. This worked fine on the PDP-11, but as C has spread to an ever-wider universe of machines, the need for stricter typing has increased. Recall the basic function portability rules:

- FUNC2: *The actual and formal parameters of a function should have the same types.*

- FUNC4: *The type of a return expression should be the same as the return type of the function.*

These rules are important for pointers because C performs no implicit conversion

of pointer types. These function rules enhance the specific rules for pointer portability by carrying their effects across function boundaries.

The specific rules for portable operations related to pointers follow. The
operations to be discussed are:

- Type casts (conversions)

- Address operation ($\&$)

- Pointer arithmetic (pointer + integer, pointer − integer, etc.)

- Member-access operators (-> and .)

- Pointer subtraction (pointer − pointer)

- Pointer comparison (==, !=)

- Pointer relational comparison (<, >, <=, >=)

- Indirection ($\ast$)

- Assignment (=, +=, −=)

7.3 Conversions between pointer and integer

Most portability problems with pointers arise in the context of pointer conversions. Programmers, especially programmers on machines like the VAX, often
assume that all pointers are the same size, that casting from one pointer type to
another involves no value conversion, that pointers and `int`s are the same size,
that the null pointer has value "all bits zero," that the machine has a uniform
address space, that there are no alignment restrictions for any data object. For
each of these assumptions there are machines for which it is false.

By following the rules listed in this chapter, you can avoid depending on any
false assumptions about the nature of pointers.

Consider the following three examples, each of which involves conversions
between pointers and integers. See if you can identify the portability problems in
each example. (You may recognize the first example: it already appeared in
§3.2.2.) The first example turns off buffering for the file `fp`. The second example
invokes the **ls** command with arguments. The **execl** function takes a variable
number of pointers, each pointing to a command line argument; the end of the
list of arguments is shown by a null pointer. The third example attempts to allocate a chunk of heap storage, and detects a failure by the return of the value −1.

```
#include <stdio.h>
extern int *sbrk();
FILE *fp;
char *p;

...
/* Example: turn off buffering */
setbuf(fp, 0);
...
/* Example: invoke the ls command */
execl("/bin/ls", "ls", "-l", "/usr", 0);
...
/* Example: allocate heap storage */
if ((int)(p = sbrk(BLOCKSIZE)) == -1) ...
```

Note that the second two examples use UNIX system calls; hence their portability is limited to UNIX environments. Instead of the UNIX-dependent **sbrk**
system call, it is more portable to use the standard library function **malloc** when
possible. There is no similar way to replace **execl** with a standard library function, since its functionality is not part of the standard library. (See the discussion
on libraries in §9.1.)

The first two of these examples suffer from the same (commonly occurring)
problem. We are passing an integer (0), intended for use as a null pointer, to a
function or system call that expects a pointer as an argument.

```
/* Example: turn off buffering */
setbuf(fp, 0);
...
/* Example: invoke the ls command */
execl("/bin/ls", "ls", "-l", "/usr", 0);
```

This practice works on machines where pointer and int are the same size (such
as PDP-11, VAX, Sun3) but fails on machines where pointer and int are *not* the
same size (e.g., 80286 under the "large" model, Motorola 68000 under certain
compilers). The problem on these machines is that we pass an int by pushing,
say, two bytes on the stack, but the function or system call expects, say, *four*
bytes on the stack. So the function pulls garbage bytes from the stack. The problem is solved by adhering to Rule FUNC2: *The actual and formal parameters of
a function should have the same types.* See also §7.3.2 on pointers and the null
pointer.[2]

---

[2] Note that the first example will work in ANSI C environments since **stdio.h** is included, which contains the
prototype declaration for **setbuf**. The prototype will look like

The second example follows the (erroneous) model suggested by the Unix Programmer's Reference Manual for **execl** in all but the most recent editions of the Reference Manual.[3]

Portable versions of the first two examples are:

```
/* Example: turn off buffering */
setbuf(fp, (char *)0);
...
/* Example: invoke the ls command */
execl("/bin/ls", "ls", "-l", "/usr", (char *)0);
```

In the third example,

```
/* Example: allocate heap storage */
if ((int)(p = sbrk(BLOCKSIZE)) == -1) ...
```

we are trying to test if the pointer returned from **sbrk** is equal to −1. (The return value of −1 indicates an error while executing the system call **sbrk**.) The trouble arises again on machines where int is not big enough to hold the value of a pointer. In such a case, it is possible (in theory at least) for a pointer that does not equal −1 to, when truncated to an int, equal −1. For example, on an Intel 80286 machine under the large model, a 4-byte pointer with hexadecimal value 0020FFFF would truncate to a 2-byte int with hexadecimal value FFFF, which will be treated as the number −1.

A more portable version of the third example is

```
/* Example: allocate heap storage */
if ((p = sbrk(BLOCKSIZE)) == (char *)-1)
```

[ANSI] specifies, "An arbitrary integer may be converted to a pointer. The result is implementation-defined." This solution still depends on the ability of the environment to distinguish (char *)-1 from any legitimate value returned by **sbrk**, but that is a problem inherent in the definition of the **sbrk** system call.

```
extern void setbuf(FILE *stream, char *buf);
```
The presence of the prototype will coerce the actual parameter 0 to type (char *).

The same cannot be done with the **execl** example, since there is no way to specify in an ANSI prototype the argument types of a function with a variable number of arguments. There is no choice but to cast the actual parameter explicitly to the correct type here.

[3] The erroneous model occurs up through and including the Programmer Reference Manual of System V Release 2. It is corrected in the Programmer's Reference Manual of System V Release 3. The error also appears in the 4.2BSD Programmer's Manual, and in the Sun OS 3.5 Programmers Manual.

7.3.1 Pointers and integers: the rule

In portable C, it is valid to convert from a pointer to an integer and vice versa, but the size of integer required to represent the full range of pointer values is implementation-dependent. There may be machines on which *no* integer size is big enough to represent the range of pointer values, at least for some pointer types.[4]

Since you cannot know in advance the type of integer needed to hold a pointer value, we recommend the use of a parameterized type such as PTRINT which you define in your own header file **environ.h** by

```
typedef int PTRINT;
/* or long, depending on the environment */
```

PTR1: *Use the typedef'd type* PTRINT *as the integer type for conversions to and from pointer types.*

Using this rule provides another way to write a portable version of the **sbrk** example above:

```
/* Example: allocate heap storage */
if ((PTRINT)(p = sbrk(0)) == -1) ...
```

If the largest integral type is not large enough to hold a pointer, this solution will not work. The original solution, casting −1 as char *, may, however, still work in this case, and is the preferred solution.

Rule PTR1 is useful also in the following example of a pointer hashing macro. We sometimes need to take various pointers and hash them to indices into an array of hash buckets. For example, the UNIX operating system hashes pointers to various objects in order to get an "event" to sleep on. Given a pointer, let us define a macro hash that will yield an index into an array of NBUCKETS entries. The hashing is implemented as follows:

1. Cast the pointer to convert it to type PTRINT (since we cannot perform ordinary arithmetic or bitwise operations directly on the value of a pointer).

2. Shift out some low order bits (due to alignment restrictions, these may always be 0 or certain other repetitive values).

---

[4] "A pointer may be converted to any of the integral types large enough to hold it. Whether an int or a long is required is machine dependent .... An object of integral type may be converted to a pointer. The mapping always carries an integer converted from a pointer back to the same pointer, but is otherwise machine dependent." [K&R], p. 210. (The latter observation is true only if the integral type is large enough.)

3. Take the result modulo the number of buckets.

We can now write the `hash` macro as it would appear in a header file **hash.h**.

```
#define NLOW     3        /* low order bits to throw away */
#define NBUCKETS    128 /* must be a power of 2 */
#define hash(ptr)    ( ((PTRINT)(ptr)>>NLOW) & (NBUCKETS-1) )
```

Notice that the macro hash follows Rule BIT6: it is permissible to right shift a bit pattern that may be of signed type (PTRINT), since we mask the result to the desired number of bits. Since NBUCKETS is a power of 2, the masking expression n & (NBUCKETS-1) is a more efficient way of saying n % NBUCKETS.

The only integer value that can be portably assigned to any pointer is 0. The attempt to use other distinguished values for a pointer can cause portability problems. C guarantees only that 0 can be converted to a distinguished "null" value for a pointer. The UNIX system call interface uses several other distinguished values for pointers. For instance, **sbrk** and **shmat** return (char *)-1 upon failure. This specification will only work on machines for which the value of (char *)-1 is not a pointer value which may be legitimately returned by the system call.[5]

Pointer alignment assures that the low order bits of pointers are generally 0 on some machines. Some code relies on this fact to cram status information into those bits. Such code is nonportable.

Any code that attempts to assign a particular nonzero integer value to a pointer is nonportable. Such code may be useful, for example, in establishing a memory-mapped I/O register for a device driver, but is also inherently machine-dependent. The best you can do in such a case is to give the constant a preprocessor-defined name, to make the intent of the code clearer to the reader. You may put the definition of the preprocessor-defined name in a header file to isolate machine dependencies from the rest of the source code.

7.3.2 Pointers and the null pointer

Before stating the rules for the portable use of the null pointer, let's return to the example we encountered in the Introduction.

---

[5] For example, (char *)-1 is a legitimate pointer value on the PDP-11, but it is not a legitimate return value for **sbrk**.

```
main(argc, argv)
int argc;
char *argv[];
{
    /* if first command line argument is an option,
     * process it
     */
    if (argv[1][0] == '-')
        . . .
```

Recall that the problem with the code was that it may de-reference a null pointer if the user provides no arguments on the command line, and that a portable version would be

```
if (argv[1] && argv[1][0] == '-')
    . . .
```

A second example that demonstrates a common misuse of null pointers is open_log, a function that opens a logfile whose name has an optional suffix.
    Look for a nonportable statement in open_log.

```
#include <stdio.h>
#include <stdlib.h>
#include <string.h>
#define LFNSIZE 30

/* open a logfile with optional suffix */
FILE *
open_log(suffix)
char *suffix;
{
    FILE *logp;
    char logfilename[LFNSIZE];

    strcpy(logfilename, "logfile");
    logp = fopen(strncat(logfilename, suffix,
                        sizeof(logfilename) - 1), "w");
    if (logp == (FILE *)0) {
        fprintf(stderr, "open_log: can't open %s\n",
                logfilename);
        exit(EXIT_FAILURE);
    }
    return logp;
}
```

```
main()
{
    FILE *lp;

    lp = open_log((char *)0);
    ...
}
```

This example will fail in most C implementations. On a Sun 3 system it produced the message

```
Segmentation fault (core dumped)
```

The problem results from a common confusion between the null pointer
((char *) 0) and the null string ("") in the call to open_log:

```
lp = open_log((char *)0);
```

The specification for the **strncat** routine does not say what **strncat** does when
given a null pointer argument. Suppose **strncat** is implemented by the following
code:

```
char *
strncat(s1, s2, n)
register char *s1, *s2;
register int n;
{
    char *os1 = s1;

    while(*s1++ != '\0')
        ;
    s1--;
    while(n-- > 0 && (*s1++ = *s2++) != '\0')
        ;
    if (n == -1)
        *s1 = '\0';
    return os1;
}
```

Then supplying a null pointer argument to **strncat** will result in de-referencing
the null pointer, which, as we have seen, is not allowed in portable C, and which
will cause an exception on many machines.

The correct code should read

```
lp = open_log("");
```

To summarize the lesson learned from the two examples just seen, we have rule

PTR2: *Never de-reference the null pointer!*

Thus, always test a pointer for "null"ness before attempting to access the data object it points to. Do not assume that $*$(char $*$)0 is '\0'. This is true only for some machines and is definitely not portable!

7.3.3 Null pointer, null character, and null string

It is essential to understand the difference between the null pointer, '\0', and "".

Null pointer is a pointer whose value is distinguished from all legitimate pointers to data objects. In C, the null pointer is denoted by the integer constant 0. When 0 is assigned to any pointer or cast to any pointer type, the result is a null pointer. Most implementations define NULL in a header file as 0 and then use the macro name NULL to designate the null pointer.

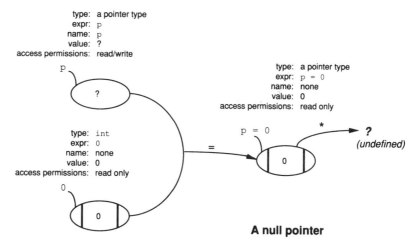

A null pointer

The C-World picture above shows the creation of a null pointer by the assign-ment of 0 to the pointer variable p. The expression p = 0 denotes a short-lived constant pointer which is a null pointer (it doesn't point to any data object). It could be used in an expression such as

    q = p = 0;

The execution of p = 0 also results in a side-effect not shown in the picture: variable p becomes a null pointer.

'\0'   is the *null character*, a character constant used in C to denote the end of a string and for application-specific purposes. Its encoding is the integer 0, that is, "all bits 0."[6]

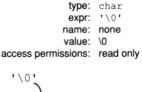

The null character

""   is the *null string*, simply a string of length 0. Since all strings in C are terminated with a null character (*'\0'*), the null string is stored as an array of one character containing the null character.

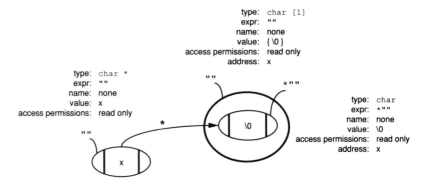

The null string

The C-World picture of *""* illustrates the two possible meanings of the expression. Like all string constants, *""* refers to an array of chars. Like all expressions referring to an array, *""* may denote the array itself or—more often—a pointer to the first element of the array, depending on context.

Some programmers follow an erroneous custom that mixes up some of these uses, for instance using NULL for the null character. While NULL and *'\0'* both

---

[6] By coincidence, the ASCII name for this value is "NUL."

evaluate to a zero-valued integer in most environments, it is *not* good form to mix up their usage.

A more dangerous error is the assumption among some VAX programmers that `*NULL` is `'\0'`. As we have seen, this is *not* a portable assumption.

Style suggestion: *In your code, for the null pointer use 0 cast to the appropriate pointer type.*

In initializers, for the null pointer use 0 without a cast, since casts in initializers are nonportable.

For example, the portable versions of the examples already shown follow this convention:

```
setbuf(fp, (char *)0);
execl("/bin/ls", "ls", "-l", "/usr", (char *)0);
```

In these two examples, the use of (char *)0 is more than a style suggestion: it is required by Rule FUNC2 so the actual parameters will have the same type as the corresponding formal parameters.

Another example that follows the style suggestion is

```
struct node *head, *tail;

/* initialize to null ptr */
head = tail = (struct node *)0;
```

If we wrote the above example using an initializer in the declaration, it should read

```
struct node *head = 0, *tail = 0;
```

Note that the initializers are written without a cast.

It is actually not necessary to explicitly cast 0 to a pointer type in assignment statements (as in the above example) or in equality comparisons (as in the following):

```
if ((p = malloc(NODESIZE)) == (char *)0)
    perror("");
```

We could write

```
head = tail = 0
```

and

```
if ((p = malloc(NODESIZE)) == 0)
```

The compiler would perform the appropriate conversion without the cast. Since the case of actual parameters is the only one where a cast is strictly necessary, it is possible to formulate a less noisy strategy for null pointers: Use NULL, with no cast, for all null pointers, except for actual parameters, which require a cast. However, we recommend that for ease of remembering and consistency of style, you nonetheless follow the style suggestion in all contexts. It also avoids any strangeness that may exist in the definition of the NULL macro.

Portable C also allows the "abbreviated" form of the above example as an acceptable style alternative: as already seen, portable C allows a pointer to be used as a Boolean variable

```
if (!(p = malloc(NODESIZE)))
    perror("");
```

although this form can be confusing to read.

We recommend using 0 cast to a pointer type rather than using the macro name NULL because in order to define NULL correctly (as 0) you may run into conflicts with the definition of NULL in **stdio.h**. Suppose you make your own definition of NULL in your **environ.h** as

```
#ifdef NULL
#undef NULL
#endif
#define NULL 0
```

then you would have to make sure your **environ.h** was always included *after* **stdio.h** in all your source files.

Some environments define NULL as (char *) 0. This definition will work on all machines (provided you then cast NULL to the appropriate pointer type before using it), but may cause **lint** to complain when you cast to the appropriate type. For example, if we define NULL as (char *) 0 and then say,

```
struct direct dir, *dp;
if (dp == (struct direct *)NULL) ...
```

lint may complain "possible pointer alignment problem."

It does not suffice to define NULL as (char *) 0 without casting to the appropriate pointer type when we use it. For example, consider the UNIX **wait** system call, which takes an integer pointer as its argument. If we say

```
wait(NULL);
```

this would be wrong on machines where integer pointers and character pointers are different sizes.

7.3.4 Environments with nonzero null pointer

The assignment of 0 to a pointer does not necessarily yield a pointer whose value is all bits 0! It yields a pointer whose value is *distinguishable* from a pointer to any object.[7]

Certain Prime computers use a value different from all-bits-0 to encode the null pointer. Also, some large Honeywell-Bull machines use the bit pattern `06000` to encode the null pointer. On such machines, the assignment of 0 to a pointer yields the special bit pattern that designates a null pointer. Similarly, `(char *) 0` yields the special bit pattern that designates a null pointer.

In those environments where the null pointer is not stored as all bits 0, the assignment

```
int *p;

p = (int *)0;
```

or

```
p = 0;
```

will initialize p with whatever special value is used to denote a null pointer. Similarly, the common C shorthand

```
if (p)
```

should work as usual since it is short for

```
if (p != 0)
```

This expression will be false if and only if p has the special bit pattern associated with null pointers.

Thus, the expression

```
if (p)
```

which uses a pointer as a Boolean value, is acceptable in portable C, even in environments where the null pointer is not all-bits-0.

However, most C environments initialize static and external variables to all-bits-0. In such an environment, if the null pointer is *not* all-bits-0, a static pointer would not be initialized to null. Hence, it is better to initialize all variables explicitly. (See Rule INIT1 in §9.6.) The same problem exists for heap objects created by **calloc**.

---

[7] "It is guaranteed that assignment of the constant 0 to a pointer will produce a null pointer distinguishable from a pointer to any object."[K&R], p. 192.

7.4 Pointer equality operators

Two pointers are *equal* in portable C if and only if they both point to the same data object or are both null pointers. Data objects are "the same" if they are of the same type and coincide in storage space. In other words, two pointers are equal if and only if they have the same type and the same value. We assume, as always, that the pointers both point to live data objects.[8]

Two pointers may compare equal in a given environment without being equal in the abstract machine of the C World. Two pointers are equal portably if they point to the same data object independent of the environment, i.e., independent of the size and layout of the data objects they point to. For example, given the fragment

```
int n, *q;
char *p;

q = &n;
p = (char *)q;
```

is `(char *)(q + 1)` equal to `p + 4`? They have same type and, in some environments, the same value. But we cannot say they are equal in a portable sense, since their equality is dependent on the size of an `int` in the environment.

We insist that two pointers have the same value *and* type to be equal. This is to avoid the earlier bad practice of treating all pointers as one generic type: "pointer." We insist that only pointers of the same type be compared for equality. Equality (`==`) and inequality (`!=`) are undefined in portable C for operands that are pointers of different types. For example, in the following fragment, it is undefined whether `cp` and `ip` are equal in the C-World.

---

[8] Clearly, data objects that are the same have the same value, the same address, and the same name, if any. Live data objects overlapping in storage space have the same lifetime. Thus, data objects that are the same also have the same lifetime.

Different expressions may refer to the same data object. By the definition just stated, given the union

```
union {
    int a;
    int b;
} u;
```

the expressions `u.a` and `u.b` denote the same data object.

Since data objects that are the same have the same type, equal pointers have the same type. Indeed, pointer comparison is constrained to pointers of the same type; pointers of different types cannot be compared in a portable way.

In ANSI C, types are called the same when they are the same except for type qualifiers. A `char *` and a `const char *` can point to the same data object. The type `char *` permits a change in value of the data object pointed at, while the type `const char *` forces that data object to be treated as a constant.

```
char *cp;
int *ip, i;

ip = &i;
cp = (char *)ip; /* are cp and ip equal? */
```

cp and ip may have the same value on many machines but they do not point to the same data object. Thus we cannot say whether they are equal or not equal in the C-World. It is necessary to cast one pointer to the type of the other in order to make the comparison. (See §7.5.) On some machines, like Tandem and Data General Eclipse, such type conversion may also cause a value conversion.

Similarly, given the two-dimensional array

```
int table [3][5];
```

are table and table[0] equal? No, because table (in most contexts) has type int (*)[5] (pointer to an array of five ints) while table[0] (in most contexts) has type int *.

There is no special rule in portable C for the equality operators on pointers, == and !=, besides the general pointer rule PTR3: *Pointer operands of an operator must match in type. Use a cast, if necessary, to ensure this*. Rule PTR3 will be formally introduced in §7.5.3.

7.5 Conversions between different pointer types

The basic idea behind the rules for pointer conversions is to eliminate operations that attempt to access improperly aligned data objects.

As an introduction to pointer conversions, consider the following example that arose in a financial application in which multiple processes communicate via messages. A server task reads a message into an input buffer, discerns its message type, then processes it accordingly. The primary data object is msg, of type MSG. The server task uses the data in msg by viewing it as one of a variety of structures, each appropriate to a different message type. Thus we wish to overlay various structures on top of this primary data object.

Can you find anything nonportable in the code?

```
/* Server routine:
 * receive incoming messages and act on them
 * Use a buffer to hold one msg that may be
 * of several possible types,
 * each with a corresponding structure
 */
typedef struct {
    char m_type;
    char m_buf[BUFSIZ];
} MSG;
typedef struct {
    int a_n;
    ...
} MSGA;
#define TYPEA 100
/*
 * ...definitions for MSGB, MSGC, ...
 * ...definitions for TYPEB, TYPEC, ...
 */
MSG msg;
void proc_a(), proc_b(), ..., proc_z();

main()
{
    ...
    msg_receive(&msg);   /* a msg arrives */
    switch (msg.m_type)
    {
        case TYPEA: proc_a((MSGA *)msg.m_buf); break;
        case TYPEB: proc_b((MSGB *)msg.m_buf); break;
        ...
        case TYPEZ: proc_z((MSGZ *)msg.m_buf); break;
    }
    ...
}

void
proc_a(p)          /* process message type MSGA */
MSGA *p;
{
    int i;
    i = p->a_n;
    ...
}
...
```

The potential portability problem is that msg.m_buf may not be aligned properly to allow various structures to be successfully overlaid on top of it.

Because some of the structures MSGA, MSGB, ... may have different alignment restrictions than msg.m_buf, an attempt to inspect the data in msg using those structures as templates could yield a hardware exception or an incorrect pointer.[9]

Moreover, even if msg.m_buf is aligned so that referencing MSGA, MSGB, ... on top of it does not result in an exception or incorrect pointer, it may nonetheless happen that msg.m_buf is not aligned to give the most efficient code when referencing other structures on top of it.

The best way to coerce the alignment of msg.m_buf to the most general possible alignment is to put it in a union with a dummy object of type ALIGN. (You must typedef ALIGN as a type with the strictest *alignment policy* in your particular environment.)

For example, on a VAX, you might declare

```
typedef long ALIGN;
```

in your own header file **environ.h**.

With this method, references to m_buf become a little more involved to code since it is one level deeper in the structure. This added complexity can be hidden in a macro such as message below. However, there should be no performance penalty and the improvement in alignment can *benefit* performance.

A portable version of the previous example now requires only a change in the declaration of MSG:

```
typedef struct {
    char m_type;
    union {
        char u_buf[BUFSIZ];
        ALIGN u_dummy;
        /* aligns u_buf on the most general boundary */
    } m_u;
} MSG;

#define message    msg.m_u.u_buf
...
```

---

[9] For example, on a machine such as a Tandem where character pointers and word pointers are represented differently, the cast

```
(MSGA *)msg.m_buf
```

could yield a pointer which is actually pointing at a different place in storage than msg.m_buf.

```
main()
{
    ...
    switch (msg.m_type)
    {
        case TYPEA: proc_a((MSGA *)msg.message); break;
        case TYPEB: proc_b((MSGB *)msg.message); break;
        ...
        case TYPEZ: proc_z((MSGZ *)msg.message); break;
    }
    ...
}
```

Note that on the VAX or the Intel 80286, the original code would actually work without this fix. The code would work because those machines have no *alignment restrictions*. A structure can be referenced starting at any address without causing an exception. However, if msg.m_buf is aligned on a random address, it may not yield the most efficient code when referenced via various structure types, hence the need to align it using ALIGN.

7.5.1 Alignment and pointer conversion

It is important to understand the difference between the *alignment restrictions* of a machine and the *alignment policy* of a compiler.

The alignment restrictions of a machine constitute the narrower notion. The alignment restriction of type *t* is the set of values that a pointer of type *t* * can have that will permit us to de-reference the pointer. For each type, its alignment restriction is the set of address boundaries that objects of that type must lie on so as not to cause a hardware exception when referencing them.

Some machines, like the Tandem, have different representations for character pointers and word pointers. For such a machine, casting a character pointer to a word pointer may yield a pointer to a different place in storage, unless the character pointer is aligned according to the alignment restrictions for word pointers.

Some machines, like Intel 80*x*86 and VAX, have no alignment restrictions. Data objects of any type can be referenced at any address boundary without causing a machine exception. Even on such machines, however, data access may be more efficient at certain alignment boundaries.

For each type, the alignment policy of the compiler determines what addresses the compiler will use in placing data objects declared to be of that type. The compiler implementer's freedom in choosing an alignment policy is limited by the alignment restrictions of the hardware. The alignment policy may be stricter than the machine's alignment restrictions for reasons of efficient access.

A machine may be able, for instance, to access a long integer beginning at any byte boundary, yet it may access `longs` more quickly if their first byte's address is a multiple of 4.

The alignment policy of a compiler determines for each type the addresses at which the compiler places data objects of that type:

- as static variables

  Knowing the alignment policy for static variables is of no use to the programmer because we cannot portably assume any relation between separate static variables. (Cf. §7.6, Rule PTR5.)

- as automatic variables

  You can use knowledge about the alignment policy for automatic variables to implement the **varargs** macros if someone hasn't done so already. (See §3.3.3.) However, aside from this limited use, understanding the alignment policy for automatic variables is not necessary, for the same reason as for static variables; we will not discuss it here.

- within a structure

  Henceforth, when we speak of alignment policy, we refer to the alignment policy within structures. We use the alignment policy within structures to decide what type `ALIGN` should be in a given environment. Alignment policy is also a source of concern when trying to write structures for communication between different machines. (See §8.3.)

  Some compilers have flags that specify "no padding" of structures. Such an option is easiest to implement on machines with no alignment restrictions; presumably, it will incur some runtime inefficiencies. It may be useful for creating structures designed for data portability between such machines—if both machines have such an option. It is perhaps a weakness of C that the programmer has limited control over the padding in structures.

In general, the alignment policy must be at least as strict as the hardware's alignment restrictions.[10] However, different compilers for the same machine may have different alignment policies. Each compiler must choose an alignment policy based on the trade-off of space efficiency vs runtime efficiency for the given type of machine.

To fully describe the alignment restrictions and alignment policy of an environment would require a description of the requirements for each scalar type, then for arrays, structures, and unions containing various types. Fortunately, for

---

[10] The Sun-4 C compiler gets around this restriction with a -misalign option, allowing for out-of-alignment references, even though the hardware does not.

the purpose of writing portable C, it suffices to specify the most stringent align-ment policy. We do so by defining the type ALIGN, whose actual implementa-tion is environment-dependent. Further, we observe that the alignment policy for a structure is the same as the most stringent alignment policy for its members—at least in all the machines we know of.

ALIGN is a typedef'd type that you should define in your **environ.h**. A data object of type ALIGN should have the strictest alignment policy. The following definition should work for all environments:

```
typedef double ALIGN;
```

However, in a given environment, the best choice for ALIGN is the smallest type among those with the strictest alignment policy. A structure with a member of type ALIGN will be aligned at the most general and efficient boundary known to *your* compiler. Here is the suggested value of ALIGN for some common machines; these values work for most compilers on the given machines.

Alignment Policy	
machine	ALIGN
VAX	long
PDP11	short
68000, 68020	short
8086, 80286	short
3B	long
IBM370	double
Sparc	double

In order to explain the rules for conversion from one pointer type to another, it is necessary to define the data objects with strictest and least strict alignment policies.

In portable C, the data objects of strictest alignment are:

- Data objects of type ALIGN

- Compound data objects (structures, unions, arrays) containing a member of strictest alignment

- Data objects created as result of a call to **malloc, calloc,** or **realloc** ("heap objects")[11]

---

[11] Despite the specification of **malloc,** you can rely on heap objects to have strictest alignment only if they are more than half the size of an ALIGN.

In portable C, the data objects of least strict alignment are `chars` (or `unsigned chars`) and arrays (of any number of dimensions) of `chars` or `unsigned chars`.

In ANSI C, a pointer to an object of least strict alignment is said to be of type `void *`, a "generic" pointer. Since `void *` is not part of pre-ANSI C, we do not recommend using it in portable C. Instead, we recommend the use of `char *` to denote a pointer to an object of least strict alignment.[12]

7.5.2 Casts and pointer conversion

In portable C, all conversions from one pointer type to another must be explicit operations using the cast operator. A cast is an operation that yields a nonmodifiable short-lived data object whose type is the target type of the conversion. When the cast operator is applied to a pointer, the operand and the result point to objects that share the same first grid character. For example, the following C-World picture shows the short-lived constant that results from the cast `(long *) p`, where p points to a data object a of type `ALIGN`.[13]

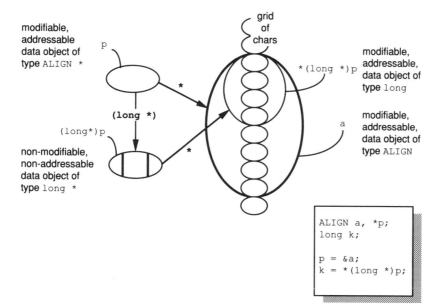

```
ALIGN a, *p;
long k;

p = &a;
k = *(long *)p;
```

---

[12] What about the prevalence of `void *` as a formal parameter type in ANSI library routines? This is not a problem, since any pointer type may be passed as the actual parameter, as long as a prototype of the library function is in scope.

[13] Of course, the size of `ALIGN` and of `long` in bytes is environment dependent, so the picture cannot be environment independent.

C does not perform implicit conversions on data objects of different pointer types whether they are operands of an operator, actual parameters, or return expressions of a function. Consider the code

```
struct xact *xp;
char *p;
p = xp;
```

In [ANSI] and some non-ANSI compilers, this code is rejected by the compiler because p and xp have different types. [K&R] allow such code but make no value conversions: p will have the same bit-pattern representation as xp after the assignment.[14] Such compilers rely on the fact that in many environments pointer conversions require no value change. The handling of the above code is quite different from the handling of the following assignment:

```
int i;
double d;
...
d = i;
```

In this case, C compilers perform a conversion from int to double before making the assignment.

7.5.3 Rules for conversions: pointer to pointer

Since there are no implicit pointer type conversions in portable C, only cast operations can perform pointer type conversions. Before stating Rule PTR3, we repeat the importance of observing the general function portability rules FUNC2 and FUNC4. Following rules FUNC2, FUNC4 and the other rules listed here will help overcome several problems: in some environments, pointers of different types may have different addressing schemes. (For example, on some Tandem machines and on the Data General Eclipse, character pointers and integer pointers have different numbering schemes, thus representing the same location by different values.) In some environments, pointers of different types have different sizes (for example, some CDC machines which lack a native character pointer). In such environments, pointer to pointer conversion may require value conversion.

Pointers to functions cannot be portably converted to other kinds of pointers. We restrict the discussion here to pointers to data objects that are not functions. Function pointers are discussed in §3.4.

---

[14] [K&R], p. 192.

PTR3: *Pointer operands of an operator must match in type. Use a cast, if necessary, to ensure this.*

This rule applies to all operations that take more than one pointer operand, except for the comma operator, | |, and & &. The operators in question are: assignment (=), pointer subtraction (−), pointer equality (==, ! =), pointer comparison (<, >, <=, >=), and the rightmost operands of the conditional operator (? :).

Use of a cast in an initializer is not portable since some compilers will not accept casts in this context. Therefore, the pointer variable to be initialized and the initializer should match in type, or an assignment statement should be used instead.

Rule PTR3 shows the necessity for pointer conversions in certain situations. But how do we know which pointer conversions are portable? Rule PTR4 will specify.[15]

PTR4: *The following are portable casts for pointers that do not point to functions:*

1. *Any pointer can be converted into a pointer of type* char *.
   That is, any pointer can be converted into a pointer to an object of least strict alignment. Hence (char *)p is a portable cast for any pointer p. The result of the cast (char *)p points to the first byte of the data object pointed to by p.[16]

---

[15] We wish to make the rule describing portable pointer conversions simple, safe, and mechanical. The following observations provide a technical background to Rule PTR4. They could be used by a mechanized reasoning tool to verify portability of casts.

Assume p and q are non-null pointers (that is, expressions denoting data objects of pointer type) and t and s are pointer types.

Observation 1. If (t)p is a portable cast, then p and (t)p point to data objects that coincide in their first byte of storage space.

Observation 2. If p equals q and (t)p is a portable cast, then (t)q is a portable cast.
(From Observation 1 it follows that (t)q and (t)p are equal.)

Observation 3. (t)(s)p is a portable cast if and only if (t)p and (s)p are portable casts.
(From Observation 1 it follows that (t)(s)p and (t)p are equal.)

Observation 4. If p is of type t, then (t)p is a portable cast.
(From Observation 1 it follows that p and (t)p are equal.)

Observation 5. A compound data object and its first member or element coincide in their first byte of storage space. Moreover, a union and *all* its members coincide in their first byte of storage.

If p is of type t and (s)p is a portable cast, then from Observations 3, 4, and 1, it follows that (t)(s)p is a portable cast and equal to p.

[16] A more precise formulation of this rule is: (t)p is a portable cast for any p, where t is char * or unsigned char * or a pointer to a single or multi-dimensional array of chars or unsigned chars.

2. *A pointer to a data object of strictest alignment can be converted into a pointer of any type.*
   That is, if p points to a data object of type `ALIGN` or any other data object of strictest alignment, then $(t)\,p$ is a portable cast for any type t.[17]

3. *A pointer to a compound type (structure, union, or array) can be converted to a pointer to the type of any member or element of that compound type.*
   A structure, union, or array has no "hole" or padding at the beginning. A pointer to a structure or array, converted to a pointer to the type of the first member or element, points to the first member or element.

It is *not* true that a pointer of type `char *` can be converted to any pointer type. On some machines, if we convert a random `char *` pointer to another type pointer, we might violate the alignment restrictions of the machine.

Exercise 7-1: Pointer conversion rules (advanced). Use Observations 1 to 5 to prove that if p is a pointer to the first member of a data object of compound type t, then $(t \ *)\,p$ is a portable cast and points to the compound data object. □

Solution to Exercise 7-1. Let q be a pointer to a compound data object of type t and s the type of its first member.
1. $(s \ *)\,q$ is a portable cast (Rule PTR4),
2. $(t \ *)\,q$ is a portable cast (Observation 4),
3. $(t \ *)\,(s \ *)\,q$ is a portable cast (Observation 3 and steps 1 and 2),
4. $(s \ *)\,q$ points to the first member of $*q$ (Observations 1 and 5 and step 1),
5. p equals $(s \ *)\,q$ (Definition of pointer equality),
6. $(t \ *)\,p$ is a portable cast (Observation 2 and steps 3 and 5),
7. $(t \ *)\,p$ points to the compound data object (Observations 1 and 5). □

Now we will look at some applications of the rules on pointer conversions. [ANSI] defines **memcpy** with the prototype

```
#include <string.h>
void *memcpy(void *s1, const void *s2, size_t n)
```

and says "The **memcpy** function copies n characters from object pointed to by s2 into the object pointed to by s1."

---

[17] Clearly, `(char *)p` is a portable cast (by part 1 of this rule). But then, `(t) (char *)p` is a portable cast (Observation 3). This is the idea behind the implementation of a storage allocation routine like **malloc**. Storage is allocated in units of strictest alignment. A pointer to such a unit cast to `char *` is returned. The resulting pointer can be cast into any pointer type.

Consider the following two examples. Is there anything nonportable about them?

```
int n;
char buf[BUFSIZ];
struct dir dir;

/* Example: copy an int into a character buffer */
/* perhaps to avoid structure padding in a write buffer */

memcpy(buf, &n, sizeof(n));

/* Example: write out a structure by viewing it
 * as a character array */

fwrite((char *)&dir, sizeof(dir), 1, fp);
```

The first example could occur when trying to pack an integer into a character buffer to circumvent the alignment restrictions of the environment (see §8.3 on portable structure design). The second example involves writing out a structure onto a file `fp`.

The first example violates Rule FUNC2 because the type of the second actual parameter differs from the type of the formal parameter.

```
    memcpy(buf, &n, sizeof(n));
```

The actual parameter `&n` has type `(int *)`, while the formal parameter has type `(char *)`. While on many commonly used machines this causes no problem (e.g., VAX, PDP-11, 680x0, 80x86), it will cause a problem on a Tandem machine or a Data General Eclipse and other machines that require a value conversion between character and integer pointers.

Note that if you wrote this code using an ANSI C compiler and included the header **string.h**, then the function prototypes in the include file would cause `&n` to be converted to the type of the formal parameter, in this case `(void *)`. So in all ANSI-conforming environments, this code would work portably. Nonetheless, for widest portability, we recommend you follow Rule FUNC2.

Following Rule FUNC2 yields the following portable version of the first example:

```
    memcpy(buf, (char *)&n, sizeof(n));
```

Note that the cast `(char *) &n` is portable because of Rule PTR4, "Any pointer can be converted into a pointer of type `char *`." The cast may cause a necessary change in value in some environments.

The second example is portable as written, because of the same rule.

```
fwrite((char *)&dir, sizeof(dir), 1, fp);
```

In fact, since there is only one **fwrite** routine, and it expects a character pointer to tell it where to begin writing out, it is *necessary* to view the structure we wish to write as coinciding with a grid of characters.

Note that in the ANSI standard library, **fwrite** takes a void * generic pointer argument as its first formal parameter. Thus, if using an ANSI compiler, you could pass *any* kind of pointer as the first argument to **fwrite**, as long as you've included **stdio.h**, which has the prototype. However, for greatest portability, we recommend you pass a char * pointer as above; this will work in both ANSI and pre-ANSI compilers.

7.6 Pointer arithmetic and member-access operations

To achieve portable pointer arithmetic, we wish to avoid operations that attempt to access non-existent memory and could cause a program to trap and abort. We introduce Rule PTR5, which is the only constraint on pointer arithmetic and member-access operations (->, .) in portable C. Intuitively, for pointer arithmetic to work in portable C, the operation must not lead us far from the original primary data object. The pointer resulting from a pointer arithmetic operation must not point *before* the primary data object associated with the operand pointer, nor far *beyond* it.

Note that these constraints specify what values a pointer can assume; they do *not* specify which pointers can be de-referenced.

PTR5: *The first byte of a data object must lie within or just beyond the associated primary data object, independent of the environment.*

A pointer points *within* a primary data object if it points to a data object whose first byte lies inside that primary data object. The data object pointed to may be real or may be imaginary. It is imaginary if it lies partly outside the primary data object.

A pointer points *just beyond* a primary data object if the first byte of the pointed-to data object coincides with the grid character immediately following the last grid character of the primary data object.[18] The data object to which such a pointer points is imaginary.

---

[18] This rule is a slight generalization of [ANSI], which guarantees that pointers can point "one past the last member" of an array.

When we say *independent of the environment*, we mean it is not sufficient to show that a given operation remains within the associated primary data object; you must show that the operation remains within the primary data object *regardless* of size and layout of the object.

Rule PTR5 states what kind of data objects are allowed in portable C. But implicitly the rule constrains what kind of values pointers can take in portable C: if p points to a data object forbidden by Rule PTR5, then *p denotes the forbidden object. Since *p is forbidden, p must be forbidden, too. Thus a corollary to Rule PTR5 is "*no operation may yield a pointer that points to a data object forbidden by Rule PTR5.*"

Assuming p is a pointer and i is an integer, by Rule PTR5, p + i is a permissible expression in portable C only if p + i points within or just beyond its associated primary data object. The same is true for p - i.

For example, given

```
int k[3];
```

k, k+1, k+2, k+3 are acceptable pointers in portable C, while k-1 and k+4 are not, because k-1 points before the array, and k+4 points too far beyond it.

As a result of Rule PTR5, *all* pointers in portable C will point to data objects that lie within or just beyond their associated primary data object.

Why is it portable to point just beyond a primary data object but not before one? There are several practical answers. Obviously much C code depends on pointers looping upwards through an array. At the end of any such loop, the pointer must point to an imaginary data object just beyond the array. So makers of existing compilers must make sure that an array cannot be the last valid object in memory; there must be at least another byte of address space beyond it. This practical observation is made explicit in ANSI C. However, such is not the case in reverse. Given an array

```
BLOB a[ASIZE];
```

the pointer &a[ASIZE] points to an imaginary data object that begins with the grid char immediately beyond the array a. But &a[-1] points to an imaginary data object that coincides with a grid character that is sizeof(a[0]) grid chars before the array a. The bigger the type BLOB is, the more unlikely that a[-1] would lie within the address space of the program. There is no way a compiler can guarantee that all such references would be within the address space of the program. Hence, we cannot portably address a[-1].

7.6.1 Pointer arithmetic

We now examine several examples that illustrate the use of Rule PTR5. Look at the following example. The macro `CTOI` is defined in §5.3.2. Can you find anything nonportable in the code?

```
#include <stdio.h>
#include "environ.h"

/* write out an integer n,
 * a character at a time
 */
putint(n)
int n;
{
    char *p;
    char *q = ((char *)&n) + 4;

    for (p = (char *)&n; p < q; p++)
        putchar(CTOI(*p));
}
```

The example works in environments with 4-byte integers but not in environments with 2-byte integers.

```
char *q = ((char *)&n) + ▮4;
```

Why? because in an environment where `int`s are 2 bytes long, the pointer p will point to imaginary data objects that lie totally outside their associated primary data object n. To make things worse, in such an environment, we then dereference a pointer to an imaginary data object. That is why the phrase *independent of the environment* is part of Rule PTR5: the result of the addition `((char *)&n) + 4` lies just beyond the primary data object n on a VAX, but not in all environments.

The cure to this portability problem is to change the constant 4 into a more portable parameterized constant: `sizeof(n)`. Thus a portable version of the above example is

```
/* write out an integer n,
 * a character at a time
 */
putint(n)
int n;
{
    char *p;
    char *q = ((char *)&n) + sizeof(n);

    for (p = (char *)&n; p < q; p++)
        putchar(CTOI(*p));
}
```

This version of putint is consistent with Rule PTR5. We could also write the initialization as

```
char *q = ((char *)(&n + 1);
```

Now for a second example. Can you find anything nonportable in the following code?

```
typedef struct {
    ...
} BIGSTRUCT;
...
BIGSTRUCT ba[MAXBIGS], *p;

/* process an array of BIGSTRUCT objects,
 * from last to first */

for (p = &ba[MAXBIGS - 1]; p >= ba; p--)
    process(p);
```

The problem with the example is that the last time around the loop, p has the value &ba[-1], which is the same as ba - 1. This is not portable since we are pointing *before* the associated primary data object ba. The code breaks Rule PTR5.

```
for (p = &ba[MAXBIGS - 1]; p >= ba; p--)
    process(p);
```

How could this lead to problems? Suppose that array ba were located near the bottom of memory. Then ba - 1 might underflow to a large number (assuming that the machine does not complain about pointer underflow—most machines do not, and that the machine uses unsigned arithmetic for pointer comparisons). The comparison p >= ba would be true, and the loop could go on indefinitely, or would produce strange results for unexpected values of p. This problem may seem unlikely, but on the 80*x*86 it becomes more likely, since under most data models each data object lies within a 64K segment and pointer arithmetic is done just within the segment.

This problem is called *pointer wraparound*. There are several solutions to the portability problem of pointer wraparound.

1. Use indexes for looping downwards rather than pointers.

```
BIGSTRUCT ba[MAXBIGS];
int i;

for (i = MAXBIGS - 1; i >= 0; i--)
    process(&ba[i]);
```

Index i can take negative values without causing any problems because int is a signed type. Is this solution "less efficient" than the nonportable version above? Programmers often assume that pointers are "more efficient" for looping in C, but this is not necessarily the case. Indexing through an array can often yield clearer code as well.

2. Loop from bottom to top of the array.

```
BIGSTRUCT ba[MAXBIGS], *p;

for (p = ba; p <= &ba[MAXBIGS - 1]; p++)
    process(p);
```

This solution will only work if the function process doesn't care about the order in which it proceeds through the array ba. If process *does* care, it may be necessary to rearrange the data structure itself.

Although at the end of the loop, p has the value &ba[MAXBIGS] (i.e., ba+MAXBIGS), which points to an imaginary data object, this imaginary data object lies *just beyond* the associated primary data object ba, and is explicitly allowed in portable C, by Rule PTR5. Note that we do not *access* the value of ba[MAXBIGS]—it is not permissible to access an imaginary data object.

7.6.2 Member-access operations (->, .)

We have shown how Rule PTR5 constrains pointer arithmetic in portable C. The next example shows how Rule PTR5 constrains member-access operations in portable C. The example shows that you can use an imaginary structure member, as long as you access only its real part.[19]

The example uses the Berkeley UNIX library functions for accessing directory entries. In a Berkeley directory, filename entries have varying lengths and occupy only as many bytes as needed (each filename is rounded up to hold a multiple of 4 bytes). The function **opendir** opens a directory, allocates storage to hold all the directory entries, and returns a "directory stream" pointer of type DIR *. To access a filename in the directory, you can repeatedly call **readdir** using the directory stream pointer. The function **readdir** will return a pointer to the next entry in the directory, a structure of type struct direct.

```
#define MAXNAMLEN 255

struct direct {
    ...
    u_short d_namlen;       /* length of string in d_name */
    char d_name[MAXNAMLEN + 1];
};

struct direct *readdir();
```

Suppose that in our environment, **opendir** allocates just enough storage to hold the actual size of the directory. Suppose we are reading a directory named logdir, which contains no files. By Unix convention, the directory nonetheless has two entries, named "." and "..".

```
    #include <sys/types.h>
    #include < sys/dir.h>

    DIR *logdirp;
    struct direct *dp;

        logdirp = opendir("logdir");
        if (logdirp == NULL)
            errexit();
        dp = readdir(logdirp);
        dp = readdir(logdirp);
```

The picture looks like

---

[19] Imaginary and real data objects are defined in §6.3.

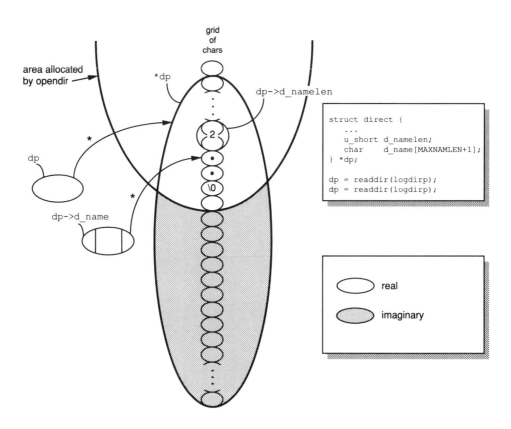

```
struct direct {
    ...
    u_short d_namelen;
    char    d_name[MAXNAMLEN+1];
} *dp;

dp = readdir(logdirp);
dp = readdir(logdirp);
```

The data object pointed to by dp is imaginary because it exceeds the size of its associated primary data object, the allocated area allocated by **opendir**, which is only big enough to hold the actual size of the directory. Nonetheless, this style of programming is portable, and works fine as long as you only reference the real part of the imaginary data object. Thus dp->d_namlen is a valid data object by Rule PTR5; it lies inside the allocated primary data object; dp->d_namlen is a real member of the imaginary structure *dp. What about dp->d_name? Clearly the data object itself is imaginary since it is bigger than the associated primary data object. However, we do not need to access all of the array dp->d_name. In the example shown in the picture, dp->d_name contains the string "..". It is permissible to access this string since it lies within the allocated area.

The data object pointed to by dp is imaginary, since its size is at least 268 bytes, while the size of the allocated primary data object is only 32 bytes in our implementation. Thus dp points to an imaginary data object some of whose constituents are real. As long as we don't access the imaginary parts of that data object, the code is acceptable in portable C.[20]

7.7 The address operator &

PTR6: *Don't apply* & *to an array expression or to a function name expression.*

That is, if we declare

```
char a[ASIZE];
int b[ROWS][COLS];
```

then it is not portable to write &a, nor is it portable write &b[1].
  Similarly, if we declare

```
extern char *f();
```

then it is not portable to write &f.
  For an array expression a or function name f, use a and f instead of &a and &f to refer to the address of those data objects. Some compilers allow &a and &f; others do not. Some compilers define &a to be the same as a, while others—including [ANSI]—define &a to mean "the address of array a."[21]

7.8 Pointer minus pointer

Since the difference of two pointers, p − q, is defined as the integer n such that q + n equals p, there is a connection between pointer subtraction and pointer arithmetic. Before considering the rule for pointer subtraction in portable C, we examine the following example, based on code found in a text formatting program. The code seeks to write out all the external variables, to be stored on file tempfile. Can you find anything nonportable in the code?

---

[20] Certain runtime environments for C can detect attempts to access imaginary data objects. This ability is very useful in debugging code. One such environment is the Saber C interpreter.

[21] In [ANSI], the type of &a above would be char (*)[10] "a pointer to an array of 10 characters."

```
struct a1 a;
struct b1 b;
struct c1 c;
  ...
struct z1 z;

f()
{
    ...
    /* write out the state of all global variables */
    fwrite((char *)&a, (&z + 1) - &a, 1, tempfile);
}
```

Though this code works in many environments, the subtraction is not portable.

```
fwrite((char *)&a, (&z + 1) - &a, 1, tempfile);
```

The code is not portable because (&z + 1) - &a violates Rule PTR3: *Pointer operands of an operator must match in type. Use a cast, if necessary, to ensure this.* However, even if we write the pointer subtraction as

```
(char *)(&z+1) - (char *)&a
```

we are making assumptions about the layout in storage of separate primary data objects. In portable C, we allow arithmetic within a single primary data object but not between separate primary data objects (Rule PTR5).

Certainly if we used similar code to write out a series of variables declared consecutively as automatic variables within a function, the results would be highly nonportable, since the ordering of automatic variables in storage varies more between machines than the ordering of external variables.

While it is true that on almost all machines, the structures in the current example would be laid out in increasing storage locations, on a segmented architecture (like 8086 using the "large model") the structures might lie in different segments and hence pointer subtraction between them would make little sense. If we were using an interpreter to run this code, again we could not assume that the external variables would be laid out in consecutive storage locations.

A more portable approach would be to declare a structure containing all the variables that we wish to store. Then we can perform a pointer subtraction *within* a primary data object, which is a more portable operation.

```
struct globals {
    struct a1 a;
    struct b1 b;
    struct c1 c;
    ...
    struct z1 z;
} globals;

f()
{
    ...
    /* write out the state of all global variables */

    fwrite((char *)&globals.a,
        (char *)(&globals.z+1) - (char *)&globals.a,
        1,
        tempfile);
}
```

However, even here we don't solve all the problems. It could be that the type for holding pointer differences is not big enough to hold possible pointer differences inside of a structure.[22] It could be that a given compiler may not allow the declaration of arbitrarily large structures. (For example, an 8086 compiler under the large model will not allow a structure larger than 64K in size.)

7.8.1 Rule for pointer subtraction

Need we limit pointer subtraction to pointers that point within the same array, as ANSI does? Portable C is able to state a slightly more relaxed constraint on pointer subtractions.

PTR7: *In order to subtract two pointers, they must*

- *be of the same type,*

- *point to data objects associated with same primary data object,*

- *and be viewable as pointing to elements of the same array (derivable from each other by pointer arithmetic), independent of the environment.*

That is, independent of the size in bytes and layout of the primary data object. The constraint that the two pointers be derivable from each other by pointer

---

[22] See §7.8.2 on `ptrdiff_t`.

arithmetic allows more situations than the requirement that they point within the same array. For example, the two pointers could point within a **malloc**'d storage area, or within a structure. So what does "viewable as pointing to elements of the same array" mean? Every data object can be viewed as part of a virtual array of data objects of the same type extending both before and beyond the original object. If the two pointers that we wish to subtract can be viewed as pointing to elements of such a virtual array, even if that array is not a declared array, then the constraint is satisfied.

For example, the following code is portable:

```
struct{
    char c;
    double d;
    int e;
} y;

/* write out 1st 2 elements of struct */

fwrite((char *)&y,
    (char *)&y.e - (char *)&y.c, 1,
    tempfile);
```

One use of pointer subtraction is to write out or copy a part of a structure. The example shows a portable use of pointer subtraction for such a purpose. The example is portable because it satisfies our rules: the pointers point within the same primary data object (y), have the same type (char *), and can be viewed as pointing to elements of a character array (the "grid of characters" array underlying the data object y).

The following nonportable example is admittedly unlikely, but illustrates Rule PTR7.

```
struct{
    long a;
    int b;
    long c;
} x;
int n;

n = &x.c - &x.a;
```

The expression &x.c - &x.a attempts to view x.c and x.a as if they were part of an imaginary array of longs. On some machines this would be the case, because int could be the same size as long, or because int is padded in a structure to the same boundary as a long. But on some machines, it is impossible to view x.a and x.c as belonging to a single array of longs. Thus we cannot view x.a and x.c as members of an imaginary array, *independent of the environment*. The code may execute, but the result is undefined.

7.8.2 Type `ptrdiff_t`

The distance between two pointers can be larger than the maximum value of a pointer difference in a particular implementation. That is, the distance might exceed the maximum value of ptrdiff_t, ANSI C's typedef'd name for the type of a pointer difference. In a non-ANSI environment, you should put the typedef for ptrdiff_t for your environment in your **environ.h**, or in your own **stddef.h**. In [K&R], the type of the result of subtracting two pointers is int. In some implementations, the result of subtracting two pointers is long.

For maximum portability, values for the results of pointer subtraction should be limited to the range [−32767..32767]. But clearly, there are instances, especially on 32-bit machines, where such a restriction is too tight. As always, violations should be clearly documented through comments, typedefs, and #defines.

The type ptrdiff_t is related to the type size_t, ANSI's typedef'd name for the type that the sizeof operator yields. Since (by Rule PTR7) two pointers can be subtracted if they lie within the same primary data object, it would be desirable if the range of ptrdiff_t includes the range of size_t (although this is not always the case). The portable range of size_t is [0..32767], but once again, you may need to exceed this range. For example, you may not wish to limit the size of all your data objects to 32767 bytes, as the portable range of size_t would require.

7.9 Pointer relational operators

The relational comparison operators are <, >, <=, and >=. We define relational comparison for pointers in terms of pointer subtraction:
Definition: For pointers p and q, $p < q$ if and only if the value of (char *)q − (char *)p is greater than zero.

PTR8: *A relational comparison on two pointers requires that both*

- *have the same type, and*

- *are associated with same primary data object,*

independent of the environment.

The constraints on relational comparison for pointers are less strict than for pointer subtraction, even though relational comparison for pointers is defined in terms of pointer subtraction.

For an example that follows Rule PTR8, consider

```
struct{
    long a;
    int b;
    long c;
} x;

if (&x.a < &x.c)
    printf("true");
```

In the example, `&x.a` clearly is less than `&x.c`, even though `&x.c - &x.a` is undefined in portable C, as shown in the previous section. Fortunately, `(char*)&x.c - (char*)&x.a` is always defined for any members of the same structure since, as we have observed, all data objects lie on top of a common grid of characters in the C-World.

Why is the constraint for the relational operators (PTR8) more stringent than the constraint on the equality operators (PTR3)? Because portable C only admits relational comparisons between pointers to data objects within the same primary data object, while *any* two pointers of the same type can be compared for equality. This makes sense since there is no environment-independent relationship between addresses of different primary data objects.

We do *not* require that the two pointer operands of == be associated with the same primary data object. Such a requirement would be too restrictive. For example, suppose you **malloc** individual nodes of a tree and then want to find out whether two pointers point to the same node. It is a reasonable demand, yet the two pointers are associated with different primary data objects. Thus we need to be able to compare *any* two pointers of the same type for equality.

7.10 Assignment

The only constraint on pointer assignment is Rule PTR3: *Pointer operands of an operator must match in type. Use a cast, if necessary, to ensure this.* While some compilers allow the assignment of a pointer of one type to a pointer of another type, ANSI specifically disallows this practice.

7.11 Indirection

We wish to avoid accessing imaginary data objects. Doing so results in nonportable behavior, possibly in a hardware exception of some kind. Nonetheless, we do not need to constrain the use of $*$ itself at all! Instead, we say that you cannot *use* an imaginary object in any further operation. Indirection ($*$) on a pointer to an imaginary data object does not necessarily cause the data object to be accessed. Suppose we declare

```
char a[ASIZE], c, *p;

p = &a[ASIZE];
```

The expression `a[ASIZE]` is equivalent to `*(a + ASIZE)`. The expression `a + ASIZE` denotes a pointer that points to an imaginary data object of type `char`. Neither the indirection operator ($*$) nor the subsequent application of the address operator ($\&$) cause the value of the imaginary object to be accessed. Hence `p` is a valid pointer in portable C. If we said

```
c = *p;
```

then that would be nonportable access to the value of an imaginary data object.

Moreover, $*$ cannot yield any data object that is forbidden by Rule PTR5 (*the first byte of a data object must lie within or just beyond the associated primary data object, independent of the environment*) since if it could, its pointer operand would already be forbidden.

So if $*$ has no constraints, the obvious question is, how do we constrain the use of data objects?

7.12 Using and copying data objects

The rules of this chapter tell which pointers are allowed in portable C. But what about the objects they point to—when can *they* be used? The answer in brief is: you can use the value of a data object as long as you view it as having the same type as the type you used when giving it its value. But does this exclude the use of pointers for type punning, to view data objects in a way other than the way they were declared? Most of the time, the answer in portable C is yes—except for copying a data object by viewing it as an array.

Many operators access the value of an operand. How does a data object get its value? A constant is created with its value; not so for a variable. Either an initialization, an assignment, an I/O operation, or a binding of an actual parameter to its formal counterpart causes a variable to get a value. Variables may overlap in storage. It is therefore possible that a variable gets a value as the result of an assignment to another variable.[23] Are we allowed to use such a value?

When the operands of an assignment operator are of the same type, the value of the right hand operand is read but not manipulated in any way. We make a distinction between *copying* a value and *using* a value. The value of any real data object can be copied, but there are additional restrictions for use of a value. Intuitively, we only want to use the value of a data object in portable C if we can trace that value back to a point where it was assigned a value of the same type as that data object.

PTR9: *A data object must be used with the same type with which its value was stored.*

A data object's type defines a set of values. In portable C, the value of a data object can only be used if it was previously put there as a value belonging to the set of values defined by the type of that data object. A data object can get a value of the right type as the result of initialization, assignment, or parameter binding. It is also possible that such a value can be put in the data object as the result of a byte by byte memory copy or I/O copy operation. That value can be used as long as it is an exact copy of the value of another data object of the same type. For values acquired through binary I/O, this implies that the input must be the result of prior output on the same or a similar system. All this is of course merely an elaboration of the key principle of portable C, Rule PORT2: *do not rely on the representation of the value of a data object.*

Every value can be traced back to constants and to values obtained from text input. Text input, as opposed to binary input, is the input of characters belonging to a codeset through functions such as **getc** or **scanf**. That means that every value is the result of manipulations on values from constants and/or text input values.

Operators that do not inspect the value of their operand are the only operators that can take imaginary data objects as operands. The following are the only such operators:

- The structure or union member-access operator . does not inspect the value of its left-hand operand. (The right-hand operand has no value since it is not a data object.) The . operator looks at the type and perhaps also at the address of its left-hand operand.

- The sizeof operator only looks at the type attribute of its operand.

---

[23] How can variables overlap in storage? Through the use of unions, or as the result of pointer operations.

- The address operator & only looks at the address attribute of its operand.

All other operators inspect the values of their operands.

Exercise 7-2: Multiple message buffer. This exercise allows you to apply many of the rules we have seen for pointer operations. It is similar to the earlier example of message buffering (§7.5), only this time we want a send routine to take a message and its numeric type, and to buffer the message if there's room, otherwise to send the buffer. The receive routine will unpack all the messages squeezed into the buffer and process each one according to its type. The desire is to cram several messages into one buffer so as to economize on the number of writes over an expensive communications medium. Each message type corresponds to a different message structure, known to both sending and receiving processes. Each message structure may be a different size. The sending and receiving environment is the same, so there is no data portability problem. What is nonportable in this code?

```
/* Want to cram several msgs of varying size into a buffer
 * for writing out.
 * Use one buffer to hold several msgs that may be of
 * several possible types,
 * each with a corresponding structure
 */
typedef struct {
    char m_nmsgs;      /* # of msgs crammed into this buffer */
    short m_types[NMSGS];
    char m_buffer[BUFSIZ];
} VMSG;

int size[] = {sizeof(TYPEA), sizeof(TYPEB), /* ... */ };


    void
    send(mtype, mbuf)
    int mtype;
    char mbuf[];
    {
        static VMSG vmsg;
        static char *endp = 0;   /* byte after end of msgs
                                     in buffer */
```

```
    if (endp == 0)                /* initialize it */
        endp = (char *)&vmsg;
    if (endp - (char *)&vmsg + size[mtype] > sizeof(vmsg))
    {
        sendvmsg(&vmsg, &endp);
        initvmsg(&vmsg, &endp);
    }
    vmsg.m_types[vmsg.m_nmsgs++] = mtype;
    memcpy(endp, mbuf, size[mtype]);
    endp += size[mtype];
    if (vmsg.m_nmsgs == NMSGS)
    {
        sendvmsg(&vmsg, &endp);
        initvmsg(&vmsg, &endp);
    }
}


/*
 * the receiving process reads the message,
 * unpacks its constituent msgs,
 * and processes each according to its type
 */
receive()
{
    VMSG vmsg;
    int i;
    char *p;

    rcvvmsg(&vmsg);               /* get msg buffer */
    p = vmsg.m_buffer;
    for (i = 0; i < vmsg.m_nmsgs; i++)
    {
        switch(vmsg.m_types[i])
        {
            case TYPEA:
                proc_a((MSGA *)p); p += sizeof(MSGA); break;
            case TYPEB:
                proc_b((MSGB *)p); p += sizeof(MSGB); break;
            ...
        }
    }
    ...
```

□

Note that the pointer arithmetic in this example is all portable since it conforms to PTR5: p always points inside its associated data object vmsg. Note also that in send, we initialize endp by an assignment because using a cast in a declaration initializer is nonportable.

As in §7.5, the problem is one of alignment. There is no problem in the send process, but the receive process performs a cast from char * to a structure pointer, which is not included in the list of portable cast operations in Rule PTR4.

```
receive()
{
    ...
            case TYPEA:
                proc_a((MSGA *)p); p += sizeof(MSGA); break;
            case TYPEB:
                proc_b((MSGB *)p); p += sizeof(MSGB); break;
            ...
    ...
}
```

Intuitively, we have crammed together a variety of structures in one buffer with no regard for their alignment. When we attempt to impose a view of that buffer as a series of structures, alignment problems may arise.

Solution to Exercise 7-2.

Solution 1. Use a **memcpy** to copy the bytes of each structure back into a suitably aligned structure.

```
            proc_a(msgp)
            MSGA *msgp;
            {
                MSGA tmp;

                memcpy ((char *)tmp, msgp, sizeof(MSGA));
                /* now process the data in tmpa */
                ...
```

Solution 2. Define every message structure as a union containing a data object of type ALIGN. Have type VMSG include a union of m_buffer with a member of type ALIGN.

```
typedef struct {
    int m_nmsgs;      /* # msgs crammed
                         into this buffer */
    short m_types[NMSGS];
    union {
        char m_buffer[BUFSIZ];
        ALIGN m_dummy;
    } m_u;
} VMSG;

typedef union {
    ALIGN a_dummy;
    struct msga a_msga;
} MSGA;
 ...
```

□

## CHAPTER 8

PORTABLE USE OF COMPOUND DATA TYPES

This chapter discusses the portable use of *compound* data types, also called *aggregate* data types: arrays, strings, structures, and unions. We also discuss enums here, although they are actually scalar types. The chapter begins with the portable initialization of compound data types.

The subject of structures leads to a discussion of data portability and the best way to design structures for use in communication between diverse machines. The issue of sending structures between machines brings us back to the subject of alignment policy within structures, which was introduced in §7.5.1. We show how to determine the alignment policy of a given environment, which can be useful in achieving data portability between specific environments.

The manner in which C stores strings is sometimes misunderstood. This chapter shows how C stores string constants and what operations the programmer may portably perform on them.

8.1 Initialization of compound data types

An *initializer* assigns a value to a data object in its declaration. In general, it is always best to initialize data objects explicitly, in their declarations or by assignment, rather than relying on the default initializations of the C language. We have seen that in the case of pointers and floating point variables, the default initialization to "all bits 0" may not initialize the variables to the null pointer or floating point zero in all environments. Hence it is better to say, for example

```
static float f = 0.0;
```

or

```
static float f;
f = 0.0;
```

rather than rely on the default initialization to zero of

```
static float f;
```

Portable C has three rules that affect the initialization of compound data types.

COMPOUND1: *Do not put initializers in declarations of automatic arrays or structures.*

In portable C, arrays and structures with automatic storage class must be given initial values by assignment statements.

ANSI and some non-ANSI compilers allow initialization of automatic structures and arrays, but [K&R] and many non-ANSI compilers do not allow such initialization.

Remember that static and external variables declared with initializers are initialized once—at program startup time—while automatic and register variables declared with initializers are initialized *each time* the block in which they are declared is entered.

COMPOUND2: *Do not put initializers in declarations of data objects containing unions.*

ANSI C allows initializers for unions, but many compilers do not. Even a structure containing a union cannot be portably initialized in its declaration. For example, the initialization

```
struct {
    int i;
    union {
        double d;
        char c[10];
    } u;
} = { 1 };
```

is not portable.

COMPOUND3: *Use full braces to show initialization of each substructure and sub-array.*

For each compound object contained within the primary data object being declared there should be a separate set of nested braces in the initializer. At a given level, the list of initializers need not be complete, but all levels must be indicated by braces. This rule makes the initializer list clearer to read and less prone to errors. Moreover, some compilers no longer permit [K&R]'s elided-braces initializer format.

The following example is nonportable for several reasons.

```
pr_temp()
{
    struct {
        char *mo_name;
        int mo_temperature;    /* monthly average */
    } month[12] =
        {"January",  5,  "February",  4,
         "March",  21,  "April",,  "May",};
    ...
}
```

The array `month` is by default automatic. Hence by Rule COMPOUND1, it cannot have an initializer in portable C. Even if `month` were declared static, Rule COMPOUND3 is violated since `month` is an array of structures. Each compound constituent of `month` needs braces of its own in the initializer list. That is, each element of the array, since it is itself a structure, needs its own set of braces. Moreover, the double commas (,,) in the initializer list are not allowed.

To fix the COMPOUND1 problem, there are two choices: initialize `month` by a series of assignments, or make `month` static. Since there are no structure or array literals in C, each member of each element must be given a value by a separate assignment:

```
pr_temp()
{
    struct {
        char *mo_name;
        int mo_temperature;
    } month[12];

    month[0].mo_name = "January";
    month[0].mo_temperature = 5;
    month[1].mo_name = "February";
    month[1].mo_temperature = 4;
    month[2].mo_name = "March";
    month[2].mo_temperature = 21;
    month[3].mo_name = "April";
    month[4].mo_name = "May";
    ...
}
```

Making `month` static changes the meaning of the program, since `month` will be initialized only once, rather than every time `pr_temp()` is called. If that is an acceptable change, then the code would look like

```
pr_temp()
{
    static struct {
        char *mo_name;
        int mo_temperature;
    } month[12] =
        {{"January", 5}, {"February", 4},
         {"March", 21}, {"April"}, {"May"}};
    ...
}
```

8.2 Structures

8.2.1 Portability rules for structures

STRUCT1: *In -> and . expressions, the right-hand operand must be a member name which belongs to the structure or union referred to or pointed to by the left-hand operand.*

Roughly speaking, the member name must belong to the structure. That is, the member access operators -> and . should not be used to achieve arbitrary offsets from a given place in storage, as was the early custom in C.

STRUCT2: *Use unique member names for each structure and union.*

STRUCT2 assures portability to older compilers that, following [K&R], have one name space for all member names. See §9.2 for a full discussion of name spaces.

Style suggestion: *Use a common prefix to identify the members of each structure and union.*

The common prefix convention for member names has two benefits:

- it facilitates adherence to STRUCT1 and STRUCT2, and

- it makes reading and debugging the code easier.[1]

For example, in the standard ANSI library structure tm for handling time and date information, all member names begin with the prefix tm_.[2]

---

[1] The style suggestion also makes an overlap between the structure tag name and the member names unlikely. See §9.2.

[2] See **ctime** in [ANSI], Section 4.12.3.2.

```
struct tm {
     int tm_sec;
     int tm_min;
     int tm_hour;
     int tm_mday;
     int tm_mon;
     int tm_year;
     int tm_wday;
     int tm_yday;
     int tm_isdst;
};
```

8.2.2 Structure and union assignment

[RefMan81] introduced new operations on structures and unions in C. It allowed them to be assigned, to be passed as parameters, and to be returned by a function.[3] Rule FUNC6 (§3.2.2) excludes structure parameters and return types from portable C. Should you use structure and union assignment in portable C? You must decide based on the universe of environments to which you expect your code to move. In this section, all that we say about structure assignment applies as well to union assignment. There are good reasons both for and against structure assignment in portable C.

Reasons for using structure assignment:

- Availability: structure assignment is available in [SVPG Refman], [ANSI C], and most new compilers.

- Efficiency: structure assignment can use a block move facility in hardware, if it exists.

- Elegance: the code looks simpler.

Reasons for not using structure assignment:

- Structure assignment is not in [K&R], and is missing from early C compilers.

- Structure assignment can easily be simulated by the macro ASSIGN which you can define in your **environ.h**. If your compiler can do structure assignment, then you can define ASSIGN by

---

[3] Note that there is no similar extension of C for structure comparison. No dialect of C allows you to say

```
if (s1 == s2)
```

for two structures s1 and s2. The reason is that possible holes in the structures eliminate the possibility of simple bytewise comparison. To compare structures, you must write out a memberwise comparison.

```
#define ASSIGN(a, b)   ((a) = (b))
```

Otherwise, define `ASSIGN` by

```
#define ASSIGN(a, b)   (*memcpy((char *)&(a), \
                        (char *)&(b), sizeof(a)))
```

Note that the macro `ASSIGN` will work for multiple structure assignments like s1 = s2 = s3 provided that you write it as

```
ASSIGN(s1, ASSIGN(s2, s3))
```

Based on the preceding list of reasons, portable C recommends the following rule:

STRUCT3: *For widest portability, do not use structure or union assignment.*

Use the `ASSIGN` macro, since it replicates the full functionality of structure assignment without loss of portability (even though you incur the greater overhead of a function call to `memcpy`). However, if you expect that your project's code will not be ported to older compilers, you may wish to ignore this rule and Rule FUNC6 when making your coding standards.

8.3 Structure design for data portability

Since structures are often used to write records in a file or to contain the contents of a message sent over a communications medium, we wish to design structures so they can be used for sending data between different environments. This is the *data portability* issue for structures, not easily solved in C. The basic problem is that the same C structure in two different environments may be laid out differently due to the environments' differing alignment policies.

Unlike program portability, we cannot achieve general data portability by following a basic set of rules. Ad hoc solutions which cover the particular environments involved in the communications are usually the best that can be achieved.

Following are a series of possible strategies to achieve data portability, in order of increasing ease of programming, but also increasing risk of data portability difficulties.

Method 1. *Use a character buffer and pack it yourself with fixed format ASCII data.*
The buffer will consist of a series of fixed-length "fields" that each contain a number or string in ASCII characters. This is the most portable method, but you lose the ease with which structures can be manipulated, since you have only an unwieldy character buffer, which

must be unpacked into a structure at the receiving end. Moreover, for all binary data, the conversions to ASCII will take some time, and the resulting ASCII buffer will take more space than the original binary data. But this is the price of the greatest data portability. Of course, data in this format will not port to non-ASCII machines, unless we have a filter to translate the ASCII buffer into the codeset of the receiving machine.

Method 2. *Send ASCII free-form text with delimiters.*

Instead of using a fixed-format buffer, send free-form text as if it were typed in at a terminal. That is, instead of using fixed length ASCII fields, use varying length ASCII strings separated by carriage returns, tabs, or some other delimiter. The receiving side can use **scanf** or an equivalent function to decode the text back into a structure. Method 2 incurs greater expense at the receiving side of the communication since it must read free-form text rather than a fixed-format buffer. Method 2 has the potential portability problem over Method 1 that there can be differing conventions about line termination in text between different environments. For example, MS-DOS text files end each line with carriage-return/line-feed, while UNIX machines use only line-feed as line terminator. Within a single environment, these differences can be hidden from the user who employs the standard library functions, but between environments the differences must be handled explicitly.

Method 3. *Send structures consisting of ASCII strings only.*

This method gives us the greater flexibility and readability of using C structures. However, there may be alignment differences between machines, even for structures that contain only character arrays. The safest approach is to make all the character arrays of even dimension, or more conservatively, make the array dimensions a multiple of four. This method is similar to method 1 except we use a structure to hold the data record.

Method 4. *Send structures containing binary data.*

This is the easiest approach for the programmer, but also the approach that requires the greatest care to avoid data portability problems. The encoding of numbers may differ between machines—for example, 32-bit integers vs 36-bit integers. Even on machines with the same encoding, there may be different alignment policies for the structures between the sending and receiving environments. In the next section we show a technique that can help minimize those alignment differences. Also, we may need a filter to rearrange byte-orderings of binary integers between machines (see §4.11).

Note that some environments, such as MS-DOS, need a special way to open files for reading or writing binary data. In the ANSI C library, a new flag b is introduced to signify opening a binary file, for example,

```
fopen(file, "wb");
```

However, non-ANSI libraries may not recognize such a flag.

The following example illustrates the four methods of attaining data portability between different machines. Suppose we are given a structure sale which contains the data for a sales transaction, and we wish to ship it to a computer with a different architecture. Here is the original data structure for sale, before any attempts to modify it for data portability:

```
typedef struct {
    char  da_mo;            /* in binary */
    char  da_day;           /* in binary */
    short da_yr;
} DATE;


struct sale {
    short s_invoice_no;
    long  s_amount;         /* in cents */
    DATE  s_date;
} sale;

FILE *outp;                 /* output file or device */
```

- Method 1
  Method 1 uses a simple character buffer which the sending computer must pack with ASCII data. The sending computer uses **sprintf** to create fixed-length strings with which to pack the buffer.

```
#define INV_SZ   5  /* s_invoice_no size */
#define AMT_SZ  10  /* s_amount size */
#define MO_SZ    2  /* da_mo size */
...
char wbuf[SALEBUFSZ];
```

```
sprintf(wbuf, "%*.*d", INV_SZ, INV_SZ,
        sale.s_invoice_no);
sprintf(wbuf + INV_SZ, "%*.*ld", AMT_SZ, AMT_SZ,
        sale.s_amount);
sprintf(wbuf + INV_SZ+AMT_SZ, "%*.*d", MO_SZ, MO_SZ,
        sale.s_date.da_mo);
...
fwrite(wbuf, SALEBUFSZ, 1, outp);
```

Note that the format string "%*.*d" fills in its field-width and precision from subsequent arguments, in this case INV_SZ and INV_SZ. You could alternately build format strings like "%5.5d" at runtime, using **sprintf** also.

The receiving computer must then unpack the buffer using **scanf** to recreate struct sale on its side.

- Method 2

  For Method 2, the sending computer sends free-form ASCII text without concern for fixed sized fields. The receiving computer then uses **scanf** or **atoi** or an equivalent function to recreate struct sale.

  ```
  fprintf(outp, "%d\n", sale.s_invoice_no);
  fprintf(outp, "%ld\n", sale.s_amount);
  fprintf(outp, "%d\n", sale.s_date.da_mo);
  ```

- Method 3

  Method 3 calls for the creation of new all-ASCII structures. It is possible that both sending and receiving computers could use the all-ASCII structures rather than the original binary formats. The receiving computer could convert individual fields to binary when it needed to manipulate their values arithmetically.

  ```
  typedef struct ascdate {
      char ad_mo[4];   /* leave room for \0,
                          round to even dimension */
      char ad_day[4];
      char ad_yr[6];
  } ASCDATE;

  struct ascsale {
      char as_invoice_no[6];
      char as_amount[12];
      ASCDATE as_date;
  } ascsale;
  ```

```
        sprintf(&ascsale.as_invoice_no, "%4.4d",
                sale.s_invoice_no);
        sprintf(&ascsale.as_amount, "%10.10ld",
                sale.s_amount);
        sprintf(&ascsale.as_date.ad_mo, "%2.2d",
                sale.s_date.da_mo);
        ...
        fwrite((char *)&ascsale, sizeof(ascsale), 1, outp);
```

Following the suggestions of Method 3, each field is of even dimension for greater data portability. (Using multiples of 4 would give even wider portability). Also, each field is wide enough to contain the null character as string terminator.

- Method 4

To send binary structures directly to the receiving computer, we reorder the fields to put members of the same type together. The order of fields should make no difference in the code itself. Before the sending computer writes out the structure, it may have to twiddle the bytes of the short and long structure members to achieve some canonical form (see §4.11). Similarly, the receiving computer may have to twiddle the bytes of the short and long structure members to get them into *its* binary format.

```
typedef struct {
    short da_yr;
    short da_dummy1;
    char da_mo;     /* in binary */
    char da_day;
    char da_dummy2;
    char da_dummy3;
} DATE;

struct sale {
    DATE s_date;
    long s_amount;  /* in cents */
    short s_invoice_no;
    short s_dummy;
} sale;

FILE *outp; /* file to write out to */

/* possibly twiddle bytes in short & long fields
 * into some canonical form before writing them out
 */

fwrite((char *)&sale, sizeof(sale), 1, outp);
```

8.3.1　A technique for more portable binary-data structures

If you choose Method 4 above, sending structures with binary data, then the following design technique can increase the data portability of your structures. The technique is a set of guidelines for designing structures containing binary data which must be sent between diverse machines.[4] As we have seen, it is more portable to send ASCII data only, but sometimes you want to send binary data anyway. The goal of the technique is to order the members of a structure so compilers with different alignment policies will all treat the structure the same way. It may still be necessary to twiddle the bytes of integers to accommodate machines with differing byte-orderings.

- Guideline 1: no members of type `int`, since this type varies in size on different machines.

- Guideline 2: no floating point numbers, because the encoding of floating point numbers is much less standard between machines than the encoding of integers; the latter are assumed to be encoded in binary.

- Guideline 3: order the members of the structure as follows:

  1. First, all members that are themselves structures (which must themselves follow these guidelines).

  2. Then, all members that are `long`s or arrays of `long`s.

  3. Then, all members that are `short`s or arrays of `short`s.

  4. Then, explicitly pad with a `short` if the total number of `short`s is odd.

  5. Then, all members that are arrays of `char`s.
     After each character array, pad explicitly with a `char` if array has odd dimension.

  6. Then, all members that are `char`s.

  7. Then, explicitly pad with `char`s so the total number of `char`s is a multiple of 4.

Note that in the example above for Method 4, types `DATE` and `struct sale` both follow these guidelines.

---

[4] Method suggested by R. Byer based on data portability experience in projects at the New York Stock Exchange. The technique assumes that the machines involved have 16- or 32-bit words, 8-bit bytes, and 32-bit `long`s.

This section is only an introduction to the complexities of data portability. The growth of heterogeneous computing networks will increase the need for standards in this area.

8.3.2 offsetof macro

Sometimes general strategies do not suffice for making structures portable and you need to figure out how much padding a given environment puts in a particular structure. The offsetof macro is useful in determining the alignment policy of various machines.

In ANSI C, offsetof is defined in **stddef.h**. In a non-ANSI environment, you can define it in your own **environ.h.** by

```
/* for structure type "type" and
 * member name in that structure "member"
 */
#define offsetof(type, member)  \
                ((size_t)(char *)&(((type *)0)->member))
```

Note that this macro implementation of offsetof is nonportable (it violates PTR2 by de-referencing the null pointer), but that is not a problem: the implementation of the macro can be changed in environments where it doesn't work.

To determine your environment's alignment policy for type t in a structure, execute the following program.

```
struct test {
    char c;
    t x;
};

main()
{
    printf("max padding before type t is %ld\n",
           (long)offsetof(struct test, x) - 1);
}
```

If offsetof does not work in a given environment, then the same program can be written without offsetof. We simply say

```
struct test {
    char c;
    t x;
} dummy;
```

```
main()
{
    printf("max padding before type t is %d\n",
            (char *)&dummy.x - (char *)&dummy.c - 1);
}
```

8.4 Unions

Is there anything nonportable about the following implementation of the standard library function **gets**?

```
/*
 * gets() -- get a line from stdin into buf
 */
#include <stdio.h>

char *
gets(buf)
char buf[];
{
    union {
        int u_i;
        char u_c;
    } u;

    while ((u.u_i = getchar()) != '\n' && u.u_i != EOF)
        *buf++ = u.u_c;
    *buf = '\0';
    return buf;
}
```

The situation here is similar to that in §5.3.1. **getchar** returns an integer, yet we need to append a character to buf[]. The problem is that the code attempts to use a union to achieve the conversion from integer to character. That is not portable practice, though it will work on "little-endian" machines (see §4.11.1). It will fail on "big-endian" machines like the 680x0. In Chapter 7, Rule PTR4 states that a pointer to union can be cast into a pointer to any member of the union. That means that all the members of a union start at the same address. Thus u.u_c is the *low-address byte* of u.u_i. That does not make it the least significant byte, which is what we need.

The portable solution is to use a cast rather than a union to convert the integer to a character.

```
/*
 * gets() -- get a line from stdin into buf
 */
#include <stdio.h>

char *
gets(buf)
char buf[];
{
    int c;

    while ((c = getchar()) != '\n' && c != EOF)
        *buf++ = (char)c;
    *buf = '\0';
    return buf;
}
```

In fact, if we simply say

```
    *buf++ = c;
```

the conversion is performed by implicitly.

8.4.1 Uses of unions

Unions have three uses in C:

1. *To view data in a way other than the way it was stored.*
   This use, seen in the gets example above, is the least portable use of unions. gets essentially uses a union reference to simulate a conversion from one type to another. If you are using a union reference to view a data object as an object of a different size (as in gets) or as a data object that would require a value conversion if you were using a cast, don't do it, because the results are nonportable. The only exception is that it is permissible to view a data object as the underlying grid of characters, as in the to_can example in §4.11.2, in which we viewed a long as its underlying grid of characters.

2. *To coerce proper alignment of a data object.*
   This use of unions is covered in §7.5.

3. *To provide a data object whose data type depends on other data.*
   That is, a union is a variable that at different times contains different kinds of data. We can use a union inside a structure as a kind of varying record type. This is the most portable use of unions.

8.5 Arrays

ARRAY1: *When initializing an array with a string, leave room for the null character.*

Follow Rule ARRAY1 even if your code does not make use of the null character terminator to delimit strings. Even if you don't use the null character, certain compilers require the array to be large enough to hold it. For example

```
#define MO_SIZE 9
...
static char month[MO_SIZE] = "September";
```

which is C shorthand for

```
static char month[MO_SIZE] =
          {'S','e','p','t','e','m','b','e','r','\0'};
```

is nonportable; some compilers will reject this initialization because the array month is too small to hold the string with its null character terminator. A portable version is

```
#define MO_SIZE 10
...
static char month[MO_SIZE] = "September";
```

Or let the compiler figure out the size for you itself:

```
static char month[] = "September";
```

8.6 Strings

How are string literals stored in the C-World, and are they modifiable? Before we answer the question, consider the following three alternate ways to specify the name of a UNIX-style terminal using a string literal which must be modified at runtime to specify *which* terminal is intended.

Which is the most portable way to specify a terminal to be chosen at runtime?

Version 1

```
#define TERMINAL "/dev/ttyXX"
FILE *fp;
...
strcpy(&TERMINAL[8], "03");
fp = fopen(TERMINAL, "r+");
```

Version 2

```
char *terminal = "/dev/ttyXX";
FILE *fp;
...
strcpy(&terminal[8], "03");
fp = fopen(terminal, "r+");
```

Version 3

```
static char terminal[] = "/dev/ttyXX";
FILE *fp;
...
strcpy(&terminal[8], "03");
fp = fopen(terminal, "r+");
```

String literals like "/dev/ttyXX" are stored in static storage. Their modifiability is environment dependent, so portable C assumes they are not modifiable. Whether two identical string literals are stored in the same location is compiler dependent. Portable C makes no assumption either way.

Version 1 The first version of the code makes two severe portability errors.

```
#define TERMINAL "/dev/ttyXX"
FILE *fp;
...
strcpy(&TERMINAL[8], "03");
fp = fopen(TERMINAL, "r+");
```

1. It assumes that all occurrences of the string "/dev/ttyXX" actually refer to the same storage, so that when one occurrence is modified, then all other occurrences would be modified. But portable C does not specify whether all occurrences of the same string refer to the same storage, and in many implementations, each occurrence of a string is stored separately.

   [K&R] says, "All strings, even when written identically, are distinct,"[5] though not all compilers adhere to this specification, and [ANSI C] no longer guarantees it.

2. It assumes that string literals are modifiable. This cannot be assumed in portable C. ANSI says, "If the program attempts to modify a string literal, the behavior is undefined."[6] Note that it is

---

[5] [K&R], p. 181.

[6] [ANSI], Section 3.1.4.

perfectly acceptable to write `"/dev/ttyXX"[8]`, as long as you use this expression to access a character in the string, not to modify it.

Version 2   This version is not portable because it modifies the value of a string literal.

```
char *terminal = "/dev/ttyXX";
FILE *fp;
...
strcpy(&terminal[8], "03");
fp = fopen(terminal, "r+");
```

Although many implementations allow this practice, we do not recommend it for portable C because an implementation may choose to keep string literals in read-only memory. As quoted above, [ANSI C] states that modifying a string literal has undefined results.

Version 3   This is the *correct* version for portable C.

```
static char terminal[] = "/dev/ttyXX";
FILE *fp;
...
strcpy(&terminal[8], "03");
fp = fopen(terminal, "r+");
```

Note that we are using a string to initialize a static array of characters, which we can then manipulate by name. We do not have to worry about whether it is portable to modify the value of a string literal, because what we modify is `terminal`, an array of characters, which is a variable and hence modifiable.

8.6.1 Portability rules for strings

STRING1: *Don't modify string literals.*
        Treat string literals as read-only arrays.

STRING2: *Don't assume unique storage for string literals.*
        Identical string literals may be stored in a single location, or they may not.

STRING3: *Avoid using ANSI string concatenation.*
        ANSI C allows the concatenation of string literals to form a larger string literal in order to ease program layout. For example

```
printf("number of widgets shipped is %d\n"
       "number of gizmos shipped is %d\n",
       nwidgets, ngizmos);
```

In the example, the two string literals are treated in ANSI C as if they were one long literal. While this new feature is a convenience in dealing with long strings, it is not available in pre-ANSI C implementations, and therefore it is excluded from portable C.

STRING4: *Avoid* ?? *in strings or comments.*

The double question mark ?? has special meaning in ANSI C. It is used to form ANSI *trigraphs*; see §9.8 on the preprocessor.[7]

8.7 Enums

Portable C does not recommend use of the enum data type, which was added to the C language in [RefMan81], because some compilers, adhering to [K&R], do not support it. Moreover, those compilers that do support enums differ on what operations can be performed on them. For example, given the declarations

```
#define NCOLORS 5
enum color {red, blue, white, green, yellow};
enum color paint, frequency[NCOLORS];
```

some compilers allow and some disallow the following expressions:

- red - blue
- frequency[white]
- if (paint)

The enum concept in C lacks ordering; there is no predecessor or successor function as there is in Pascal. Although the use of enums can be helpful when debugging with a good symbolic debugger, **printf** and many debuggers cannot print the symbolic value of an enum.

Since enumerations can be represented by integers without losing functionality (see §2.6.1), there is no great loss in excluding them from portable C.

---

[7] Actually, only the 9 sequences ?? (, ??<, ??/, ??', ??=, ??), ??>, ??!, and ??- are trigraphs in ANSI C. But for ease of remembering, we avoid the sequence ?? entirely. If you need to write the sequence ?? in an ANSI environment, you can use "\?\?". However, this string may not work in all non-ANSI environments.

CHAPTER 9
OTHER PORTABILITY ISSUES

The previous chapters of this book have each focused on a particular data type and the portability problems associated with it. In this chapter we treat topics that transcend particular data types, and that nonetheless are important for portability.

The biggest problem is clearly the *standard library*, which is unfortunately even less standard than the language itself. Portable C recommends the use of the ANSI standard library interface, which, unlike ANSI C itself, can be emulated in non-ANSI environments.

The choice of *names*, or *identifiers*, involves portability issues: the length of names, the number of distinct name spaces, and the set of reserved names. Also, the *scope* of a name, called in ANSI its *linkage*, can differ between environments. We explain the different possibilities for handling names of program scope, and the most portable way to declare them.

The *order* in which the compiler performs certain operations is not specified in C—it is left to the compiler implementation. It is important to know which kinds of ordering are compiler-dependent, so your code does not rely upon them.

The *preprocessor* can be a source of portability problems. We suggest a conservative use of the preprocessor to avoid differences between environments. The preprocessor can, however, be an important tool for enhancing portability by hiding environment dependencies through macro definitions and `#ifdef`'d code.

We discuss *tools and techniques* that can help you to create portable code or to port other people's code. The tools include **make** and **lint**.

The chapter concludes with *internationalization*, a description of recent efforts to provide a library which allows programs to adjust to language and national conventions at runtime.

9.1 Standard libraries

Probably the most troubling difference among environments is in the set of library functions available to the programmer. Since C relies on library functions to perform I/O, storage allocation, and string handling—activities that are incorporated into the body of some other languages—C programs are inherently vulnerable to library differences. We will examine the kinds of library differences that exist and the various attempts in progress to standardize the "standard" library.

This chapter cannot give an exhaustive list of library differences between different operating systems. Such a list can never be comprehensive and will always be outdated by newer libraries.[1] We suggest instead a strategy for dealing with library differences by emulating the ANSI standard library in environments that lack it.

9.1.1 Differences among standard libraries

Most C implementations include some version of a standard library, but these existing versions suffer from the following portability problems.

1. *Problems in the specification.* Many functions in the standard library have `int` or `unsigned` formal parameters (a less "portable" type than `short` or `long`). As seen in the **sleep** example in §4.3, portability problems arise when programmers use values outside the portable range of `int` or `unsigned` for the actual parameters. The problem is that if you work on a 32-bit machine, it is hard to restrict yourself to integers in the range $[-32767..32767]$—the natural tendency is to use the full range of available `int`s.

2. *Different names.* Some functions, identical in other respects, are known by different names in different libraries. For example, the string function **strchr**, which appears in most libraries, e.g., ANSI, is called **index** in UNIX Version 7 and in 4.2BSD. This is the easiest sort of problem to deal with. Simply code using the ANSI name, and for a Version 7 system write a header file, such as **string.h**, containing

   ```
   #define strchr  index
   ```

3. *Changes in specifications.* It is harder to deal with functions whose specifications differ in small details from one environment to another due to historical changes. The function **printf** is a good example of this problem; probably no two implementations have identical specifications. For example, earlier versions of **printf** allow the format `%D` as an equivalent format to `%ld`. However, in [ANSI] and [SVID], `%D` is not a valid format.[2]

4. *Different interfaces.* Some libraries use entirely different functions with different interface specifications to accomplish essentially the same purpose. For example, BSD UNIX's **re_comp** and **bcopy** accomplish essentially the same tasks as UNIX System V's **regcmp** and **memcpy**, though with different

---

[1] A detailed listing of UNIX operating system differences is found in [Lapin], pp. 55-190.

[2] In some early libraries, since `%D` meant "print a `long` in decimal format," `%X` meant, by analogy, "print a `long` in hexadecimal format." `%D` became disallowed so that `%X` could mean "print an `int` in hexadecimal format using ABCDE" instead of "print a `long` in hexadecimal format using abcde."

interfaces. The **re_comp/regcmp** problem is one that cannot be resolved simply by resort to the ANSI interface, since ANSI lacks the functionality of either function.

9.1.2 Standardization efforts

To address the problems of differences among standard C libraries, a number of efforts have been made to standardize the standard library:

- ANSI C (XJ311) describes a standard library interface for C language programs, based on the *1984 /usr/group Standard,* minus its UNIX-specific functions. In particular, ANSI C does not include specifications for unbuffered UNIX-style I/O routines like **open**, **close**, **read**, **write**, **lseek**. The ANSI C library is modeled on existing UNIX library interfaces, for better and for worse. Portable C follows the ANSI library interface, because it is the one likeliest to have wide implementation and acceptance.

- AT&T has published an interface specification of a C language library, including a "standard" library as well as many UNIX-specific functions, as part of the SVID (System V Interface Definition). In the future, it is likely that SVID will incorporate the ANSI library interface.

- X/OPEN bases its library interface specification on the SVID, including also **curses** terminal-manipulation library and an IPC (Inter-Process Communication) library. The IPCs are based on the SVID IPCs, but with the provision that these may be replaced at a later date.

- POSIX (IEEE Trial Use standard 1003.1) provides a UNIX-like library interface based on the *1984 /usr/group Standard.*

9.1.3 The portable C strategy

What strategy can you adopt to minimize the portability problems associated with library functions? Portable C recommends:

LIB1: *Use the ANSI standard library function interface.*

Where possible, avoid functions not included in the ANSI library.

For example, it is more portable to use **malloc** than **sbrk**. Similarly, it is more portable to use **fopen** and **fread** than **open** and **read**. It is more portable to say

```
#include <stdio.h>
...
FILE *fp;
struct record rec;

if ((fp = fopen("inputfile", "r")) == NULL)
{
    perror("can't open inputfile");
    exit(1);
}
while (fread((char *)&rec, sizeof(struct record), 1, fp) == 1)
{
    ...
```

than to use the UNIX system call version of the same code:

```
#include <fcntl.h>
...
int fd;
struct record rec;

if ((fd = open("inputfile", O_RDONLY)) == -1)
{
    perror("inputfile");
    exit(1);
}
while (read(fd, (char *)&rec, sizeof(struct record)) > 0)
    ...
```

Using the latter version makes the code dependent on the UNIX operating system.

Obviously, it is not always possible or desirable to avoid low-level non-ANSI interfaces. Sometimes non-ANSI functions have functionality unattainable by ANSI library functions. If properly used, non-ANSI functions may be more efficient than ANSI library functions. But since they are less portable, non-ANSI functions, such as system calls, should be isolated as much as possible in low-level routines of the code.

We should note that it is possible for a novice programmer to write code that is *less* efficient using low-level interfaces. In the above example, the **read** version would seem to be more efficient, since it is performed without **fread**'s extra layer of buffering. However, the **read** version is more efficient only if the size of `struct record` is a multiple of `BUFSIZ`, the natural size for I/O buffering using **read**.

Unlike ANSI C itself, it is possible to use the ANSI library interface in a non-ANSI environment. If you program in an ANSI environment, simply use the ANSI library. If you program in a non-ANSI environment, or if you have to port to one, you can try several approaches:

- Emulate the ANSI interface by implementing an interface from the ANSI specification to the local standard library. This may sound like a nontrivial task, but if it is done on an organization-wide basis, it is worth the effort. There are several ways to do this:

  1. Write or obtain your own ANSI-compatible library. It seems likely that source code should become available in the public domain to implement the ANSI C library in various common environments.

  2. Write an interface that captures the ANSI library calls and translates them, with appropriate adaptations, to your own standard library calls.

- Write `#ifdef`'d code for both your local standard library and the ANSI interface.

Here is a trick that allows you to intercept an ANSI-style function call and translate it into a call on your own library. In this example, we intercept a call to **fopen**, and if it contains the flag b, we ignore the b; then we use the usual local **fopen**. A typical use of **fopen** would be

main.c:

```
#include <stdio.h>

main()
{
    FILE *fp;
    fp = fopen("data.0729", "rb");
    ...
}
```

The interface consists of 2 files: a new **stdio.h** which you rewrite, and a file **FOPEN.c**. If you port this code to an ANSI environment, simply remove these two files.

stdio.h:

```
#define fopen    FOPEN
#include "/usr/include/stdio.h" /* use full pathname of */
                               /* standard header file */
```

FOPEN.c

```
#include <stdio.h>  /* the standard header */
#include <string.h> /* for the declaration of strchr */

FILE *
FOPEN(file, mode)
char *file, *mode;
{
    char *p;

    /* eliminate b flag */
    if ((p = strchr(mode, 'b')) != (char *)0)
        do {
            *p = *(p+1);
        } while (*(++p) != '\0');
    /* call the local fopen */
    return fopen(file, mode);
}
```

The tricky part of this technique is that when compiling **main.c**, it is necessary to tell the compiler to use the altered **stdio.h**, rather than the standard version. Supposed we keep the altered **stdio.h** in /usr/ansi/include. Then on a Unix system, we would use the −I option to tell the compiler to look in the special include directory first:

```
cc -I/usr/ansi/include main.c
```

9.1.4 Non-ANSI functionality

A harder problem is what to do about functions that are beyond the functionality of the ANSI library. For example, inter-process communication, task creation, terminal handling, and networking are all beyond the domain of the ANSI library.

One approach is to implement your own interface to important functions which you then map to local libraries. When faced with library functions whose specifications differ between environments, you can hide these differences by encapsulating the interfaces in a function of your own specification that you can store in a project library of your own creation. Your function could be a higher-level interface to the functionality than that offered by existing libraries.

For example, semaphore handling and terminal handling functions tend to vary greatly between environments. Yet often your needs are simple: to incre-ment or decrement a semaphore, say, or to set a terminal to raw mode. These needs lend themselves to an interface of your own design, implemented in terms of the existing library interfaces. (See [Lapin], p. 191.)

9.1.5 Portability issues of using the ANSI library

Using the ANSI library interface does not guarantee portability. ANSI changes the type of many formal parameters of the library functions from `int` to the typedef'd type `size_t`. This is an improvement over the original specification, but still is prone to the same problem: the range of `size_t` is environment dependent.

It is still possible to use the ANSI interface in a nonportable way. Consider the following example:

```
...
long n = 3;
short flag = 0xFFFD;

printf("value of n is %d\n", n);
printf("value of flag is %o\n", flag);
```

The code contains several portability problems.

- `%d` does not work for `long` values on a machine with 16-bit `int`s. Use `%ld` to print `long`s.

- `%o` will work for `short` in most cases, since `short` arguments are pro-moted to `int` when they are passed to a function, in this case **printf**. The only case where this can result in a problem is when printing a bit pattern in octal or hexadecimal. In such a case, the extra 1-bits due to sign-extension may show up. One way around this problem is to use `%ho`, but although this format is available in the ANSI specification for **printf**, it is not available in all versions of **printf**. A more portable approach would be to mask the desired number of bits.

  ```
  printf("value of i is %o\n", i & 0xFFFF);
  ```

  This version is portable since `0xFFFF`, and hence `i & 0xFFFF`, is an `int` constant.

Problems with the use of **printf** are not detected by **lint**!

9.2 Name spaces

In this section we consider portability issues in the choice of *names*, or identifiers, in your program. The issues include the number of distinct name spaces recognized by your translator, the set of reserved names, the length of names, and the scope of names.

The number of distinct name spaces, or name pools, differs between C compilers. For a given name space, a name within its scope denotes a unique entity. But the same name, within the same scope, can denote different entities, provided they are in different name spaces. For example, a structure tag and a structure data object can have the same name, as in

```
struct node node;
```

while the same name cannot refer to a structure tag and one of its members in portable C, as in

```
struct node {
    char *node;
    ...
};
```

Portable C has two name spaces.

| **Name spaces in portable C** ||
Name space 1	Name space 2
• structure, union, enum tags	• names of data objects • member names of all structures and unions • enum constants • labels

Portable C takes a conservative approach to name spaces, following [K&R] in specifying a single name space for tags and member names of *all* structures and unions. Most modern C compilers have a separate name space for *each* structure and union, as well as a separate name space for tags (e.g., [ANSI C], [SVPG RefMan]). Many modern C compilers (and [ANSI C]) put labels in a separate name space, but for widest portability, portable C does not.

[K&R] allows a member name to appear in two different structures as long as it has the same offset in each. Recent compilers, since they have separate name spaces for each structure, allow a member name to appear in different structures with different offsets. Portable C takes a more conservative approach; by Rule STRUCT2, *Use unique member names for each structure and union*, portable C requires that a member name be used in only one structure or union. §8.2.1 also introduced a style suggestion that is helpful in implementing STRUCT2: *Use a common prefix to identify the members of each structure and union.* Following Rule STRUCT2 assures that portable C will be compatible even with older C compilers that have a single name space for member names of all structures and unions.

For example, the following pair of declarations is not acceptable in portable C because it would not compile under a strictly [K&R]-adhering compiler.

```
struct s1 {
    int   msg_type;
    ...
};

struct s2 {
    char flags;
    int   msg_type;
    ...
};
```

The member name msg_type appears at a different offset in each structure. Apply Rule STRUCT2 to obtain a portable C version of the declarations:

```
struct s1 {
    int   s1_msgtype;
    ...
};

struct s2 {
    char s2_flags;
    int   s2_msgtype;
    ...
};
```

9.3 Scope of names

The *scope* of the name of a data object, called by ANSI its "*linkage*," determines where the name can potentially be used: in all the source files of a program, in one source file, or only within a function or block.[3] Both compiler and linker must deal with the scope of names. The conventions for specifying the scope of a

---

[3] The term "source file" includes the source files for library functions.

name differ between environments. Fortunately, there are ways to specify the scope of a name that will work in most environments.

9.3.1 Scope and lifetime

The *scope* of the name of a data object is the region of code in the source files of a program where that name can potentially be used. We say potentially because a declaration may be needed to actually use that name. For example, the scope of an external variable is the entire code of a program. To use the name, however, we may still need a declaration for that name.

We distinguish scope from the *lexical scope* of a name. The lexical scope of a name, discussed in §9.3.2, is the subregion of its scope where you can use that name without making additional declarations.[4]

The *lifetime* of a data object (§6.5) is the interval of time during which a data object exists. For example, the lifetime of an automatic variable is the invocation time of the block in which it is declared. Each time that block is entered the variable is created, and each time the block is exited the variable ceases to exist.

Lifetime is an attribute of a data object; scope is an attribute of the name of a data object. In fact, we can also talk about the scope of a name of something that is not a data object—for example, the scope of a `typedef` name, a structure member name, a label, etc.

A name can have *block*, *function*, *file*, or *program* scope.

- The name of a variable has *program* scope if declared

  1. outside any function, without the keyword `static`, i.e.,

     a. with keyword `extern`, or

     b. with no storage class keyword.

  2. inside a block, with keyword `extern`.

- The name of a function has *program* scope if declared without keyword `static`. For example,

```
void
errexit(msg)
char *msg;
{
    ...
}
```

---

[4] Our definitions of scope and lexical scope follow the definitions in [K&R]. ANSI defines "scope" as what we call lexical scope; their "linkage" is what we call scope.

Multiple declarations of a name with program scope all refer to the same data object. ANSI calls names of program scope names of *external linkage*.

- The name of a variable has *file* scope if declared outside any function, with keyword `static`.

- The name of a function has *file* scope if declared with keyword `static`. For example, the function

```
static int
hidden_func(n)
int n;
{
    ...
}
```

is usable only in the source file in which it is defined.

File scope is useful for "data hiding"—keeping variables and functions private to one source file. Data hiding is useful in defining a data structure together with functions that manipulate it, where only certain interfaces are made public to other source files, while the internal workings of the mechanism are kept hidden from other source files (see §3.1.1 on modularization).

ANSI calls names of file scope names of *internal linkage*.

- The name of a variable has *block* scope if declared inside a block, without keyword `extern`.

ANSI calls names of block scope names of *no linkage*.

Lifetime and scope		
Data object	Scope	Lifetime
external	program	program
static (declared outside a block)	file	program
static (declared in a block)	block	program
formal parameter	function	invocation time of function
automatic	block	invocation time of block

As shown in the table above, C separates the confusing syntactic notion of storage class into the categories of scope and lifetime. Part of the ambiguity surrounding scope lies in the C storage class keywords used to denote scope. The keywords `extern` and `static` both specify the lifetime of a data object as well as the scope of its name. (They both specify a lifetime equal to that of the entire program.) The keyword `static` denotes a name of file or block scope.

The keyword `extern` denotes a name of program scope. The absence of a storage class keyword in a declaration denotes either program or block scope.

The table above deals only with entities that have both a name and a lifetime. However, there are data objects without names, such as heap objects created by **malloc**. They have lifetime but no scope. Names that do not refer to data objects cannot have program scope. For example, a `typedef`'d type has file scope if declared outside a function, or block scope if declared inside a block. Similarly, a label always has function scope.

9.3.2 Lexical scope

We have defined the lexical scope of a name as the subregion of its scope where you can use that name without making additional declarations. For example, if you declare a variable as `extern` inside a block, its *lexical scope* is the rest of that block, while its *scope* is all source files of the program.

The example below is taken from §3.1.1.

```
BIGNODE *
alloc_bignode()
{
    extern char * malloc();

    return (BIGNODE *)malloc(sizeof(BIGNODE));
}

SMALLNODE *
alloc_smallnode()
{
    return (SMALLNODE *)malloc(sizeof(SMALLNODE));
}
```

The declaration of **malloc** establishes it as a name of program scope. Compilers will differ in their treatment of its lexical scope. Some compilers treat the lexical scope of **malloc** as extending from its declaration to the end of the file, some to the end of the block. ([K&R] is ambiguous here; ANSI C specifies to the end of the block.)

As in Chapter 3, the best policy is Rule FUNC1: *Declare every function in a header file.* We can generalize Rule FUNC1 as follows:

NAME1: *Declare all data objects of program scope in a header file.*

Rule NAME1 applies to variables and functions whose name have program scope.

9.3.3 Referencing and defining declarations

A data object of file or program scope can have multiple declarations that refer to it. The *defining declaration*, or *definition*, of a data object allocates storage and possibly initializes it. A *referencing declaration* does not allocate storage nor can it initialize the data object; it provides type information within its lexical scope.

The definition of a function contains the code of the function, while a referencing declaration of a function simply gives its return type (and in ANSI, the type of each argument).

When you use Rule NAME1, the declaration in the header file must be a nondefining declaration. In addition to the declaration in the header file, there must be one defining declaration in a source file. You should include the header file in all source files that use its data objects. You should include the header file even in those source files that contain the defining declarations of the data objects declared in the header file.

The following example shows declarations of a variable and functions with program scope. Header file **node.h** contains:

```
typedef ... NODE;
extern NODE *nodep;
extern int node_alloc();
```

Source file **node.c** contains:[5]

```
#include <stdlib.h> /* contains declaration of malloc */
#include "node.h"    /* contains decl of node_alloc, nodep */

/*
 * node_alloc() == allocates node. sets external pointer nodep
 * RETURNS  non-0 success
 *             0     failure
 */
int
node_alloc()
{
    return (nodep = (NODE *)malloc(sizeof(NODE))) != (char *)0;
}
```

---

[5] Another portable way to write node_alloc, perhaps unnecessarily slick, is

```
int
node_alloc()
{
    return !!(nodep = (NODE *)malloc(sizeof(NODE)));
}
```

Note that `malloc` and `nodep` have program scope. Function `node_alloc` has program scope by default since no storage class keyword appears in its definition.

The declaration of `node_alloc` in **node.c** is a defining declaration. Since the file **node.c** includes **node.h**, it contains both a referencing and a defining declaration of `node_alloc`. This is portable practice, and a beneficial style convention, as it promotes consistent declarations among different files.

9.3.4 Conventions for program scope

For functions, it is evident which declarations are defining and which are referencing; the defining declaration of a function is the one with the code. For a function of program scope, there must be exactly one defining declaration.

Four different conventions are used in C translation environments to handle multiple declarations of data objects with program scope that are not functions:

1. *Strict Ref/Def.* The keyword `extern` appears on all *referencing* declarations. There must be exactly one defining declaration, indicated by the absence of a storage-class keyword.

   Strict Ref/Def is the portable C preference, and it is endorsed by ANSI. Code written according to this model will port to the widest range of translation environments.

2. *Relaxed Ref/Def.* The keyword `extern` may be present or absent on all referencing declarations. There must be at least one defining declaration, indicated by the absence of a storage-class keyword.

   Many UNIX translation environments adhere to Relaxed Ref/Def. It is classified by ANSI as a "common extension."

3. *COMMON.* The keyword `extern` may be present or absent on all declarations. No defining declaration is necessary. The compiler will arbitrarily choose one declaration as defining.

   The COMMON approach is like Fortran's COMMON storage. It was the original intention of Dennis Ritchie to follow this model for C.[6]

4. *Initialization.* The keyword `extern` may be present or absent on all declarations. An explicit initialization is required on one declaration to make it defining. All other declarations are referencing. This model is the least appealing, since it requires many spurious initializations, and fortunately is not often encountered.

---

[6] [ANSI Rat], p.22.

Code written according to the Strict Ref/Def model for portable C will not necessarily port to a translation environment that uses the Initialization model; it is necessary to add initializations to port to such an environment.

For each of the four conventions above, we show an example illustrating how it denotes program scope of variables.[7] In each example, the program consists of two source files, **main.c** and **init.c**. Suppose **main.c** contains:

```
extern void init();

main()
{
    init();
    printf("i=%d\n", i);
}
```

while **init.c** contains:

```
void
init()
{
    i = 10;
    . . .
}
```

Both source files refer to the external variable i, which has program scope. How should the external declaration of i be phrased in each file?

Examples of program scope conventions		
Convention	source file	
	main.c	**init.c**
Strict Ref/Def (portable C approach) (ANSI approach)	extern int i;	int i;
Relaxed Ref/Def	int i;	int i;
COMMON	extern int i;	extern int i;
Initialization	int i;	int i = 0;

---

[7] This example is based on a similar example in [ANSI Rat], Section 3.1.2.2.

The rule for declaring variables with program scope is

NAME2: *Use the strict Ref/Def convention for names of program scope.*

Thus, a variable of program scope must be defined in one source file with a declaration that has no keyword `extern` or `static`. It may be referenced in other source files by declaring it with keyword `extern`, preferably in a header file.[8]

We can make a number of style suggestions for the use of variables of program scope:

- Minimize the number of variables of program scope. This is simply a conventional wisdom of well-structured programming. It is clearer to pass parameters explicitly than to rely on the manipulation of external variables.

- One can put all defining declarations of variables with program scope in a single source file. Or, alternately, one can define each variable of program scope in a file appropriate to its use.

9.3.5 Functions with file scope

We would like to use similar code to specify functions and variables of file scope. We would like to say:

```
static char *mymalloc();  /* referencing decl */
static char *nodep;       /* defining decl */

NODE *
node_alloc()
{
    return (NODE *)(nodep = mymalloc(sizeof(NODE)));
}
```

---

[8] All declarations associated with the same data object must have the same type. The compiler cannot enforce this requirement across source file boundaries, but **lint** and some linkers can detect errors of this sort. A particularly tricky instance of this error is to define in one file the external variable

```
char tempbuf[BUFSIZE];
```

and then to declare it in another source file by

```
extern char *tempbuf;
```

In one file `tempbuf` is defined as a character array big enough to hold `BUFSIZ` characters; in the other, `tempbuf` is a pointer variable, big enough to hold exactly one pointer. The code will compile and link, but will produce bad results. It is common for C programmers to make this confusion since the two declarations are equivalent for formal parameters. They are *not* equivalent for external variables! Note that this problem is not a portability problem; it is just bad code.

The referencing declaration should be

```
extern char tempbuf[];
```

```
static char *    /* function hidden from other files */
mymalloc(n)
int n;
{
    ...
}
```

This code is acceptable under ANSI C. Unfortunately, the code is not portable. The desire is that `node_alloc` should be "public"—known to other source files, but that `mymalloc` and `nodep` should be "private"—known only within this source file. The code declares `mymalloc` and `nodep` to be of file scope, and `node_alloc` to be of program scope. The first declaration of `nodep` is a defining declaration.

The first declaration of `mymalloc` is a referencing declaration at the top of the source file so that all subsequent functions can use `mymalloc`. The problem is that in some compilers, it is not acceptable to use `static` as a storage class specifier on a referencing declaration. Hence, we have Rule NAME3:

NAME3: *The keyword* `static` *should not appear in a referencing declaration of a function.*

The practical implication of this rule is that the defining declaration of a function or variable with file scope in portable C should appear before any use of the function or variable.

Thus, a portable version of the previous example would be:

```
static char *nodep; /* defining decl */

static char *        /* defining decl */
mymalloc(n)
int n;
{
    ...
}

NODE*
node_alloc()
{
    return (NODE *)(nodep = mymalloc(sizeof(NODE)));
}
```

The only problem with Rule NAME3 is that it means there is no way in portable C for two functions of file scope to each call the other (i.e., to be mutually recursive), since the defining declaration of each must precede the other.

9.3.6 Incomplete types

The problem just described of mutually referring functions of file scope does not arise with *structures*. It is possible for two structures each to reference the other in portable C. However, there is a portable and nonportable way to do it.

The nonportable approach is:

```
struct node {
    struct head *n_p;
    int         n_etc;
};

struct head {
    struct node *h_p;
    int         h_etc;
};

static struct node node;
static struct head head;
```

The declarations above are allowed in [ANSI], but are nonportable since struct head is an "incomplete" type at the time it is used in the declaration of struct node. Not all compilers allow this use of incomplete types.

A more portable approach is:

```
struct node {
    struct head {
        struct node *h_p;
        int         h_etc;
    } *n_p;
    int n_etc;
};
static struct node node;
static struct head head;
```

The structures declared in this version are identical to those in the previous version. That is, in both versions, node is a structure containing a pointer and an int as members.

9.4 Name conventions

A rose by any other name would smell as sweet, but portable C requires certain constraints on names. What will the following example print?

```
int overnight_param = 4;
int todays_qty;
double todays_price;

main()
{
    int overnight_qty = 3;

    printf("overnight_param=%d\n", overnight_param);
    printf("overnight_qty=%d\n", overnight_qty);

    todays_qty = 30000;
    todays_price = 1.5;
    printf("todays_qty=%d\n", todays_qty);
    printf("todays_price=%g\n", todays_price);
}
```

This code works fine on an ANSI-conforming compiler or on a compiler that adheres to [SVPGRefMan]. It will produce undesired results on older compilers that use only eight characters to differentiate identifier names (as permitted in [K&R]). For example, on a Version 7 UNIX compiler, the program printed:

```
overnight_param=3
overnight_qty=3
todays_qty=1086324736
todays_price=1.5
```

On such a compiler, the declaration of `overnight_param`—treated by the compiler as name `overnigh`—is overridden by the declaration of `overnight_qty`—treated by the compiler as the same name, `overnigh`, inside the block.

```
int overnight_param = 4;
...
main()
{
    int overnight_qty = 3;
    ...
```

The compiler will not complain, since an automatic variable can override an external variable with the same name inside the automatic variable's lexical scope.

This same compiler treats the external declarations of `todays_qty` and `todays_price` as declarations of the two external variables, whose names are `todays_q` and `todays_p`. However, the linker in this environment only recognizes seven character names, and treats both declarations as referring to the same variable, `todays`. (It allows multiple declarations of `todays` because it uses the Relaxed Ref/Def model for variables of program scope, §9.3.4.)

```
int todays_qty;
double todays_price;
```

These are silent but dangerous portability problems, which can occur without warning.

For greatest portability, local (non-external) variables should be unique within the first eight characters, and external variables should be unique within the first six characters. Thus the following version will work portably:

```
int ovn_param = 4;      /* overnight parameter */
int td_qty;             /* today's quantity */
double td_price;        /* today's price */

main()
{
    int ovn_qty = 3;    /* overnight quantity */
    ...
```

lint can be used to prevent such problems. If you run **lint** with a portability option set, it will check your names with an eight character limit, and external names with a six character limit.

We generalize these observations in the following rules:

NAME4: *Within its scope and name space, a name of block or file scope must be unique within the first eight characters, case sensitive.*

Because of case sensitivity, `ovn_qty` and `Ovn_qty` are distinct names in portable C, but `overnight_qty` and `overnight_param` are not. (Nonetheless, names as similar as `ovn_qty` and `Ovn_qty` should be avoided.)

Rule NAME4 follows [K&R], even though more recent compilers and standards have extended the number of characters used to establish uniqueness to 31 or more ([ANSI],[Microsoft]). In fact, [SVPGRefMan] places *no* limit on the number of characters used to distinguish identifiers.

NAME5: *Names of program scope must be unique within the first six characters, case-insensitive.*

Names of program scope are what ANSI calls names of file scope with external linkage. These are names of data objects with storage class `extern`.

Thus, `ovn_qty` and `Ovn_qty` are *not* distinct external names in portable C; `ovnght_qty` and `ovnght_param` are not distinct external names in portable

C; but `ovn_qty` and `ovn_param` are. External variables are subject to more stringent constraints because they are handled by the linker, which is often tied to particular operating system conventions that have nothing to do with the C language, such as case insensitivity.

One way to avoid the severity of Rule NAME5 is to keep all external variables in a single structure which in effect packages them into a single context. Then the individual external variables are treated as members of the external structure, and member names are governed by Rule NAME4, not NAME5.

```
struct globals {
    int     ovnght_qty;
    int     ovnght_param;
    int     todays_qty;
    double  todays_price;
    ...
};
extern struct globals globals;
```

Another strategy is to use one such structure of program scope per module, rather than per program.

9.4.1 Reserved names

As the libraries and environment associated with C grow, there is a growth in "name pollution," the reserving of certain names for use by the implementers of the environment, not the programmer. Reserved names are unavailable to the programmer. Rule NAME6 summarizes the reserved names in portable C.

NAME6: *The following names are unavailable for programmer use:*

- *Keywords of the language, including keywords of ANSI C*

- *names beginning with _ (underscore)*

- *Names of ANSI standard library functions, macros, and other external names in ANSI standard header files*

The forbidden keywords include longtime keywords such as `if` and `int`, more recent keywords such as `enum` and `void`, and ANSI keywords such as `const` and `volatile`. The exclusion of names beginning with underscore comes from ANSI.[9] The exclusion of library function names also comes from ANSI. Because

---

[9] The ANSI formulation is actually not as restrictive. Names beginning with _ are unavailable for programmer use as names of program scope. Names beginning with _ or _ followed by an upper-case letter are unavailable for programmer use. The formulation in Rule NAME6 is easier to remember.

of ANSI restrictions, we cannot redefine an ANSI library function in portable C, unless it is for the purpose of emulating the ANSI library in a non-ANSI environment.

9.4.2 Filenames

Explicit filenames appearing in a program are obvious sources of nonportability. Since filenames are highly environment-dependent, it is best to isolate them from the program code in some way.[10] For example, consider

```
#include "/usr/local/include/environ.h"
```

Rather than use the full pathname of the include file, which makes your code dependent on your particular directory structure, use a compiler option to set the pathname of the include files. For example, in a UNIX environment, the $-I$ option of the C compiler **cc** allows you to specify a directory that the preprocessor will search for include files. You could say

```
cc -I/usr/local/include test1.c
```

If you have **make**, you can say in your makefile:

```
INCDIR = /usr/local/include
...
CFLAGS = -I$(INCDIR)
```

Then in your code you need only say

```
#include "environ.h"
```

You thereby isolate the environment dependence from the code itself.

Similarly, for filenames used in the code itself,

```
fp = fopen("/c1/project2/input.0887", "r");
```

one way to make this code fragment more portable is: use #defines for filenames, keeping the actual names in a header file. For example, in **environ.h** you could say

```
#define INFILE "/c1/project2/input.0887"
```

---

[10] Even the syntax for specifying filenames is environment dependent. For example, MS-DOS filenames use \ as a separator, instead of the Unix /. Moreover, MS-DOS is not sensitive to case in filenames, while Unix is. For portability, most functions in the standard library under MS-DOS that expect a filename as argument will translate / into \. Thus it is more portable to use the Unix convention of / as delimiter, except in contexts where a filename might not be expected. Note that in C strings, the character \ must be written as "\\"; thus the filename B:\user\file1 would be written in C as the string "B:\\user\\file1".

and in your code you could say

```
fp = fopen(INFILE, "r");
```

An alternative strategy is to use **getenv** to retrieve the filename from the host *environment*. The environment here refers to an array of strings of the form VAR=value, set up by the host environment and made available to the C program at startup time. For example, in an MS-DOS environment, you could set the variable in MS-DOS by saying

```
SET OVERNIGHT_FILE=B:\C1\PROJECT2\INPUT.0887
```

Alternatively, in a UNIX environment using the Bourne shell as command processor, you could define a shell variable OVERNIGHT_FILE:

```
export OVERNIGHT_FILE
OVERNIGHT_FILE=/c1/project2/input.0887
```

In either environment, the code would say

```
char *infile;

infile = getenv("OVERNIGHT_FILE");
if (infile == (char *)0)
    errexit("OVERNIGHT_FILE undefined");
fp = fopen(infile, "r");
...
```

This method allows OVERNIGHT_FILE to be changed easily in the host environment without the need to recompile the code. The function **getenv** is part of the ANSI standard library as well as being available under UNIX and Microsoft C.

Unfortunately, there is no corresponding way to portably modify the environment from inside a C program. Microsoft has a function **putenv**, but it is not portable. Some programmers attempt to modify the environment by accessing a global variable environ, but that method is also not portable.[11]

9.5 Limits

Limits are inherent in any software. Translation software's limits become a problem for portability. The limits in the translation environment are determined by

---

[11] Of course, there is nothing portable you could *do* with a modified environment anyway, since all methods of process spawning are nonportable. See §9.6.

the amount of memory available for translation and by table sizes in the preprocessor, compiler, and linker. The limits imposed by a translation environment often are not documented anywhere but must be "discovered" the hard way—by exceeding them. Limits may also interact with one another; for example, a large set of preprocessor names may limit the number of variable names because of a common heap space used for all names in some translation environments. Following are some of the quantities subject to limits in the translation environment:

- Number of names in a block, in a source file

- Number of macro names in a source file

- Number of external names in a source file, in all source files for a program

- Number of operations in an expression

- Number of levels of nesting in control structures

- Number of parameters in a function

- Number of characters in a logical line of the source file

- Number of characters in a string literal

- Maximum size of a compound data object[12]

- Maximum size of a stack frame (which limits the total size of the automatic variables in any function)[13]

[ANSI] gives minimum values for each of these limits and others which a translator must fulfill in order to be conforming, but there is no guarantee that existing compilers satisfy ANSI's minima. We can derive one rule from the last two limits:

LIMIT1: *Large data objects should be declared with external or static storage class.*

That is, large arrays or structures of automatic storage class should be avoided in portable C.

Portable C can offer no other rules to avoid exceeding the limits of all translation environments (aside from the rules on naming conventions in §9.4). Instead, if you run into a translation limit when porting a program to a new environment, you must follow a "divide and conquer" strategy: if your source file

---

[12] For example, on an Intel 80286 machine under the large model, a data object cannot exceed 64K in size.

[13] Many architectures assume that stack frames are small. Even on a VAX, a stack frame is limited to 64K in size.

has too many names, split the source file into smaller files; if an expression has too many subexpressions, split the statement into shorter statements; if the program has too many external names, use fewer external variables, or use a single structure to contain all the external variables. This *ad hoc* approach is the best that portable C can offer.

9.5.1 Address space limitations

Limits in the runtime environment, like limits in the translation environment, are difficult to anticipate. Such runtime limits as the number of concurrent open files or the maximum size of a file are highly environment dependent. Most notable are address space limitations. *Address space limitations* are imposed by pointer size, memory size, and operating system (for instance, whether the operating system uses swapping, demand paging, or neither).

There may be separate limits on a program's stack size and heap size in certain environments. For example, in an MS-DOS environment, the programmer usually must specify the maximum stack size at compile time, while in many environments (including MS-DOS under certain options), stack and heap can compete for available memory space.

Programmers in large address space environments may be reluctant to constrain themselves to small address space programs just in order to remain portable to small address space environments. They must decide whether to exclude small address space environments from their universe of portability.

Porting a large address space program to an environment with a smaller address space is not an easy task. With the advent of microcomputers the problem arises more frequently. In a multiprogramming environment it may be possible to divide the program into separate processes that communicate via pipes, files, or some other interprocess communications mechanism. In a single process environment, it would be necessary to separate the program into a series of stages that communicate via files.

9.6 Program startup and termination

Other aspects of the runtime environment that affect portability are program startup and program termination.

Program startup is usually carried out by the operating system, which sets up the stack for the `main` function and, for example, initializes `argc` and `argv` appropriately. Some of program startup may be linked in with the program itself.

Program termination is the set of activities carried out when **exit** is called, or when the program returns from the `main` function.

The program startup routine sets up the parameters to `main` and calls `main`. Some environments set up a third argument to `main`, `envp`, an array of strings of the form "name=value", where each name is a variable set in the host environment. It is not portable to use `envp`. Instead, it is more portable to use **getenv** to obtain the value of the variables set in the host environment. **getenv** is supported in [ANSI], [Microsoft], and all Unix libraries.

The initialization of static and external variables is performed by the program startup routine. As seen previously, [K&R] and most non-ANSI compilers initialize all such variables with all-bits 0, while [ANSI] specifies that static and external pointers are initialized to the value of the null pointer, and floating point variables are initialized to floating point zero, even if these values are not all-bits-0.

The best way to handle initialization differences among environments is to initialize all variables explicitly.

INIT1: *Don't rely on the implicit initialization of variables to "all bits zero." Make all initializations explicit.*

This rule applies as well to automatic variables, since it is simply wrong to use an uninitialized automatic variable (though much code makes this mistake). Initialize all data objects using explicit initializers in their declarations, or by explicit assignment, or by input. Rule INIT1 applies also to data objects created by **calloc**, which initializes storage to all-bits-0, since it is impossible to know in advance whether this will suffice for null pointers and floating point zeros.

Part of program termination is the optional returning of a value to the command processor that invoked the program. ANSI and some non-ANSI compilers allow this to be done by saying

```
return n;
```

from `main`, where n is an integer value. It is more portable to use the function **exit** to return a value to the command processor. The function **exit** is supported in the ANSI library and is available in most existing C compilers. It can be invoked from functions other than `main`. **exit** should be used to return a small set of integer values, preferably in the range 0 to 127, which can be used to represent success and various kinds of failure. The values returned by **exit** should be parameterized. Thus it is more portable to say

```
exit(EXIT_SUCCESS);
```

or

```
exit(EPERMISSION);
```

than to say `exit(0)`, since 0 may denote success in one command processor, failure in another.[14] **exit** should not be used to return a count or other significant data to the command processor, since the portable range of its return value is only seven bits.

We summarize these insights with Rule TERM1:

TERM1: *Use* **exit** *to return a value between 0 and 127 to the invoking command processor.*

Don't use `return` to return a value from `main`.

The program termination routines may also flush partially filled buffers, close open files, and in general tidy up the runtime environment. In Unix environments, the **exit** system call can give status information to a waiting parent process. The exact mechanisms of program termination are specific to the runtime environment.

9.7 Unspecified ordering

Some aspects of the C language are intentionally left to the compiler implementer who must choose the most natural approach for the environment. The order in which side effects of an expression occur, the order of evaluation of operands of an operator, and the order of evaluation of actual parameters passed to a function are all unspecified in [K&R] and remain unspecified in [ANSI].[15]

---

[14] `EXIT_SUCCESS` is an ANSI-sanctioned name that indicates successful exit status to the host environment. ANSI also allows the parameter 0 to designate successful exit status, regardless of what value it is translated to in the host environment. ANSI allows any nonzero value to designate some type of failure. We made up the symbolic name `EPERMISSION`, defined in a header file, to designate a type of failure.

[15] The ANSI standard carefully describes which aspects of ANSI C are unspecified. The ANSI standard distinguishes four different terms for unspecified behaviors. We paraphrase their definitions here:

- *Unspecified behavior.* For correct program and data, the ANSI standard makes no requirements for what should happen (for example, the order of evaluation of arguments to a function).

- *Undefined behavior.* For incorrect program or data, the ANSI standard makes no requirements for what should happen. Maybe nothing will happen, or the program will react in a documented way—like issuing an error message, or execution will halt (for example, behavior on integer overflow).

- *Implementation-defined behavior.* For correct program and data, the ANSI standard specifies that each implementation of C will document what it will do in these circumstances (for example, propagation of the high-order bit on right shift of signed integer).

- *Locale-specific behavior.* Behavior that depends on nationality, culture, or language (for example, whether **islower** returns true for characters other than the 26 lower-case English letters).

Rule ORDER1 states that it is nonportable to rely on any ordering which is left to the implementer of the compiler.

ORDER1: *Don't rely on the order of evaluation of*

- *side effects*
- *sub-expressions*
- *function arguments.*

9.7.1 Order of side effects

The following example shows a common error of beginning programmers that violates Rule ORDER1. Some first-time C programmers will use the following code to increment variable i. Where is the nonportable code and what will the program print out?

```
main()
{
    int i = 0;

    printf("%d\t", i = i++);
    printf("%d\n", i);
}
```

On some compilers, the program will print

```
0    0
```

On others, it will print

```
0    1
```

On still others it will print

```
1    1
```

To understand this variation in behavior, we must distinguish between the *result* and the *side effect* of an operation. A side effect is a change in the value of a data object that is a by-product of the evaluation of an expression. In the statement

```
n = 2;
```

the assignment of a new value to n is technically a side effect of the evaluation of the = operator. The result of the = operation is a short-lived constant data object with value 2. Similarly, in the statement

```
n = ++k;
```

the assignment of a new value to k is a side effect of the ++ operator, while the result of the expression ++k is a short-lived constant data object. Function calls can also cause side effects.

In the example,

```
printf("%d\t", i = i++);
```

there are two side effects: i gets incremented as a side effect of the operator i++, and i gets a new value as a result of the assignment =. Since compilers are free to compute side effects in any order, and can pre-compute side effects, a variety of results can ensue from this example.

9.7.2 Order of evaluation of sub-expressions

The next example depends on another kind of unspecified ordering—the ordering of sub-expressions in an expression:

```
#include <stdio.h>
#include "environ.h"
char a[] = "ABC";
main()
{
    int n;

    n = putchar(CTOI(a[0])) +
        putchar(CTOI(a[1])) +
        putchar(CTOI(a[2]));
}
```

This program could print out

```
CBA
```

or

```
BCA
```

or any other permutation of A, B, and C, depending on the compiler used.

The reason is that C does not specify the order of evaluation of the operands of an operator, except for

- && , | | , and , (comma), which are guaranteed to evaluate their operands left-to-right.

- ? : which has a specified order of evaluation.

Parentheses cannot always be used to solve ambiguities of ordering because, counter to intuition, C is free to ignore parentheses under certain circumstances.

As seen in §4.6.3, C can rearrange the operands of successive identical operators that are commutative and associative, *ignoring the parentheses* that the programmer may have inserted! This is true for *, +, &, |, and ^.

Thus

```
n = a * (b * c);
```

can be evaluated by the compiler as if it were written

```
n = (c * a) * b;
```

To coerce an ordering, it is necessary to use two separate statements:

```
t = b * c;
n = a * t;
```

or to use the comma operator:

```
t = b * c, n = a * t;
```

Note that parentheses *do* work in statements such as

```
n = (c + a) * b;
```

where different operators (+, *) are involved.

ANSI has removed this specification of [K&R] about parentheses to make C more like other high level languages such as Fortran, particularly for floating point operations where the order of evaluation of sub-expressions makes a difference.[16] Thus in ANSI, parentheses always coerce the order of evaluation of sub-expressions. However, portable C cannot rely on this innovation in ANSI; the only portable way to coerce the order of evaluation of sub-expressions involving identical commutative and associative operators is to write separate statements as shown above.

9.7.3 Order of evaluation of arguments

What is nonportable in the following code?

---

[16] [ANSI Rat], p.37.

```
/* get a number, print its square root */

#include <math.h>    /* has declaration of sqrt */
#include <stdio.h>   /* has declaration of gets */
#include <stdlib.h> /* has declaration of atoi */
main()
{
    int i;

    printf("n=%d, square root of n=%f\n",
            i = atoi(gets()), sqrt((double)i));
}
```

On an AT&T 3B-series machine running System V UNIX, the code executes
as expected.

```
$ cc sqrt.c -lm
$ a.out
9
n=9, square root of n=3
$
```

On a PC/AT clone running a port of System V UNIX, executing this code so
troubled the operating system that it caused a system crash.

```
$ cc sqrt.c -lm
$ a.out
double panic
```

Presumably this crash is due to a bug in the port of System V to the 80286. However, even if it did not cause a system crash, the program would not print the
correct result.

The example relies on an unspecified behavior of C: the order of evaluation
of arguments to a function. Since the code assumes that the arguments are
evaluated left-to-right, it will fail on a machine where this is not the case (e.g.,
the VAX). The example violates Rule ORDER1.

```
printf("n=%d, square root of n=%f\n",
        i = atoi(gets()), sqrt((double)i));
```

To make the code portable, we take the assignment of value for i out of the
function call statement, thus eliminating any reliance on unspecified behavior of
C. The portable version is:

```
/* get a number, print its square root */

#include <math.h>    /* has declaration of sqrt */
#include <stdio.h>   /* has declaration of gets */
#include <stdlib.h>  /* has declaration of atoi */

main()
{
    int i;

    i = atoi(gets());
    printf("n=%d, square root of n=%f\n",
            i, sqrt((double)i));
}
```

9.8 The preprocessor

The preprocessor transforms source code into a different form used by the further stages of translation. It may be implemented as a separate program which passes over the source file before passing its results to the compiler, or it may be implemented as part of the compiler. Nonetheless, we can view the preprocessor as a logically separate phase of translation. Some compilers allow you to view the output of the preprocessor by specifying certain flags. This feature can be useful in debugging, though it is not universally available.

Style suggestion: *Use compiler features, where possible, in preference to prepro-*
cessor features.

For example, use `typedefs` instead of `#defines` to define parameterized types. There is a clear advantage to writing

```
typedef char *STRING;
```

rather than

```
#define STRING char *
```

For example, the declaration for two STRINGs, s and t,

```
STRING s, t;
```

is correct using the `typedef`, but incorrect using the `#define`. Compiler features are preferable to preprocessor features because

- Preprocessor code is harder to debug since some compilers cannot show the output of the preprocessor, and preprocessor tokens and macros are not accessible even in some source-level debuggers.

- Preprocessor macros are not subject to type checking or **lint** checking (or to ANSI prototype checking).

- Preprocessors vary more in behavior than do compilers.

Nonetheless, the preprocessor plays an important role in the writing of portable code by allowing for parameterized constants and the hiding of environment dependencies in header files. For example

```
#define BELL          '\7'
#define TONUMBER(d)  ((d) - '0')
```

One use of the preprocessor is particularly relevant to portability: conditional inclusion of code. It is sometimes necessary to have different versions of code depending on aspects of the hardware or software environment. While conditional inclusion of code is the least elegant solution to portability problems, it is sometimes necessary. For example, suppose we define a preprocessor flag VOID to mean that the environment supports type void.

```
#if !VOID   /* if compiler does not support void */
#define void  int
#endif
```

As a matter of style, it is best to base conditional inclusion on features of the environment, such as

```
#if SIGSETMASK
```

for systems that support the **sigsetmask** function, or

```
#if BIG_ENDIAN
```

for "big-endian" machines, rather than basing conditional inclusion on a particular architecture, such as

```
#if vax | sun
```

Conditional inclusion of code in the above manner ties in nicely with setting the variables like BIG_ENDIAN in the compiler invocation or in the makefile (see §9.9).

The following rules govern the portable use of the preprocessor.

PRE1: *Don't nest comments.*

Some C preprocessors allow nested comments, but most do not. In compilers that do not allow nested comments, the first occurrence of `*/` ends the comment.

For example, the following code is nonportable:

```
/* This code is deactivated because...
 *
int ovn_param;   /* overnight parameter */
 */
```

Instead of nesting comments, use `#ifdef` or `#if` to comment out code:

```
#if NEVER        /* This code is deactivated because... */
int ovn_param;   /* overnight parameter */
#endif
```

PRE2: *Use no white space before or after the* #.

For example, use

```
#include
```

rather than the less portable

```
#   include
```

Some preprocessors tolerate white space before or after the `#`, but the practice is not portable.

PRE3: *Avoid macro calls within a string constant or character constant.*

Macro invocations inside a string constant are not supported in [K&R] or [ANSI].

PRE4: *Do not use* #define *to redefine any C keywords, nor any function names in the ANSI library.*

Redefining reserved words is not allowed in [ANSI]. See Rule NAME6 on reserved names.

PRE5: *Avoid the ANSI extensions* #elif *and* defined, # *and* ##.

Keywords `#elif` and `defined` are supported in [SVPG RefMan], [Microsoft] but not in many pre-ANSI compilers. The new ANSI preprocessor operators `#` and `##`, used for quoting and concatenating tokens, are not supported in non-ANSI compilers.

The functionality of `#` and `##` can be achieved in a more portable fashion. To turn a macro parameter into a quoted string, use the macro STRINGIZE. The following example shows a portable definition for STRINGIZE and a sample use of it in the macro assert, a handy macro for debugging code.

```
#include <stdio.h>

#ifdef __STDC__
#define STRINGIZE(a)    #a
#else
#define STRINGIZE(a)    "a"
#endif

#define assert(expr) \
                    (expr) ? 1000 : \
                    fprintf(stderr, \
                            "File %s, line %d: <%s> fails\n", \
                            __FILE__, __LINE__, \
                            STRINGIZE(expr))
main(argc, argv)
int argc;
char *argv[];
{
        assert(argc == 1);
}
```

Note that __STDC__ is true only in an ANSI environment. The constant 1000 is a placeholder, an arbitrary value which is not used.

The functionality of ## can also be implemented portably by the macro CONCAT_TOKEN. CONCAT_TOKEN takes two arguments and turns them into a single token. A portable definition is:

```
#ifdef __STDC__
#define CONCAT_TOKEN(a,b)       a ## b
#else
#define IDENTITY_(a)a
#define CONCAT_TOKEN(a,b)       IDENTITY_(a)b
#endif

main()
{
        int j3 = 99;

        printf("CONCAT_TOKEN(j,3) = %d\n", CONCAT_TOKEN(j,3));
}
```

The example should print

```
CONCAT_TOKEN(j,3)  = 99
```

It is important that the macros IDENTITY_ and CONCAT_TOKEN be written without any additional spaces.

PRE6: *Macro definitions can extend over more than one line.*

[K&R] specifies that the preprocessor allows \ to signify a macro extending over more than one line. Although some preprocessors do not adhere to this specification, it is fair to consider them deficient. If you have to port to a deficient translation environment that does not support multi-line macros, use either nested macro definitions or change the macro to a function.

For example, suppose you wish to define a macro that will give a portably defined integer division. As we saw in §4.6.9, integer division is not portably defined on negative numbers because of the direction of truncation. We can say

```
/*
 * idiv(a, b) == returns integer division of a/b
 *              truncate towards the largest integer less
 *              than or equal to the floating point result
 */
#define idiv(a, b)    (sgn(a) == sgn(b) ? (a)/(b) : \
                      -(abs(a)/abs(b)) - (abs(a) % abs(b) != 0))
#define sgn(n)        ((n) >= 0)
```

(On some machines, idiv(a, b) can be implemented simply as (a)/(b).) If you have to port idiv to an environment that lacks multi-line macros, you could type it on one very long line, making it difficult to print, or you could say

```
#define idiv(a, b)    (sgn(a) == sgn(b) ? (a)/(b) : ndiv((a), (b)))
#define ndiv(a, b)    (-(abs(a)/abs(b)) - (abs(a) % abs(b) != 0))
```

or you could use a function to implement idiv().

[ANSI] has added *trigraphs* to the character set for C source files. Their purpose is to allow C programs to be written in translation environments that do not have a full ASCII codeset. In particular, trigraphs allow C to be written in translation environments that use the ISO 646-1083 Invariant Code Set which supports all European languages, but lacks such ASCII characters as [ ] { } ^ # | and ~. Trigraphs are three character sequences beginning with ?? that stand for the missing characters. For example, ??= stands for #, while ??> stands for }.

Trigraphs are not part of pre-ANSI C environments. If you must use them because you work in a non-ASCII translation environment, you will need to translate them to ASCII characters when porting to pre-ANSI environments. If you work in a full ASCII environment, follow Rule STRING4: *Avoid ?? in strings or comments.* The double question mark could be misinterpreted in an ANSI environment as the beginning of a trigraph.

9.9 Tools and techniques for enhancing portability

We have already encountered some of the techniques that, in addition to the rules in this book, can enhance the portability of code:

- Using parameterized types, constants, and code, which can be customized in header files to particular environments.

- Isolating environment dependencies in header files, such as **environ.h** or **limits.h**, and in certain source files, e.g., **machine.c**.

- Using **getenv** to retrieve environment-specific data.

- Using `#if` or `#ifdef` to specify alternate code for different environments.

In addition to the above techniques, the tools **make** and **lint** can be used to enhance portability of a program.

9.9.1 make

The tool **make** can be useful in making a program portable, assuming that **make** is available in the translation environments you wish to use. Several versions of **make** exist in the UNIX world; **make**-like programs have also become available in the MS-DOS and Macintosh markets. Some PC compiler makers include a **make** program with their compiler.

Very often the **makefile** contains the information about the overall packaging and construction of a software product. Since **make** is used to create the load module(s) from source files, the **makefile** is often the first file a programmer will encounter when porting a product from one environment to another. The careful programmer will therefore design the **makefile** with portability in mind, so that another person can alter environmental parameterizations when porting to his or her environment.

In the **makefile**, define macros that identify specific features of the translation and runtime environment. For example,

```
##================================
# Environment-specific parameters
##================================

# Define MSDOS if running under MS-DOS
MSDOS = 0

# VOID is   1 if your C compiler supports type void.
#           0 otherwise.
VOID =  1
```

```
# REGCMP is 1 if your system has the regcmp() function.
# This should be true for System 5.
# RECOMP is 1 if your system has the re_comp() function.
# This should be true for various BSDs.
# In a non-UNIX environment, neither may be true.
REGCMP =    0
RECOMP =    0


...
PARAMS =    "-DVOID=$(VOID)" \
            "-DMSDOS=$(MSDOS)" \
            "-DREGCMP=$(REGCMP)" \
            "-DRECOMP=$(RECOMP)"

CFLAGS = $(PARAMS) ...
```

In your C source files, use #ifdef or #if to conditionally include environment-specific code, based on the definitions set in the **makefile**.

```
#if MSDOS
    /* code for MS-DOS only */
    ...
#endif
```

Since a makefile becomes the primary packaging tool of an application for portability to various environments, it is a good idea to write the makefile itself in a portable way. While the portable syntax of makefiles is beyond the scope of this book, it suffices to say that you should use the simplest features of your local **make** and not rely on more exotic features which may not be shared by other **make**s.

If **make** is not available, the same technique can be used by invoking the C compiler directly using the appropriate defines in the compiler invocation. For example, using a UNIX-style compiler invocation:

```
cc -c -DVOID=1 -DMSDOS=0 -DREGCMP=0 source1.c ...
```

9.9.2 lint

The tool **lint** is crucial to portable C programming. **lint** exists in all UNIX environments, and **lint**-like programs have become available for MS-DOS environments. All your code should pass through **lint**. **lint** can save time and effort in making code portable, as well as in finding bugs.

TOOL1: *Make sure all your code passes through* **lint**. *Lint together all the source files of your program.*

Many recent compilers, because they perform tighter type checking, now offer some of **lint**'s warning messages as part of the compilation process. Moreover, ANSI-conforming compilers can utilize the prototypes of the programmer and the standard library to perform the most important checking done by **lint**: the comparison of formal and actual parameter types.

Some people dislike **lint**'s verbose output. It can be frustrating to distinguish **lint**'s useful messages from the rest of its output. Most versions of **lint** provide flags which allow you to specify which tests you would like **lint** to perform. Finer control can be achieved by writing your own filter program (using **awk**, **grep**, or **sed**) to extract from **lint**'s output just the material that you want to see.

Recent versions of **lint** operate in a manner similar to the C compiler; they have compile and link phases. The compile phase of **lint** operates on individual source files, while the link phase does inter-file checking. It is therefore possible to transform the compile entry in a makefile into a **lint** entry, using all the same macro definitions and include directories.

Recent versions of Unix **lint** also allow you to create your own **lint** library corresponding to a project library. There are two kinds of lint libraries: binary and text. A text lint library consists of husks for each function which show the function's return type and parameter types, but have no code in the body. For example,

```
/* LINTLIBRARY */
FILE *fopen(filename, mode);
char *filename;
char *mode;
{
}
```

Most environments provide such a lint library for the functions in the standard library. Recent versions of lint allow you to generate a binary lint library which can be used by the link phase of lint for inter-file type checking.

The most important messages **lint** offers concern the matching of the number and type of formal and actual parameters to functions, the matching of the type of return expressions and return values of functions, and the use of return values from functions. To get the most use from these messages, it is important to lint together all the source files of your program. This enables **lint** to cross-check all the function calls and declarations.

Some of the other checks **lint** performs that are useful for portability are:

- Use of uninitialized variables.

- Code that assumes char is signed.

- Assignment of long to int.

- Strict type checking.

If you use the -p option of lint, it will perform extra portability checks, which include

- Truncating all non-external names to eight characters;

- Truncating all external names to six characters, one case;

- Checking function calls against a set of standard library functions.

9.9.3 Runtime checkers

Even the best static checking done by **lint** will fail to find certain classes of errors and portability problems. Only a runtime checker is capable of detecting certain errors such as de-referencing an invalid pointer or invalid array reference. The design of such tools for C is difficult; only in recent years have serious runtime checkers become available for C. This book is based in part on the experience of writing one such checker, **bcc**. Other products, such as the Saber C interpreter, can now do a good job of runtime checking, often saving the programmer hours of time in porting code.

9.10 Porting other people's code

It is possible to port a large program written by others without understanding how it works. At most, you may have to read some small sections of code. Here is a step-by-step procedure that has proven effective in porting other people's code.

1. Look at the **makefile**(s) for the code and adjust all environment-specific settings to fit your environment.

2. Look at all the #ifs and #ifdefs in the code to make sure the flags are defined appropriately for your environment.

3. Try to make the program. Often, it will fail to compile. Make the changes necessary to get it to compile and link.

4. Lint the code. Lint all the source files together if possible. Make appropriate changes in the code.

5. Make the program again.

6. Run the program. If it dies, use a runtime checker for diagnosis, or as a last
    resort, use a debugger. Repair the program, return to step 3, and repeat.

9.11 Internationalization

Internationalization is an attempt to make a program switchable at runtime
between different national environments: human languages, time, and money
formats. Internationalization is itself a different form of portability in which the
program is expected to run in different countries. The effort to make internationalized programs is relatively new, but some library functions are proposed in
[ANSI] and [X/OPEN] to help achieve the goal. These proposed techniques rely
on a runtime binding of the language-appropriate string constants to the program.

   Internationalization, also called *localization*, is described here because it is a
form of portability: not portability of source programs, but portability of executable programs to make them adapt to different national environments. The facilities described here are library interfaces or enhancements to existing C library
calls in the [ANSI] and [X/OPEN] documents. Unlike the program portability
rules that make up most of this book, the library functions for internationalization
will work only in an ANSI or X/OPEN conforming environment. At this writing,
internationalization represents more of a goal and suggested direction than an
existing body of programs.

   The goal is to make programs adjust to local conventions *at runtime*. Local
conventions include input and output messages in native language, and country-
specific formats for date, time, numbers, and money. The use of different
languages also means that programs must handle various *codesets* with
language-specific *collating sequences*.

   For example, some variations on the standard formats for date, time and
numbers are:

Date   `1776-07-04`
         `4.7.76`
         `7/4/76`
         `4.VII.76`
         `76186`
         `04JUL76`
Time   `3:30PM`
         `1530`
         `15h.30`
         `15.30`
         `15:30`

```
Numbers 1,800,534.23
        1.800.534,23
        1800534·23
```

The *radix character*, which separates the whole part of a number from the fractional part, differs from country to country.

The *codeset* is the encoding used to represent the letters of the alphabet and other keyboard characters as binary numbers. Most C environments use a seven-bit ASCII codeset to encode the English language alphabet and special characters. However, many European languages use eight-bit supersets of ASCII. Some Asian languages require 16-bit characters. There are ISO standards for various codesets, including ISO 8859/1, an eight-bit codeset that can represent most European languages.

A given codeset may use differing *collating sequences* to determine the dictionary ordering of words, depending on the language used. Unlike English in ASCII, not all codesets have collating sequence identical with the ordering of the binary encoding of characters. In particular, in some languages, one character sorts as two characters—the German β sorts as `ss`. In some languages, two characters sort as one character—the Spanish `ll` sorts after `l`, `ch` sorts after `c`.

9.11.1 Internationalization techniques

Both ANSI and X/OPEN address the internationalization effort with a set of library functions and enhancements to existing language functions to make them more locale-independent. X/OPEN goes further than ANSI in defining an internationalization mechanism, and for obvious reasons: X/OPEN is a largely European consortium of manufacturers who wish to make a UNIX-like interface as a programming standard for all their machines, in all their countries. ANSI and X/OPEN differ in some of their library interfaces for internationalization.

An *announcement mechanism* lets a program determine the native language and country conventions to use at runtime. In ANSI C the announcement mechanism is the function **setlocale**. X/OPEN uses **nl_init**. In X/OPEN, the native language and territory can be specified in an environment variable LANG. LANG has the format `language[_territory[.codeset]]`, where the brackets indicate optional parts of the string. The "announcement" of the locale specifics can be done by setting LANG in the shell and calling

```
nl_init(getenv("LANG"));
```

or by calling **nl_init** with an appropriate string.

```
char *lang = "french_swiss.6937";

nl_init(lang);
```

In X/OPEN **nl_init**, by specifying the language/territory/codeset, thereby also chooses the associated

- collating sequence

- character classification table (for **isalpha**, **ispunct**, etc.)

- shift tables (for **toupper**, etc.)

- language-specific information header file consisting of macros for

  — days of week

  — months of year

  — date/time formats

  — currency symbol

- and message catalogues—files of output messages.

9.11.2 Library functions

In order to sort strings in dictionary order, a program must be able to use the collating sequence associated with the local native language. The collating sequence also must take into account 1-to-2 and 2-to-1 character mappings, case, and accent priority. In ANSI C, this is accomplished either by **strcoll** or by a two step method: **strxfrm** transforms the original string to be ready for **strcmp**. X/OPEN uses a single function **nl_strcmp** which does string comparisons directly using the collating sequence of the language specified by **nl_init**.

ANSI C uses **strftime** to format date or time in a locale-specific way. In X/OPEN **nl_cxtime** and **nl_ascxtime** print date or time using D_T_FMT, which is a locale-specific macro-defined format string. In X/OPEN's **langinfo.h**, native-language macros are defined such as DAY_1, MON_1 for Sunday, January in native language.

In X/OPEN and ANSI, the *radix character* that separates the whole part from the fractional part of a number is locale-specific. X/OPEN also introduces **nl_printf**, which has an expanded format specifier that can specify in what order the arguments are printed. For example, %3$d means print the *third* argument, in decimal format. This can be useful, for example, in printing the date, since different countries order the month, date, and year differently. Thus, by varying the format string at runtime, it is possible to change the order in which the arguments are printed out.

9.11.3 Message catalogues

X/OPEN introduces *message catalogues*, text files used to store output messages separately from the rest of the source program. Message catalogues allow the choice of native language output to be made at runtime. The native language for the messages is specified by the announcement mechanism, **nl_init.**

To print a message from a message catalogue, all you need is its number. The message catalogue is a file consisting of numbers and strings. Each message has a number. **catopen** is used to open the appropriate catalogue. Once the catalogue is opened, messages are extracted from the catalogue by **catgets.**

```
nl_catd catopen(a, b);
char *catgets(catd, set_num, msg_num, default_msg);
nl_catd catd;
int set_num, msg_num;
char *default_msg;
```

catd   is the catalogue descriptor returned from **catopen**

msg_num   is the number of the desired message

default_msg   is the message to return if there is no catalogue entry for the current language and message number.

The following example shows the use of some features of the X/OPEN library for internationalization. The program prints the date in the native language and format of the user's locale.

```
#include <stdio.h>
#include <nl_types.h>
#include <time.h>

#define DATE_MSG     1

main()
{
    nl_catd catd;    /* catalogue descriptor */

    nl_init(getenv("LANG"));
    catd = catopen("dateprog", 0);
    /* if catopen fails, default msgs will print */

    printf(catgets(catd, 1, DATE_MSG, "Today's date is %s"),
        nl_asctime(time((long *)0)));

    catclose(catd);
}
```

If LANG is not set explicitly in the shell, or whatever program calls this program, then this program prints the default message:

```
Today's date is Fri Jul 31 11:18:26 1987
```

On the other hand, if in the shell you say,

```
LANG=french
```

then the output is something like

```
C'est aujourd'hui ven le 31 juil 11:18:26 1987
```

SUMMARY OF RULES FOR PORTABLE C

A.1 Basic rules

PORT1: *Be explicit; don't rely on defaults of the language.*

PORT2: *Don't rely on the representation of the value of data objects.*[1]

PORT3: *Identify, isolate, and parameterize environment-dependent code and definitions in separate source or header files. Include* **environ.h** *in every source file.*

A.2 Rules for the portable use of functions

FUNC1: *Declare every function in a header file.*

FUNC2: *The actual and formal parameters of a function should have the same types.*

FUNC3: *The number of actual and formal parameters of a function must match.*

FUNC4: *The type of a return expression should be the same as the return type of the function.*

FUNC5: *Define every function with an explicit return type.*

FUNC6: *Don't use structures or unions for argument types or return types.*

A.3 Rules for numbers

NUM1: *The value of a data object of arithmetic type must lie within the portable range of that type.*
See §4.5.2 for the table of portable ranges.

NUM2: *A value to be converted must lie within the portable range of the type converted to.*

NUM3: *Arithmetic operations must not overflow the portable range of the resulting type.*

---

[1] One exception to this principle is that portable C *does* assume the binary encoding of positive integers.

NUM4: *In portable C we view a binary operator as if it promotes the operand of "smaller" type to the type of the operand of "larger" type, where "smaller" and "larger" are defined by the following two hierarchies:*

```
char, short, int, long, float, double
```

and

```
unsigned char, unsigned short, unsigned,
unsigned long
```

In portable C we view unary operators as if they perform no implicit conversions; thus we view the type of the result as the same as the type of the operand.

NUM5: *Don't mix signed and unsigned types in operations on numbers.*

NUM6: *Number constants of type* long *should be written with an* L *suffixed to the decimal, octal, or hexadecimal format.*

NUM7: *The integer division operators (*/ % /= %=*) require non-negative operands.*

A.4 Rules for bit patterns, Booleans, floating point

BIT1: *The bitlength of a bit pattern represented by a data object of integral type must not exceed the portable bitlength of its type.*
See table, §4.7.1.

BIT2: *Signed and unsigned integral types can represent bit patterns, and can be mixed in expressions, though unsigned types are preferable. We view a binary bitwise operator as if it promotes the operand of "smaller" type to the type of the operand of "larger" type, where "smaller" and "larger" are defined by the following hierarchy:*

```
char
```
or unsigned char,
```
    short
```
or unsigned short,
```
    int
```
or unsigned int,
```
    long
```
or unsigned long

BIT3: *Beware of bit patterns of bitlength 8 or 16.*

BIT4: *Append an* L *to bit pattern constants of bitlength greater than 16. Where possible, cast constants to unsigned types. Use octal or hexadecimal formats for bit pattern constants—don't use decimal format.*

BIT5: *For the shift operators (`<< >> <<= >>=`), if the type of the left operand is in the left column, then the right operand should be in the range specified by the right column.*

Left Operand	Right Operand
`char` `unsigned char`	[0..7]

`short`
`unsigned short`
`int`
`unsigned`
	[0..15]

`long` `unsigned long`	[0..31]

BIT6: *For `>>` with a left operand of signed type, either*

- *Mask the result to the desired number of bits, or*

- *Cast the left operand to the appropriate unsigned type.*

BIT7: *Use integral types, instead of bit-field structure members, to represent bit patterns.*

BOOL1: *Any integer or pointer type can be used as a Boolean, but floating point types cannot.*

BOOL2: *For the Boolean operators (`&&` and `||`), pointer and integral operands can be mixed.*

FLOAT1: *Explicitly initialize all floating point variables.*

A.5 Rules for the portable use of `char`

CHAR1: *The* **getchar** *family of routines,* **getchar**, **getc**, *and* **fgetc**, *all return an* `int`; *use an* `int` *variable to store the return value of any of them.*

CHAR2: *Use an* `int` *whose value is representable as an* `unsigned char` *or* EOF *as the argument to the* **ctype** *routines.*

CHAR3: *Use single-quoted constants for codeset characters and bytes. In portable C, a single-quoted constant is treated as if it has type* `char`. *Where possible, use character representation rather than octal representation for single-quoted constants.*

CHAR4: *Don't compare bytes or codeset characters with* `int`*s. Rather, when using the* `==` *or* `!=` *operators, make sure both operands are* `int`*s or both are* `char`*s.*

CHAR5: *Don't apply arithmetic, relational comparison, or bitwise operators to codeset characters or bytes. Use* **ctype** *macros where possible.*

A.6 Rules for the portable use of pointers

PTR1: *Use the typedef'd type* `PTRINT` *as the integer type for conversions to and from pointer types.*

PTR2: *Never de-reference the null pointer!*

Style suggestion: *In your code, for the null pointer use* 0 *cast to the appropriate pointer type.*

PTR3: *Pointer operands of an operator must match in type. Use a cast, if necessary, to ensure this.*

PTR4: *The following are portable casts:*

- *Any pointer can be converted into a pointer of type* `char *`.

- *A pointer to a data object of strictest alignment can be converted into a pointer of any type.*

- *A pointer to a compound type (structure, union, or array) can be converted to a pointer to the type of any member or element of that compound type.*

PTR5: *The first byte of a data object must lie within or just beyond the associated primary data object, independent of the environment.*

PTR6: *Don't apply* & *to an array expression or to a function name expression.*

PTR7: *In order to subtract two pointers, they must*

- *be of the same type,*

- *point to data objects associated with same primary data object,*

- *and be viewable as pointing to elements of the same array (derivable from each other by pointer arithmetic), independent of the environment.*

That is, independent of the size in bytes and layout of the primary data object.

PTR8: *A relational comparison on two pointers requires that both*

- *have the same type, and*

- *are associated with same primary data object,*

independent of the environment.

PTR9: *A data object must be used with the same type with which its value was stored.*

A.7 Rules for the portable use of compound data types

COMPOUND1: *Do not put initializers in declarations of automatic arrays or structures.*

COMPOUND2: *Do not put initializers in declarations of data objects containing unions.*

COMPOUND3: *Use full braces to show initialization of each substructure and sub-array.*

STRUCT1: *In -> and . expressions, the right-hand operand must be a member name which belongs to the structure or union referred to or pointed to by the left-hand operand.*

Roughly speaking, the member name must belong to the structure.

STRUCT2: *Use unique member names for each structure and union.*

Style suggestion: *Use a common prefix to identify the members of each structure and union.*

STRUCT3: *For widest portability, do not use structure assignment.*

ARRAY1: *When initializing an array with a string, leave room for the null character.*

STRING1: *Don't modify string literals.*

STRING2: *Don't assume unique storage for string literals.*

STRING3: *Avoid using ANSI string concatenation.*

STRING4: *Avoid ?? in strings or comments.*

A.8 Other rules

LIB1: *Use the ANSI standard library function interface.*

NAME1: *Declare all data objects of program scope in a header file.*

Rule NAME1 applies to variables and functions whose name have program scope.

NAME2: *Use the strict Ref/Def convention for names of program scope.*

NAME3: *The keyword* static *should not appear in a referencing declaration of a function.*

The practical implication of this rule is that the defining declaration of a function or variable with file scope in portable C should appear before any use of the function or variable.

NAME4: *Within its scope and name space, a name of block or file scope must be unique within the first eight characters, case sensitive.*

NAME5: *Names of program scope must be unique within the first six characters, case-insensitive.*

NAME6: *The following names are unavailable for programmer use:*

- *Keywords of the language, including keywords of ANSI C*

- *names beginning with _ (underscore)*

- *Names of ANSI standard library functions, macros, and other external names in ANSI standard header files*

LIMIT1: *Large data objects should be declared with external or static storage class.*

That is, large arrays or structures of automatic storage class should be avoided in portable C.

INIT1: *Don't rely on the implicit initialization of variables to "all bits zero." Make all initializations explicit.*

TERM1: *Use **exit** to return a value between 0 and 127 to the invoking command processor.*

ORDER1: *Don't rely on the order of evaluation of*

- *side effects*
- *sub-expressions*
- *function arguments.*

Style suggestion: *Use compiler features, where possible, in preference to preprocessor features.*

PRE1: *Don't nest comments.*

PRE2: *Use no white space before or after the* #.

PRE3: *Avoid macro calls within a string constant or character constant.*

PRE4: *Do not use* #define *to redefine any C keywords, nor any function names in the ANSI library.*

PRE5: *Avoid the ANSI extensions* #elif *and* #defined, # *and* ##.

PRE6: *Macro definitions can extend over more than one line.*

TOOL1: *Make sure all your code passes through* **lint**. *Lint together all the source files of your program.*

APPENDIX B
BIBLIOGRAPHY

The C Journal, Vol. 1, No. 4, Winter 1986 Portability Issue.

The C Users Journal, Vol. 7, No. 1, Dec./Jan. 1989 Portability Issue. Good articles on MS-DOS/UNIX portability and UNIX/VAX portability.

"Draft Proposed American National Standard for Information Systems—Programming Language C," X3J11/88-159, December 7, 1988. [ANSI]

Harbison, Samuel P., and Guy L. Steele, Jr., *C, A Reference Manual* (2nd ed.), Prentice-Hall, Inc., Englewood Cliffs, N.J., 1987. [H&S]

IEEE Std 1003.1, "Draft American National Standard, IEEE Trial-Use Standard Portable Operating System for Computer Environments (POSIX)," April 1986. [POSIX]

Johnson, S. C., and D. M. Ritchie, "UNIX time-sharing system: portability of C programs and the UNIX system," *Bell System Technical Journal*, 57:2021-48. [J&R]

Kernighan, Brian W., and Dennis M. Ritchie, *The C Programming Language*, Prentice-Hall, Englewood Cliffs, N.J., 1978. [K&R]

Kernighan, Brian W., and Dennis M. Ritchie, *The C Programming Language*, Second Edition, Prentice-Hall, Englewood Cliffs, N.J., 1988. [K&R2]

Lapin, J. E., *Portable C and Unix System Programming*, Prentice-Hall, Englewood Cliffs, NJ, 1987. [Lapin]

MacLennan, B. J., "Values and objects in programming languages," *SIGPLAN Notices*, Vol. 7, No. 12, December, 1982.

Microsoft C Compiler for the MS-DOS Operating System: Language Reference, Microsoft Corporation, 1986.

"Rationale for Draft Proposed American National Standard for Information Systems: Programming Language C," X3J11/88-151, November 14, 1988. [ANSI Rat]

Rosler, L., "The Evolution of C--Past and Future," *AT&T Bell Labs Technical Journal*, Vol.63, No.8, October 1984.

Spafford, Eugene H., and John C. Flaspohler, "A Report on the Accuracy of Some Floating Point Math Functions on Selected Computers," Technical Report GIT-ICS 85/06, Georgia Institute of Technology, School of Information and Computer Science, January 10, 1986, reprinted in *;login:*, Volume 11, Number 2, March/April 1986, pp. 31-55. [Spaf&Flas]

Stroustrup, Bjarne, *The C++ Programming Language*, Addison-Wesley, 1987. [Stroustrup]

Stroustrup, Bjarne, "What is Object-Oriented Programming?," *IEEE Software*, May 1988, pp. 10-20. [StrOop]

System V Interface Definition, Spring 1985, Issue 1, AT&T. [SVID]

Tilson, Michael, "How Portable is C?," *Microsystems*, November, 1984, p.84.

Unix Programmer's Manual, 4.2 Berkeley Software Distribution, Virtual VAX-11 Version, August, 1983, Computer Science Division, University of California, Berkeley, California.

"UNIX System V Programmer's Guide, Release 2.0," Chapter 2: C Language definition. [SVPG 5.2 RefMan]

"UNIX System V Release 3 Programmer's Guide," AT&T, Chapter 17: C Language. [SVPG RefMan]

X/OPEN Portability Guide, Vol. 4, "Programming Languages," pp. 3.1-4.9, and Vol. 3 "XVS Supplementary Definitions: XVS Internationalisation," Elsevier Science Publishers B.V., Amsterdam, 1987. [X/OPEN]

"A Guide for Writing Portable C Programs," AT&T Bell Laboratories internal document, 1984.

"C Reference Manual," AT&T Bell Laboratories internal document, 1981. [RefMan81]

INDEX

V

W

X

Z